CANADIAN IMMIGRATION PATTERNS
FROM BRITAIN AND NORTH AMERICA

UWE
BRIS

Th
s

SN

The International Canadian Studies Series
La Collection internationale d'études canadiennes

The *International Canadian Studies Series* offers a unique collection of high-quality works written primarily by non-Canadian academics. The Series includes conference proceedings, collections of scholarly essays, and various forms of reference works. The Series publishes works written in either English or French.

La *Collection internationale d'études canadiennes* présente des ouvrages de premier ordre, rédigés surtout par des universitaires non canadiens. Elle comprend des actes de colloque, des recueils d'articles et divers types d'ouvrages de référence. La collection publie en français et en anglais.

Editorial committee / Comité éditorial
Chad Gaffield
Guy Leclerc

ISSN 1489-713X

International Canadian Studies Series
Collection internationale d'études canadiennes

CANADIAN MIGRATION PATTERNS
FROM BRITAIN AND NORTH AMERICA

Edited by
Barbara J. Messamore

International Council
for Canadian Studies

UNIVERSITY
OF OTTAWA
PRESS

LES PRESSES DE
L'UNIVERSITÉ
D'OTTAWA

Université d'
University of
Ottawa

Institut d'études canadiennes
Institute of Canadian Studies

National Library of Canada Cataloguing in Publication

Canadian migration patterns from Britain and North America /
edited by Barbara J. Messamore.

(International Canadian studies series)
Includes bibliographical references.
ISBN 0-7766-0543-7

1. Canada – Emigration and immigration – History. 2. Great
Britain – Emigration and immigration – History. 3. North America –
Emigration and immigration – History. I. Messamore, Barbara Jane,
1959- II. Series.

JV7220.C35 2004   325.71'09   C2002-904407-3

University of Ottawa Press gratefully acknowledges the support extended
to its publishing programme by the Canada Council and the
University of Ottawa.

We acknowledge the financial support of the Government of Canada
through the Book Publishing Industry Development Program (BPIDP)
for our publishing activities.

 UNIVERSITY OF OTTAWA
UNIVERSITÉ D'OTTAWA

Printed and bound in Canada

Acknowledgements

This collection of essays represents a selection of the papers presented at the 1998 Migration conference at the Centre of Canadian Studies at the University of Edinburgh. Dr Colin Coates, Director of the Centre, and Professor Ged Martin wish to thank all of the participants of the conference for their contributions to the event and the valuable exchange of ideas. The Centre of Canadian Studies at the University of Edinburgh receives substantial funding from the Foundation for Canadian Studies in the United Kingdom thanks to the generosity of Standard Life plc.

The task of editing has been greatly lightened by the encouragement and assistance of Professor Ged Martin and Dr Colin Coates. Their help in this project is but one example of the ongoing support that has made my association with the Centre of Canadian Studies so enjoyable.

Contents

Introduction:
Canada and Migration: Kinship with the World

Barbara J. Messamore

"IT IS A DULL SUBJECT, AT LEAST TO ME," JAMES STEPHEN REMARKED IN 1839 ON emigration.[1] Yet migration has been the single most powerful force in shaping the traditions and history of Canada. From the earliest contacts between aboriginal Canadians and newcomers to the emergence of a modern multicultural society, the history of Canada has been a history of migration.

Canadians tend to identify themselves according to their ethnic origin, and it is not uncommon to hear Canadians who have never set foot in the British Isles describe themselves as "Scottish." With the obvious exception of Native people, it is difficult for Canadians within their own country to claim to be simply "Canadian" without being pressed for more detail, especially if they are members of a "visible minority." Canadian travellers have been known to experience a moment's uncertainty when asked to complete a landing card on international flights, their pens hesitating over the box marked "nationality." With few having an unqualified claim to pure Canadian nationality, there is little stigma attached to immigrant status. "It is meaningless to call anyone a foreigner in this country," observed John Marlyn's fictional Hungarian-Canadian. "We are all foreigners here."[2]

Since the arrival of the six thousand or so French immigrants who had formed the nucleus of New France by the second half of the seventeenth century, the character of Canada has been shaped by successive waves of immigration. Even after the conquest of New France by the British and the influx into British North America of tens of thousands of Loyalists fleeing the American Revolution in 1783, the steep rate of natural increase among Canadiens ensured the heterogeneous nature of the population.

The end of the Napoleonic Wars in 1815 opened the floodgates for an unprecedented surge of migration to North America from the British Isles.[3] The million newcomers from Ireland, Scotland, and England before 1850 exercised an irresistible force in shaping the development of British North American society. Of course, their arrival was not seen in an altogether positive light by those already established in the colonies. Some in Britain regarded colonial possessions as the ideal dumping ground for the mother country's superfluous population—a safety valve for social discontent in an era of economic strain. In spite of a few short-lived experiments with government-assisted pauper emigration,[4] most arrivals were not part of any organized scheme. The development of the British North American timber trade may have played a role in the burgeoning of immigrant traffic as timber ships were hastily fitted out to transport human ballast on the otherwise unprofitable journey west across the Atlantic. Disease was rampant, and many did not survive the passage of several weeks in conditions of squalid overcrowding. Cholera also made its appearance in the towns to which the migrants gravitated, in 1832 decimating the population of the ports of Quebec and Montreal. Perhaps the best-known episode of this era is the exodus of Irish immigrants from the potato famine of the 1840s. In 1847, the peak year, the number of immigrants to British North America jumped to almost ninety thousand, almost triple the number of those in the years immediately preceding.[5] Canada's Executive Council complained that "Intending settlers possessed of wealth or means are . . . few in number" and that the ships were crowded with "the decrepit, the maimed, the lame, the subjects of chronic disease, widows with large families of tender age, and others [with] infirmities or confirmed habits [who] were incapable of maintaining themselves at home by their own labour."[6] More than ten thousand died that season either en route to British North America or in hospital once they had arrived, mainly falling victim to typhus. A further thirty thousand were reported ill at the end of the shipping season.[7] Resentment in the colonies over Britain's lax regulation of the immigrant traffic[8] was further fueled by outbreaks of typhus among Canadian residents. In a leading article entitled "Horrors of the Exodus to Canada," the London *Times* reported that more than nine hundred residents of Montreal, excluding newly arrived immigrants, had succumbed to disease in a nine-week period.[9]

After this mid-century surge in immigration—a mixed blessing—the number of newcomers soon began to dwindle. Canada's Department of Agriculture, in both the pre- and post-Confederation periods, sought to recruit settlers in Britain and western Europe for the sparsely populated west. The group migration of settlers from some non-traditional sources in the decade following Confederation made a permanent impact on the developing character of the prairie west. Most notable of these groups were the Icelandic settlers in the area centred around Gimli, on Lake Winnipeg, and Mennonites who took up land grants in what would become Manitoba and Saskatchewan. Yet overall immigration figures were disappointing. From Confederation to the mid-1890s, immigration did not even keep pace with the outflow of population to the United States.[10] Even when Canadian settlers did not choose to cross the border, they frequently sought to better their prospects by relocating away from areas of most concentrated settlement, and these "hopeful travellers," as David Gagan terms them, are an important feature of Canada's migration history.[11] In the nineteenth century, as in the twentieth, migration within the country was part of the life experience of many Canadians.

The advent of Laurier's Liberal government in 1896—and, more specifically, the appointment of Clifford Sifton as minister of the interior—has often been seen as a watershed in Canadian immigration history. Sifton's proverbial "stalwart peasant in a sheepskin coat"[12] represented a new ideal, a fanning out to eastern and central Europe in the quest for farmers to till the Canadian prairies. Immigration did rise by the turn of the century, from a low of 16,835 in 1896, to 138,660 by 1903, and to over 400,000 just before the outbreak of the First World War.[13] While some credit is certainly due to Sifton's aggressive recruitment policies and to more systematic administration, world conditions—a European population boom, rural overcrowding, the persecution of ethnic minorities, and the draw of employment opportunities and higher wages—no doubt contributed more to the influx. The conspicuous presence of large numbers of non-Anglo-Saxon groups, such as Ukrainians in the prairie west, tended to mask the fact that most immigrants to Canada continued to come from the United States and the British Isles.

What is more, nativist reaction tended to favour groups who would blend in most readily with the Anglo-Saxon majority. Even the most enlightened observers took it for granted that assimilation was necessary and desirable. While calling on Canadians to "divest ourselves of a certain arrogant superiority and exclusiveness" and reminding them that "many of the world's greatest and best men were from the very countries which our immigrants call home," J. S. Woodsworth asserted that "non-assimilable elements are clearly detrimental to our highest national development, and hence should be vigorously excluded."[14] Reactions to Chinese immigrants are illustrative of Canadian ambivalence. The vital role of Chinese labourers in the construction of the transcontinental railway has been well documented. Yet, in 1885—a date which coincides with the completion of the railway—an ungrateful federal government succumbed to pressure from British Columbia and imposed a head tax on Chinese immigrants. Attitudes toward foreign workers reveal a paradox: shunned by many trade unionists as a threat to wage rates and working conditions, foreigners were also targeted as the source of dangerous radical ideas, especially after the Bolshevik Revolution of 1917. Wartime tensions added another source of discrimination for aliens from enemy nations, and during both the First and Second World Wars, these immigrants faced persecution, internment, or deportation. Deportation was also used as an economic tool during the Great Depression, with thousands who had unwittingly become a "public charge" forced to leave Canada. A similarly hard-nosed policy was applied to would-be refugees with the outbreak of the Second World War, and Canadian immigration officials forced desperate Jews to return to meet their fate in Nazi Germany.[15] During the early 1940s, in fact, the total annual number of immigrants to Canada dipped into four figures for the first time since Confederation.[16]

The end of the Second World War signaled a new era in immigration, with more than two million coming to Canada between 1945 and 1961. Increasingly, these newcomers were from continental Europe, especially Germany, Italy, and the Netherlands. This new influx changed the complexion of many Canadian cities, transforming a "staid and complacent British" Toronto, in the words of W. L. Morton, "into a varied and vivacious cosmopolitan metropolis."[17] Toronto alone absorbed ninety thousand Italian immigrants from 1951 to 1961.[18]

The late 1960s and early 1970s seemed to usher in a shift from the assimilationist assumptions of the past. In 1967, new immigration regulations did away with entrenched race and colour biases. A points system would determine a potential immigrant's suitability based on such criteria as education, fluency in English or French, occupational demand, age, and personal characteristics. This system, along with provisions for reuniting family members and humanitarian considerations, would be incorporated into the Immigration Act of 1976. The emphasis was no longer on the immigrant's ability to blend in with Canadian society. The announcement of the federal policy of official multiculturalism in 1971 seemed to complement this new approach. Attempts to recognize and protect the language and culture of French Canada spurred the realization that other ethnic groups might benefit from similar recognition and encouragement, and that it was no longer accurate to see Canada as merely bicultural.

Increasingly, new Canadians have come from non-traditional sources: Africa and the Middle East, the Caribbean, and especially Asia. A more generous refugee policy contributed to the arrival of some 77,000 "boat people" from Indochina between 1975 and 1981.[19] In the 1980s, in fact, Vietnam was the single greatest source of immigrants to Canada, with 92,873 arrivals, closely rivaled by the United Kingdom (91,025), India (87,117), and Hong Kong (77,752).[20] New regulations in 1986 made provision for an "entrepreneurial" class of immigrants, who would be admitted on the condition that they make significant investments in Canada. The "yacht people" from Hong Kong were frequently admitted under this provision. Official multiculturalism notwithstanding, immigrants who are members of visible minority groups occasionally experience difficulty in winning acceptance and may be the target of resentment, especially during times of economic strain.

The struggle to adjust to life in a new country has long been a key theme in Canadian literature. From the humorous and heartbreaking trials of Susanna Moodie, a Victorian gentlewoman pioneer in the backwoods, to Robert Service's fictional Sam McGee, who "left his home in the South to roam round the Pole,"[21] the centrality of migration to the Canadian experience has been well established. Contemporary literature is also rich with works dealing with the theme; a new generation of Canadian writers, many of them immigrants themselves, have revitalized Canada's literary tradition with fresh perspectives drawn from varied experiences. The British Columbia–based poet Thuong Vuong-Riddick has devoted a collection of poetry, *Two Shores/ Deux Rives*, to her migration from Vietnam, to France, to Montreal, and at last to the Pacific coast, where "the country I left behind is there / in front of me."[22] Her work is both a lament for what she has left behind, and a celebration of the "human warmth / of the country / I belong to."[23] In "He Covered Me With a Blanket," Vuong-Riddick writes with tender gratitude of her Canadian-born husband:

When my family arrived from France,
Ma, Na, Mi, Kieng, Tchieng, Te, Ti,
he covered them all
with his signature.[24]

In "Poudrerie," she is touched and surprised when she is invited to socialize with her students and finds friendship in the midst of a cold Quebec winter.

> Never had I imagined
> winter could be cheerful,
> warm . . .[25]

To migrants, "globalization" is more than a buzzword. With their consciousness shaped by the country they have adopted and the ones they have left behind, theirs is truly a global outlook. "I belong," writes Vuong-Riddick,

> to a country of the mind
> with friends and relatives
> scattered in Canada, America, France, Australia,
> Vietnam.[26]

Even while forging strong bonds of affection with the country chosen as home, the immigrant carries ties and traditions which span continents and oceans. Canada, drawing its population from every country of the world, is linked by these ties, which radiate out in every direction. Such a population is unlikely to embrace a chauvinistic nationalism, yet, more meaningfully, can adopt a genuinely global perspective, born of kinship with all the world.

*   *   *   *   *

The essays that make up this collection address various aspects of migration in Canada. They have been drawn from a number of papers presented at the 1998 conference on the theme of migration hosted by the Centre of Canadian Studies at the University of Edinburgh. While the majority of the papers are historical in perspective, this is a multidisciplinary collection, including contributions by geographers, economists, and sociologists, and works devoted to literature and even music. The chronological range is likewise broad, ranging from the eighteenth century to the 1990s. Not surprisingly, such a wide range of works presents a number of challenges to previously held views of migration in Canada.

The opening essay, by Marjory Harper, provides a historiographical survey of migration studies, examining the sometimes-conflicting views which have informed studies of migration. She further considers the mechanics of trans-Atlantic migration, how immigrants were recruited, and the ties—personal and ideological—which bound those who left to those who remained behind. While optimistic about the new interest in migration history that has been spurred by the desire to research family origins, Harper offers a caveat about how to use this climate of enthusiasm to advantage.

Two of the essays which follow focus directly on exploding long-established myths in Canadian migration history. Peter Marshall's essay considers the widespread use of the term "late Loyalist" for immigrants to Upper Canada from the United States in the decades after the American Revolution. While explaining the contradictions inherent in the term, Marshall offers some insights into the economic and ideological currents of early Upper Canada which help to account for its adoption. Ronald Stagg also takes issue with historical accounts of a widely accepted phenomenon: the supposed migration of thousands of disgruntled Upper Canadians to the United States after the failure of the rebellion of 1837. By extrapolating from available statistics, Stagg presents a convincing case that challenges views based on anecdotal evidence.

Three contributions to this collection offer new interpretations and a fuller picture of the "invisible" English immigrants to Canada in the nineteenth century. Bruce Elliott points out that these migrants tend to be overlooked amid the more dramatic stories of the Highland Scots driven from their homes by the clearances and the Irish fleeing the potato famine. Elliott contrasts the pattern of English migration with that of the Irish, before concentrating his attention on the pre-Confederation period when English immigrants were less numerous. He is able to provide a detailed picture of the nature of English pre-Confederation immigration by analysing the areas in which they settled, and those from which they were drawn. Wendy Cameron's essay provides an important piece in the pre-Confederation English migration puzzle, through her analysis of a specific instance of parish-assisted emigration. This study of the Petworth emigration scheme of the 1830s is a valuable vehicle for acquiring greater insight into the fortunes of assisted immigrants and the social and economic tensions which gave rise to such a project. Terry McDonald further develops the picture through a study of published letters of Wiltshire and Somerset emigrants to Upper Canada in the early 1830s. McDonald argues that such letters were considered very valuable in the bid to win over prospective immigrants, and he shows how publishers might misrepresent details concerning the correspondents in order to exploit the propaganda value of the letters.

While McDonald's work serves to remind us that they must be used with caution, letters form the most valuable research tool available for those who seek to trace the history of the migration of a particular family or individual. Four papers in this collection have used correspondence to do just that. By providing specific examples of immigrant stories, they put flesh on the bones of migration research, enabling us to use our imaginations to enter into the world of the migrant. Kathleen Burke traces the fortunes (and misfortunes) of two families with early links to Upper Canada. From the late eighteenth century, the Smith and Pilkington families kept alive a sense of connection to Canada that would contribute to a "trans-generational" pattern of migration. Duff Crerar tells the story of the "quest for independence" of a Highland family in the nineteenth and twentieth centuries, the strategies they adopted, and proactive approach they took to improving their circumstances. While they did not always succeed, these immigrants, Crerar finds, were far from passive victims. Joan Bryans considers the migration within Canada—from Nova Scotia to British Columbia—of two sisters in the late 1880s. Approaching their story from the context of feminist philosophy, Bryans describes the sisters' divergent strategies for coping with the loss of the "significant others" who were so vital to their sense of self. Excerpts from the sisters' letters home provide a vivid picture of their struggles to adapt. Donald F. Harris likewise recounts the challenges met by a family migrating to British Columbia around the turn of the century. A genteel English family, the Lees experienced some culture shock in the "odd country" that they adopted as their home. Harris draws particular attention to the absence in British Columbia of the kind of social restraints such a family would have expected, based on their experiences in England.

The migration of ideas is an important aspect of migration studies, and two papers in this collection consider the flow of information and attitudes from old country to new, and vice versa. John F. Davis finds that prospective immigrants "From Eastern England to Western Canada" in the early twentieth century had a variety of resources at their disposal to help them make an informed decision about emigration. Newspaper advertisements and reports, exhibitions, and lectures by farmer delegates were all available, and Davis provides a sampling of the sort of information that was circulated. Information was seldom value-neutral, of course, and Richard Dennis looks at another aspect of migration: the reactions of established Canadians around the turn of the century to foreigners in their midst. Focusing on William Lyon Mackenzie King's work as a journalist and would-be reformer in the slums of Toronto, Dennis analyses King's attitudes toward various immigrant groups and his proposals for solving the attendant problems. Interestingly, Dennis finds that the degree of one's perceived "foreignness" was not necessarily determined by the length of one's residency in Canada.

Among the most important considerations in any study of migration is the question of why people choose to relocate. An analysis of the factors that push immigrants from their countries of origin and pull them toward a new one pervades all of the papers in this collection to a greater or lesser extent. Three of the essays, however, have focused specifically on these factors. Tracey Connolly has tackled the much-neglected field of Irish migration to Canada in the 1950s. She explains the reasons behind the huge exodus and explores the differences that distinguish Irish immigrants of this era from other groups, and indeed Irish immigrants to Canada from those who went elsewhere. Sebastián Escalante's essay addresses the controversial topic of refugees in Canada. By focusing on the specific plight of those who flee Mexico because of domestic violence or persecution over their sexual orientation, Escalante is able to explore the wider issue of attitudes toward refugees. Gary L. Hunt and Richard E. Mueller consider the role played by economic incentives in decisions about migration within North America. Using census data from 1990 and 1991 for the United States and Canada, Hunt and Mueller assess the importance of an area's mean wage and the value of returns to skills in an individual's decision to migrate.

Leaving hard data aside, there is a more impressionistic aspect to migration studies. Migration has long been an important theme in the realm of the arts, and two of the papers included here consider how the migration experience has been conveyed. Christopher J. Armstrong examines a selection of post–Second World War literature of Atlantic Canada with special attention to the theme of mobility. Armstrong surveys a number of novels before focusing on the work of Paul Bowdring. Armstrong finds in Bowdring's fiction a sense of the tension which exists between the protagonist's attraction to the world of the cosmopolitan urban intellectual and his nostalgia for his home in Newfoundland. Karen Clavelle shares a number of "Songs of Love and

Longing" which she has compiled. These migration songs, many of them old and familiar, evoke the complex, and often contradictory, emotions associated with the experience of making a home in a new, distant land.

As these various essays demonstrate, migration is a central theme in the history and contemporary life of Canada. The ties that Canadians feel to other nations of the world, and to other regions within their own country, are an important feature—perhaps even the defining feature—of the Canadian identity. Migration is not merely a historical phenomenon, but a key issue in Canada's social, economic, political, and cultural life. By addressing aspects of the migration phenomenon—from refugee policy to migration songs—the contributors to this collection have added greater depth and clarity to our understanding of the Canadian identity.

Notes

1. James Stephen to Macvey Napier, 10 August 1839 in Macvey Napier, ed. *Selections from the Correspondence of the late Macvey Napier, Esq.* (London: Macmillan, 1879), 295.
2. John Marlyn, *Under the Ribs of Death* (Toronto: McClelland and Stewart, 1971), 24.
3. For a useful overview of immigration in this period, see Helen I. Cowan, *British Emigration to British North America. The First Hundred Years* (Toronto: University of Toronto Press, 1961), and W. S. Shepperson, *British Emigration to North America. Projects and Opinions in the Early Victorian Period* (Oxford: Basil Blackwell, 1957).
4. See H. J. M. Johnston, *British Emigration Policy, 1815–1830: 'Shovelling out Paupers'* (Oxford: Clarendon Press, 1972).
5. The Colonial Land and Emigration Office reported 89,927 immigrants to British North America during the first six months of 1847, compared to 32,593 for the same period in 1846. See *British Parliamentary Papers Relating to Canada, 1847–48*, vol. 17, 367.
6. "Extract from a Report of a Committee of the Executive Council . . . on the subject of the Emigration of the present year," 7 December, 1847, *British Parliamentary Papers Relating to Canada, 1847–48*, vol. 17, 383–4.
7. Report of G. M. Douglas, Medical Superintendent, *British Parliamentary Papers Relating to Canada, 1847–48*, vol. 17, 385.
8. See Oliver Macdonagh, *A Pattern of Government Growth 1800–60: The*

Passenger Acts and Their Enforcement (London: MacGibbon & Kee, 1961).

9. *The Times* (London), "Horrors of the Exodus to Canada," 17 September 1847.

10. Reg Whitaker, *Canadian Immigration Policy Since Confederation* (Ottawa: Canadian Historical Association Booklet, no. 15, 1991), 4.

11. David Gagan, *Hopeful Travellers: Families, Land, and Social Change in Mid-Victorian Peel County, Canada West* (Toronto: University of Toronto Press, 1981).

12. Quoted in Valerie Knowles, *Strangers at Our Gates: Canadian Immigration and Immigration Policy, 1540–1990* (Toronto: Dundurn Press, 1992), 64.

13. For statistics on immigration in this era, see David J. Hall, "Room to Spare," *Horizon Canada*, 76 (1986): 1803.

14. J. S. Woodsworth, *Strangers within Our Gates* (1909) (Toronto: University of Toronto Press, 1972), 240, 232.

15. Whitaker, *Canadian Immigration Policy*, 13.

16. See statistical tables in Knowles, *Strangers at Our Gates*, 189–90.

17. Quoted in Howard Palmer, "Reluctant Hosts: Anglo-Canadian Views of Multiculturalism in the Twentieth Century," in Gerald Tulchinsky, ed., *Immigration in Canada: Historical Perspectives* (Toronto: Copp Clark Longman, 1994), 314.

18. Franca Iacovetta, "From Contadina to Worker: Southern Italian Immigrant Working Women in Toronto, 1947–62," in Tulchinsky, *Immigration in Canada*, 381.

19. Knowles, *Strangers at Our Gates*, 166.

20. Douglas Francis, Richard Jones, and Donald Smith, *Destinies: Canadian History since Confederation* (Toronto: Holt, Rinehart and Winston, 1992), 459.

21. Robert Service, "The Cremation of Sam McGee," in *Collected Verse of Robert Service*, vol. 1 (London: Ernest Benn, 1960), 48.

22. Thuong Vuong-Riddick, "For My Father," in *Two Shores/Deux Rives* (Vancouver: Ronsdale Press, 1995), 116.

23. Thuong Vuong-Riddick, "He Covered Me With a Blanket," in *Two Shores/Deux Rives*, 160.

24. Ibid., 158.

25. Ibid.

26. Thuong Vuong-Riddick, "Searching," in *Two Shores/Deux Rives*, Preface.

Crossing the Atlantic:
Snapshots from the Migration Album

Marjory Harper

RESEARCHING MIGRATION IS AKIN TO COMPILING A GIANT, MULTIDIMEN-sional snapshot album. In recent years, thanks to an international upsurge of interest in demographic studies, several pictures have been added by a growing body of scholars, and continuing enthusiasm for the subject is reflected not only in research and publication, but also, unsurprisingly, in teaching at both tertiary and secondary levels, as well as in the popular arena. This paper seeks, first, to chart the historiography of migration studies in a British-Canadian and Scottish-Canadian context, incorporating some reflections on the paradoxes and tensions which have characterised the debate throughout its modern history. The historiographical skeleton will then be fleshed out through an evaluation of some of the major recurring mechanisms of transatlantic migration over the past two centuries, again with particular reference to Scotland, and the study will conclude by anticipating future developments in the enduring saga of migration research.

The Historiography of Migration

Historiographical paradoxes with respect to migration are exemplified by the contradictory observations of Sir Charles Dilke and Robert Service, both penned in the era of fervent new imperialism which preceded the First World War. Dilke's perception that "British emigrants do not as a body care whether they go to lands under or not under British rule, and cross the seas . . . at the prompting not of sentiment but of interest"[1] was in sharp contrast to the upbeat imperialism of Robert Service:

If you leave the gloom of London and you seek a glowing land,
Where all except the flag is strange and new,
There's a bronzed and stalwart fellow who will grip you by the hand,
And greet you with a welcome warm and true;
For he's your younger brother, the one you sent away,
Because there wasn't room for him at home;
And now he's quite contented, and he's glad he didn't stay,
And he's building Britain's greatness o'er the foam.[2]

This disparity highlights just one of many paradoxes in the complex mosaic of migration in the age of Empire. While a study of statistics clearly confirms Dilke's assertion, demonstrating unequivocally that for most of the nineteenth century the best-trodden migrant path was that to the United States,[3] the weight of information and recommendation in the national and provincial press, in journals and guidebooks, and in the records of migration societies consistently points toward Canada as the most-favoured and best-publicised destination for British migrants.[4] Other features which have characterised the often heated emigration debate since at least the mid-eighteenth century include the question of whether it represented a threat or an opportunity to both donor and destination countries and different perceptions about the calibre of migrants. Not only have policy-makers struggled to promote imperial colonisation while discouraging foreign emigration, particularly to the United States; they have also been bombarded with contradictory accusations from each side of the Atlantic that they have stripped Britain of the brain and sinew of its population yet simultaneously populated Canada with paupers, social misfits, and political agitators.

Migration historiography reverberates with the conflicts and conundrums which have repeatedly beset demographic upheaval, particularly since the late eighteenth century. During that mercantilist era, public and political opposition to migration centred on the damaging repercussions for the nation's health and security of a depletion of economic and military manpower, particularly from the Scottish Highlands and Ireland, areas whose most industrious, rather than surplus, people were, it was perceived, haemorrhaging away across the Atlantic. The Westminster government, Highland landlords, travelogue writers such as John Knox and Samuel Johnson, and periodicals such as the *Scots Magazine* all deplored emigration, although Johnson was somewhat ambivalent in his reference to emigrants both as "rays diverging from a focus" and as people who "changed nothing but the place of their abode."[5] By 1815, mercantilism was giving way to Malthusianism, as population pressure, aggravated by a tide of demobilised soldiers, brought the spectre of massive unemployment, pauperism, and social conflict. Migration in the depressed 1820s therefore came to be perceived by policy-makers in seventeenth-century terms, as a safety valve rather than a threat, until economic revival in the 1830s allowed Edward Gibbon Wakefield to implement his policies of systematic colonisation and positive empire settlement.[6] The "safety valve" argument—and the accompanying clamour for state-aided migration—then re-emerged during the 1870s depression, in strident assertions that the twin problems of overpopulation in Britain and a colonial labour deficit could be solved by state funding.[7] Those arguments fell on deaf ears until 1922, when the Empire Settlement Act marked the government's capitulation to the case for state funding, in a rearguard attempt to retain the settler colonies' umbilical attachment to the "Old Country."[8]

Although particular migration policies were dominant at different periods, they were never unanimously endorsed. Mercantilist opposition to migration, particularly among Highland landlords, was fuelled by the recruitment activities of a number of emigration agents, notably Lord Selkirk,[9] and by the British government's reluctance to condemn imperial migration wholeheartedly after it had lost the thirteen colonies and recognised the vulnerability of its Canadian frontier. But Malthusian policies were also criticised in the press and in Parliament either as expensive and ineffective or as unethical, while Wakefield was blamed in Britain for promoting an exclusive policy which took away the best and left the most needy.[10] The Empire, however, with Canada in the vanguard, tended to dispute British claims that it was receiving the pick of the population, particularly during times of depression in Britain. Canadian accusations of settlers' unworthiness, along with a refusal to accept Britain's unwanted population, became more vociferous at the end of the nineteenth century, as growing powers of self-government enabled federal and provincial authorities to deny entry to migrants whom they regarded as unsuitable.

These paradoxical attitudes are reflected in both contemporary and modern historiography. Confident imperialism, superseded by defensive imperialism, was the hallmark of a plethora of filiopietistic histories in the late nineteenth and early twentieth centuries, antiquarian hagiographical roll-calls of the achievements of individual emigrants, which side-stepped any investigation of the overall economic, social, cultural, or political impact of the ethnic group.[11] It was also the hall-mark of inter-war publications which viewed emigration history through the window of the Cabinet Office or Colonial Office, with very little reference to the local circumstances, private inducements, and regional networks which really shaped the movement. Books published in the 1920s exuded a Whiggish confidence in the government's new inter-ventionism, which, it was predicted, would fill up the dominions with British settlers and confer the benefits of civilisation and economic development on passive colonial societies.[12] One of the few negative notes was sounded by W. A. Carrothers, who claimed, with regret, that the Empire Settlement Act had failed to live up to its promise.[13]

Meanwhile, in Canada, although there was never a consensus, sentiments were much more biased toward a negative interpretation of migration from the "Old Country." If British imperial historiography was bullish in the late-Victorian era, Canada was more ambivalent about the benefits of sponsored colonisation, as policy-makers tried to reconcile the demand for competent prairie farmers (to offset American competition) with the supply of what they perceived to be an excess of delinquent juveniles or impecunious loafers from urban-industrial back-grounds. Then, at the turn of the century, Clifford Sifton's courtship of the "stalwart peasant in a sheepskin coat" produced a nativist backlash, which was fuelled not only by the Protestant British but also, ironically, by French-speaking Catholic Quebec. These contradictions continued into the inter-war period, when the federal government tried to modify the transportation companies' relentless pressure for unrestricted im-migration. Restriction was supported by organised labour and the churches, but opposed by some sections of the press and public opin-ion, which thought that a parsimonious approach to empire settlement would enable other dominions to steal an edge over Canada. By 1928, however, a fairly universal reaction had set in against heavy expendi-ture on what it was claimed was the importation of misfits and pau-pers, not least in the notorious harvesters' scheme of that year.[14]

As in modern British migration historiography, over-simplified ste-reotypes have continued to affect Canadian perceptions of migration and settlement during the twentieth century, not least with respect to Irish migration. Only in recent years has the focus shifted away from the victims of potato blight to serious study of those relatively affluent pre-famine Irish, 55 per cent of them Protestant, who came to British North America as agricultural pioneers, in much larger numbers than their destitute compatriots after 1845.[15] Similarly, perceptions of Scottish migration continue to be shaped by images of Highland clearance, even though by the later nineteenth century Highlanders constituted a minority of Scottish migrants, many of whom came from the commercialised rural lowlands and even more from the urban-industrial central belt.[16] As for the English, whose crucial influence has so often been obscured by more visible or voluble ethnic groups, only now are they undergoing rehabilitation in Canadian migration historiography.[17]

On both sides of the Atlantic, but particularly in Britain, the second half of the twentieth century has seen a clear shift away from viewing emigration only through the policy-makers' eyes; as the sun has set on the Empire, so it has also set on the Whiggish imperialistic approach which characterised Victorian, Edwardian, and inter-war publications. Since the 1960s there have been both quantitative evaluations of the socio-economic background and motives of the emigrants and debates about their settlement and assimilation overseas, while the development of an international comparative approach, spearheaded by Charlotte Erickson and Dudley Baines, has encompassed a growing recognition of the complexity of migration.[18] Recent research has also demonstrated a tendency to move away from "victim history," stressing the positive, well-thought-out motives and the adaptability of the migrants, both male and female, often through archivally based studies of particular ethnic groups.[19]

Scottish migration historiography displays many of the phenomena which characterise the wider international tapestry, particularly the competing claims of victim history and calculated entrepreneurship. In nineteenth-century Scotland, the fire of enforced diaspora was stoked by men like Hugh Miller, Donald Macleod, and Alexander Mackenzie, polemicists who depicted emigration exclusively as an outflow of unhappy Highlanders who had been driven into exile by clearance and eviction, and who sought to reconstitute their disrupted lifestyles overseas.[20] But this dominant image of the impoverished exile, despite its undoubted validity in many a Highland and Hebridean context, tended to impede recognition of how multidimensional and widespread Scottish emigration actually was.

Although in the 1920s Margaret Adam, writing in the *Scottish Historical Review*, produced one of the first empirically based investigative studies of Highland emigration,[21] it was not until 1966 that the publication of Gordon Donaldson's book, *The Scots Overseas*, laid a broader basis for the study of Scottish emigration in all its diversity.[22] Two years earlier, Donaldson, in his inaugural lecture as professor of Scottish

history at Edinburgh University, had advocated the study of "neglected" subjects such as Scotland's overseas connections, a plea which has been answered in the last three decades by numerous published investigations of the social and economic roots and repercussions of Scottish emigration, and by an enduring interest in the subject at the undergraduate and research levels.[23] Much of the focus has continued to rest on Highland emigration, for since the 1970s especially there has also been a vibrant interest in Highland history, literature, and folklore, and it is impossible to write about the modern Highlands without writing about emigration. But on neither side of the Atlantic is there unanimity of opinion about the reasons for the exodus. The emphasis of writers such as Ian Grimble, John Prebble, and James Hunter on the social tragedy encompassed in Highland emigration was challenged in the 1980s by Eric Richards's economic study of the clearances, and by J. M. Bumsted's argument that eighteenth-century Highlanders migrated for positive entrepreneurial reasons, a view which has in turn been contested by Marianne McLean and David Craig.[24] Both T. M. Devine and A. I. Macinnes have emphasised the varied and complex nature of the Highland emigration tapestry, the former in a detailed study of the evidence surrounding the famine of the 1840s, and the latter by demonstrating the entrepreneurial ambitions of Highland emigrants as early as the seventeenth century.[25] Meanwhile, a lowland perspective has also been added to the picture, initially by Malcolm Gray, who in the 1970s demonstrated the links between the commercialisation of Scottish agriculture and emigration and suggested that the dramatic episodes of Highland emigration were paralleled by an equally significant, but neglected, exodus from the rural lowlands.[26] Over a decade later, the present author developed Gray's thesis with particular reference to north-east Scotland, and four years later a seminar series at Strathclyde University took further the theme of an emigration mosaic, emphasising the importance of setting demographic movement within the context of the society which produced the emigrants.[27]

Bridging the Atlantic

What does such a weight of source material reveal about the major recurring mechanisms of transatlantic emigration during the last two centuries? The following brief survey of the emigrant transportation business, the significance of professional propaganda, the development of recognisable settlement patterns through personal and community

networks, and the psychological assimilation of emigrants draws primarily on evidence from northern Scotland, but many of the examples can be replicated in other parts of the British Isles.

Mechanisms of Transportation

Migrant transportation was undoubtedly a business even in the eighteenth century. As far as Scotland was concerned, the parliamentary union of 1707 opened up unprecedented opportunities to trade across the Atlantic, and shipowners and agents soon harnessed migration to their commercial involvement with the mainland American colonies and the Caribbean. The Jamaica Streets and Virginia Streets of our cities' docklands are not so named by accident, and the shipping columns of provincial newspapers reflect the vibrancy of a transatlantic trade in human cargoes as well as tobacco, sugar, and other colonial commodities.

> That any young Man bred a Taylor, who is good at his Business and can cut and shape well, who will engage for 3 or 4 Years, and go over to Virginia, let them apply to John Elphinston Mercht. in Aberdeen, who will enter into an Indenture with them, and oblige himself to pay them 10£. Ster. yearly, with Bed, Board and Washing: And in case they don't like the Country, when there, he shall oblige himself to bring them back to Aberdeen on his own Charge.
>
> If there is any other Trades Men, such as Smiths, Wrights, Bricklayers &c has a mind to engage, let them apply as above, and he will give them very great Encouragement; and dare venture to say that there's Scarce a Trades-man in this Country that can make near so much free money yearly with his own Hand.[28]

With the loss of the American colonies and the subsequent French revolutionary and Napoleonic wars, the focus of emigrant transportation shifted, as a trade in timber from New Brunswick and the St Lawrence developed around Britain's ports, and with it a reciprocal trade in human freight. Passages on timber traders were widely advertised in a range of provincial newspapers, not least the *Aberdeen Journal*, which advertised up to sixteen ships each year until the mid-nineteenth century, not only from the port of Aberdeen itself, but from smaller harbours elsewhere in the region.[79] Although by the 1850s the eclipse of sail by steam had terminated the emigrant trade of all but a few ports, the action simply shifted from the docks to the railway stations, and the fortuitous development of the railway network at the same time as emigrant shipping became concentrated on Glasgow and Liverpool made it relatively easy for passengers to travel to these major embarkation centres. Large shipping companies such as the White Star, Anchor, Allan, and Dominion lines advertised regularly in the national and provincial press, and by the turn of the century, such was the demand for emigrant passages that special "colonist cars" were attached to some Glasgow- and Liverpool-bound trains, and leave-takings were major public events, regularly reported in the newspapers.[30] By no means were all those departing permanent settlers, for another dimension of migration that was made possible as a result of the way in which the railway and steamship revolution had shrunk the world was an increasing trend toward episodic, seasonal movement, particularly among tradesmen who had secured temporary contract work in North America.[31]

Although records of shipping movements improved in the course of the nineteenth century, it was not until 1895 that full lists of passengers' names, places of origin, and occupations were recorded by the authorities. Unfortunately for the passengers, the glowing recommendations of advertisers all too often disguised the harsh realities of seasickness, storms, and—at worst—shipwreck and death, for a transatlantic passage, even in a steamship, was an endurance test rather than a luxury cruise, particularly for the majority of emigrants, who were crowded into the steerage. Shipboard diaries and letters can add a crucial extra dimension to the unvarnished statistics of the Colonial Land and Emigration Commission or its successor, the Board of Trade, particularly in respect of mortality at sea. In 1846 Alexander Robertson, from the village of Monymusk in Aberdeenshire, embarked with his wife and seven children at the port of Aberdeen, but less than two weeks into the voyage, the birth and death of a premature baby were followed almost immediately by the death of Robertson's wife. The family's anguish was articulated both in thirteen-year-old Charles Robertson's diary and in a letter sent by Alexander Robertson to his wife's family back in Scotland.

> I take up my pen to acquaint you with the dreadful affliction that has befallen me in the death of my wife. . . . She grew ill as we left the point of the pier with sickness and continued to grow worse as we went further on. Some days she was a little better and able to be on

deck, and often did we flatter ourselves that she would soon be better, but the weather grew bad and she was taken with dysentery, which reduced her to great weakness, when one dreadful night she was taken with the pains of labour. There was two midwives on board and she was safely delivered of a female child on Wednesday April 29 about 12 at night. The child was alive but very small. . . . It lived the next day and through the next night or morning, when it died. . . . My wife was still in a fair way on Sunday [but] that day she grew worse, ere about nine o'clock at night, when her soul took its flight to that pure land where there will be no more sorrow nor trouble and where I long to follow. Oft since then I have lain beside my poor children and looked back to the many happy nights we have spent together, never, never to be recalled. The children do not feel their want—it is me alone that does suffer, but their time will come. I often wish that we would be driven against some rock, that we might all have the same grave.[32]

Stimulating an Interest: Professional Propaganda

Emigrant activity did not come about by accident. People still had to be persuaded to leave, and advised on where and how to proceed. The linchpins in this process were the emigration agents, a veritable army of men, and a few women, who came in many guises and used various devices to entice emigrants to what they convincingly promised was a more encouraging environment on the other side of the Atlantic.

Highland tacksmen who recruited their sub-tenants to fill up Canadian land grants made to them after the Seven Years' War, land speculators such as Thomas Talbot and Lord Selkirk around 1800, and the nineteenth-century shipmasters who sought a human cargo for their returning timber ships—all were, in different ways and for different reasons, emigration agents, as were the multitudes of anonymous individuals who, by sending home encouraging letters and remittances, played a crucial part in stimulating and sustaining secondary migration.[33] But these individuals had their own limited agendas to fulfil. What was needed, the Canadian authorities decided, was a co-ordinated campaign to allow Canada to compete effectively with both the United States and the Antipodean colonies. Upper Canada led the way, appointing English settler Thomas Rolph as its first official agent in 1839 in an attempt to revive emigrant interest after the 1837 Rebellions. For three years, Rolph was employed as an itinerant agent in Britain, but the momentum was not sustained, and it was only in 1854 that the

Canadian legislature made its first budget grant toward immigration, mainly to support a publicity campaign in Britain.[34] Five years later, an information office was opened in Liverpool, then after Confederation the much higher profile given to agency work led to resident agents being stationed in various ports and other strategic towns throughout the British Isles, with their work co-ordinated and supervised from a head office in London.

The resident agents were the eyes and ears, as well as the mouthpieces, of the Ottawa-based immigration authorities, and it was largely on the basis of their reports and recommendations that the federal government decided overall migration strategy, then relied on the selfsame agents to implement its policies. They were carefully chosen with reference to local needs and connections. W. L. Griffith, who was sent from Manitoba to North Wales in 1897, was a Welsh-speaking native of Bangor, whose cousin controlled a syndicate of Welsh newspapers and was therefore most useful in the propaganda war; Henry Murray, appointed to Glasgow at the same time, had previously been a purser with a transatlantic shipping company; and John Maclennan, appointed to the new northern Scottish agency in 1907, was a Gaelic-speaking Canadian of Highland descent. The territorial agents were therefore generally either emigrants themselves, first-generation Canadians who had roots in the area to which they were sent, or men who had some specialist knowledge of emigration procedure.[35]

The biggest surge of activity—and spending—came between 1896 and 1906, when four million dollars were injected into the federal immigration budget in an attempt to boost prairie land settlement, through a heightened lecturing and publication campaign, as well as the continuing payment of commissions to shipping companies and booking agents. This initiative was largely the result of the concern of the Dominion government and the transcontinental railway companies to populate the vast western prairies, for reasons of, respectively, national unity and economic viability, although at the same time, it fuelled—and was also fuelled by—an upsurge of imperialist enthusiasm for Canada in late-Victorian Britain.

There was a huge network of booking agents across the country—almost two hundred in north-east Scotland alone by 1900, though not all were active.[36] They were responsible for organising lectures and interviews in their areas, and sometimes accompanied emigrant parties overseas themselves. But just as some booking agents could be dormant, newspapers—another key propaganda tool—could be both friend and foe. In north-east Scotland, the Liberal *Aberdeen Free Press* was given financial help from Ottawa with the publication of occasional special issues which advocated emigration, on the advice of the Dominion government's London-based Superintendent of Emigration that "there is no better friend to Canada than this newspaper."[37] The Conservative *Aberdeen Journal*, on the other hand, was condemned by the resident agent in the north of Scotland for having "poisoned the public mind" against Canada, in its attempt to dissuade farm servants from emigrating.[38]

By the 1920s, the Canadian Immigration Department was being urged by its field officers to modernise its literature and recruitment tactics in response to the increasing sophistication of would-be migrants. London-based J. Obed Smith, who had overall charge of agency work in Europe, warned his superiors in 1920 that recruitment tactics had not been modernised in response to the increasing sophistication of would-be emigrants.

> I should point out that the class of person seeking to go to Canada in these days in no sense is the same as in the early days of emigration. In the days of steerage passage on a passenger liner, sleeping and eating among the anchor chains and bilge water, the emigrant of those days sought relief and a living overseas as a forlorn hope. The reverse is now the case. Times have changed. Children have been educated and people live well in the British Isles, and, there being little or no destitution, Canada has to make her appeal to the best blood and sinew of the homeland in the cradle of the British race. An inquirer now is one who asks fifty questions, whereas an emigrant of years ago asked only one, and that was probably how much his ticket would cost.[39]

Not all agents were employees of the Canadian government or railway companies. Some were independent maverick operators, such as William Brown, captain of one of the Anchor Line's transatlantic steamships, who recruited over seven hundred emigrants from northeast Scotland to create a "Scotch Colony" in the depths of the New Brunswick forest in 1872.[40] Equally influential, in a different way, were those representatives of the late Victorian network of evangelical charity who channelled their efforts into setting up societies to promote the migration of vulnerable or disadvantaged groups, notably women and destitute children, in what became some of the most controversial aspects of the whole migration movement. The roll-call of philanthropic emigration agents included individuals like Dr Barnardo, Maria Rye, Ellen Joyce, William Quarrier, and William Booth of the Salvation Army, while the organisations that they directed have generated a wealth of archival material on both sides of the Atlantic, much of it reflecting the particular tensions inherent in the organised emigration of the disadvantaged.[41]

Sustaining a Trend: Personal Contacts and Emigrant Networking

Although agents, in various guises, clearly had a formative role in generating and shaping migration patterns, their impact was limited by the fact that most of them were not personally known to those whom they recruited. One of the main reasons that they were so successful, particularly in a Canadian context, was that their work was often underpinned by the more crucial encouragement—and sometimes the practical assistance—given to pioneer migrants by friends, relatives, and acquaintances. Correspondence, visits home, and remittances were the most potent mechanisms of personal persuasion. While some migrants asked for their letters to be published in the press as a general encouragement, correspondence more often remained unpublished, though it might well be passed around in the extended family and community and could thus act as a catalyst for secondary movement. In Aberdeenshire, for example, a substantial chain migration of farmers from the upper Deeside parish of Logie-Coldstone to southern Ontario, from the 1830s to the 1870s, was based largely on persistent personal encouragement in the pioneer migrants' letters, as well as an emphasis on farming opportunities, which were much better than the deteriorating prospects at home.[42] Farther down the same valley, in the parish of Aboyne, baker James Thompson's emigration to Canada in 1844 was followed twelve years later by that of his father and three other family members, after the pioneer emigrant had made enough money at his trade not only to fulfil his original ambition of purchasing a farm, but to pay the passages of his relatives who had fallen on difficult times at home.[43]

Care has to be exercised when using migrant letters as a source, since they tend to be biased toward recording success, and perhaps toward exaggerating achievements. Letter-writers who advocated secondary emigration were probably less prone to overstatement, as it would not be in their interests to paint misleading images and then have to cope later with the wrath or failure of a disillusioned or destitute migrant. But sometimes there was a hidden agenda, as in the case of John McBean, who went from the family farm in Nairn to Manitoba in 1902, and who, although he lived only until 1906, sent home at least seventy-four letters to his brother and sister during a three-and-a-half-year sojourn on the prairies. McBean had been led to migrate partly out of curiosity—he said he wanted to resolve conflicting accounts of Canada's prospects which were circulating in Scotland—and partly because he too was looking for greater independence and advancement than he could find in Scottish tenant farming, or in his bi-employment as an occasional journalist. His career in Manitoba was fraught with the problems of illness, accident, and insecure employment, and although in general he urged farmers to emigrate, at first he clearly tried to dissuade his brother Andrew from following his example, presumably fearful that he would become a millstone around the pioneer emigrant's neck. Until early 1905, he consistently argued that Andrew was not of a sufficiently resilient character to overcome the hardships of pioneering on a dreary, isolated prairie homestead, and when he changed his mind, it was simply because he needed his brother's money, rather than because of any new confidence in Andrew's ability or adaptability. Specifically, he wanted Andrew to go into partnership with him in the purchase of a farm which he could not afford to buy on his own, and plans for Andrew's emigration were well in hand when they were aborted by John's death in spring 1906.[44]

The Export of Ideas

While there were numerous practical mechanisms by which the Atlantic was bridged, no less important were the psychological ethnic anchors put down by migrants, and the ways in which those anchors facilitated their assimilation into an unfamiliar environment. There is a telling phrase in a novel by Frederick Niven in which an unwilling exile comforts himself and his family with the assertion, "We'll take Scotland with us—a kingdom of the mind."[45] Such an attitude was characteristic of many migrants who, while they certainly wanted to better themselves and their families, still needed the reassurance that they would not be abandoning all the familiar associations of home. For that reason, they sought destinations to which they believed their lifestyles and institutions could be most readily transplanted, and, for Scots in particular, Canada, with its long history of Scottish settlement, was an obvious choice, boasting not only relative proximity, good wages, and land in abundance, but "good living among kindred people, under the same flag."[46]

Among the institutions which migrants transplanted or sought to re-establish, the most prominent were usually the church, the school, and the ethnic association. Parent churches at home were generally willing to meet their responsibilities in terms of funding and man-power, as far as they were able. When in 1834 George Elmslie of Aberdeen was sent out to purchase land in southern Ontario on behalf of a group of fellow-townsmen, he was instructed not only to assess its farming potential, but also to ensure that church and school were within "reasonable distance," and within a year of the foundation of the Aberdonians' Bon Accord Township, St Andrew's church had opened in nearby Fergus. Thirty-two years later Charles Farquharson was persuaded to emigrate from Logie-Coldstone to Chatham at least partly because he had been reassured about the proximity of those two key institutions.[47] Similar priorities were evident in William Brown's Scotch Colony in Victoria County, New Brunswick. Within four years, four schools had been built, and thriving mutual instruction classes had been started in imitation of similar institutions at home. In 1878 a church was opened with the aid of a grant from the Colonial Committee of the Free Church of Scotland, and in 1896 the Scotch Colonists called as their minister the Reverend Gordon Pringle, a native of Aberdeenshire, who was to hold the charge for almost fifty-two years.[48]

Anchoring institutions could also be secular, non-intellectual, and charitable. Burns Night was the highlight of the social calendar in the Scotch Colony, as it was in many other places. Other mechanisms for cultural transfer included sporting and piping associations, St Andrew's societies and Caledonian clubs, and more localised bodies such as the Aberdeenshire, Kincardineshire and Banffshire Association of Winnipeg.[49] Some of these societies had both a charitable and a social purpose, a function for which the Scotch Colonists had cause to be grateful, when they fell on hard times during their first winter in Canada, and had to be rescued from looming destitution by a $100 donation from the St Andrew's Society in Saint John.[50]

The Way Ahead?

What should be the priorities of future research? Clearly there is a demand for migration studies at the popular and academic levels alike, some of which stems from the undying interest in "roots" generated by family history societies on both sides of the Atlantic. In academic circles, four Scottish universities are currently offering honours courses which focus either exclusively or partially on migration, and a similar trend is evident in Canada.[51] Since 1991 the Association of European Migration Institutions has provided a forum for various people with an interest in migration—academics, museum curators, archivists, and tourist officers—to share ideas and, in the case of the Ellis Island Museum and the Ulster American Folk Park, to develop a collaborative project to identify, interview, and build a database of migrants who returned to Ireland from the United States.[52] The North American Association of Migration Institutions, created in 1996 as an offshoot of the original association, should clearly play a key part in facilitating future research and the dissemination of information, in Canada as well as in the United States, perhaps by promoting neglected but crucial themes such as return migration, along with the influence of the invisible English, who formed up to 25 per cent of the total migrants to Canada in the nineteenth century and orchestrated the transformation of pre-Confederation Canada into an integral, integrated, and loyal part of the British Empire.[53]

Although migration is a theme which clearly lends itself to popular writing, it should not fall victim to populism, stereotyping, or the pitfalls of hidden agendas, whether in respect of contemporary official policy, statistics, and propaganda, or the disingenuous motives of modern commentators with a case to prove or an axe to grind. Some of the dangers of antiquarianism, one-dimensional myopia, and facile assumptions can be avoided by encouraging in research and publication as many sources and approaches as possible, and an increasing stock of rigorous, archivally based investigations over the last twenty years has done much to endow the subject with scholarly credibility. While the migration album will always remain incomplete, there is opportunity not only to sharpen the resolution of the existing pictures, but also to add a few new ones.

Notes

1. Charles Dilke, *Problems of Greater Britain*, vol. 1 (London, 1890), 26.
2. Robert Service, "The Younger Son," in *Collected Verse of Robert Service*, vol. 1 (London: Benn, 1960), 70.
3. N. H. Carrier and J. R. Jeffrey, *External Migration: A Study of the Available Statistics 1815–1950* (London: HMSO, 1953).

4. See, for instance, Marjory Harper, "Images of Canada in Early Emigrant Literature," *British Journal of Canadian Studies* 7, no. 1 (1992): 3–14.

5. Samuel Johnson, *A Journey to the Western Islands of Scotland*, ed. R. W. Chapman (Oxford: Oxford University Press, 1924), 87, 119. See also *Scots Magazine*, vol. 37 (Sept. 1775): 523, vol. 64 (Aug. 1802): 705–6; John Knox, *A View of the British Empire, more especially of Scotland; of some proposals for the improvement of that country, the extension of its fisheries and the relief of the people*, 3rd ed., 2 vols. (London, 1785); Parliamentary Papers 1802–3 (45) IV 1: Thomas Telford, *A Survey and Report of the Coasts and Central Highlands of Scotland* (1802); Parliamentary Papers 1802–3 (80) IV 29: Report from the Select Committee on the Survey of the Coasts etc of Scotland, Relating to Emigration; Alexander Irvine, *An Inquiry into the causes and effects of emigration from the Highlands* (Edinburgh, 1802).

6. H. J. M. Johnston, *British Emigration Policy, 1815–1830. 'Shovelling out Paupers'* (Oxford: Clarendon Press, 1972); E. G. Wakefield, *The Collected Works of Edward Gibbon Wakefield*, ed. M. Lloyd Prichard (London: Collins, 1968); Ged Martin, *Edward Gibbon Wakefield. Abductor and Mystagogue* (Edinburgh: Ann Barry, 1997).

7. Howard Malchow, *Population Pressures. Emigration and Government in Late Nineteenth Century Britain* (Palo Alto, Calif: Society for the Promotion of Science and Scholarship., 1979).

8. Stephen Constantine, ed., *Emigrants and Empire. British Settlement in the Dominions between the Wars* (Manchester: Manchester University Press, 1990).

9. Thomas Douglas, Earl of Selkirk, *Observations on the present state of the Highlands of Scotland, with a view of the causes and probable consequences of emigration* (London, 1805).

10. *Westminster Review*, vol. 6 (Oct. 1826), 342–73; *Hansard's Parliamentary Debates*, 6 April 1843, col. 522 (Charles Buller).

11. See, for instance, Peter Ross, *The Scot in America* (New York, 1896); John Murray Gibbon, *The Scot in Canada: A run through the Dominion* (Aberdeen, 1907).

12. E. A. Belcher and J. A. Williamson, *Migration within the Empire* (London: W. Collins, 1924); J. W. Gregory, *Human Migration and the Future. A Study of the Causes, Effects and Control of Emigration* (London: Seeley Service, 1928).

13. W. A. Carrothers, *Emigration from the British Isles, with Special Reference to the Development of the Overseas Dominions* (London: P. S. King & Son, 1929), viii, 273, 287–304.

14. Reg Whitaker, *Canadian Immigration Policy Since Confederation* (Ottawa:

Canadian Historical Association, 1991), 7, 12–14. I am indebted to Marilyn Barber of Carleton University for drawing my attention to this pamphlet, and for sharing with me her perceptions of Canadian attitudes toward immigration in the inter-war era.

15. Phillip Buckner, *English Canada—The Founding Generations: British Migration to British North America 1815–1865* (Canada House Lecture Series, no. 54, 1993), 11. See also Bruce S. Elliott, *Irish Migrants to the Canadas: A New Approach* (Kingston: McGill-Queen's University Press, 1988).

16. T. M. Devine, ed., *Scottish Emigration and Scottish Society* (Edinburgh: J. Donald Publishers, 1992), 2–3, 9.

17. In *English Canada*, Buckner demonstrates how British North America's imperial bonds were forged by unprecedented British migration in the period 1815–65.

18. Charlotte Erickson, *Invisible Immigrants: The Adaptation of English and Scottish Immigrants in Nineteenth-century America* (London: London School of Economics and Political Science; Weidenfeld and Nicolson, 1972); Charlotte Erickson, ed., *Emigration from Europe, 1815–1914: Select Documents* (London: A. and C. Black, 1976); Dudley Baines, *Emigration from Europe, 1815–1930* (Houndmills: Macmillan, 1991).

19. In Canada, the Multicultural History Society of Ontario has been instrumental in commissioning many such ethnic studies.

20. See, for instance, *The Witness*, 1840–63; Donald Macleod, *Gloomy Memories in the Highlands of Scotland* (Toronto, 1857); Alexander Mackenzie, *The History of the Highland Clearances* (Inverness, 1883).

21. Margaret I. Adam, "The Highland Emigration of 1770," *Scottish Historical Review* 16 (1919): 280–93; idem, "The Causes of the Highland Emigrations of 1783–1803," *Scottish Historical Review* 17 (1920): 73–89; idem, "The Eighteenth-Century Highland Landlords and the Poverty Problem," *Scottish Historical Review* 19 (1921): 1–20, 161–79.

22. Gordon Donaldson, *The Scots Overseas* (London: Hale, 1966).

23. Gordon Donaldson, *Scottish History and the Scottish Nation* (University of Edinburgh inaugural lecture no. 20, 4 May 1964), 14–15.

24. Ian Grimble, *The Trial of Patrick Sellar. The Tragedy of Highland Evictions* (London: Routledge and Kegan Paul, 1962); John Prebble, *The Highland Clearances* (London: Secker & Warburg, 1963); James Hunter, *The Making of the Crofting Community* (Edinburgh: Donald, 1976); Eric Richards, *A History of the Highland Clearances*, vol. I, *Agrarian Transformation and the Evictions* (London: Croom Helm, 1982); vol. 2, *Emigration, Protest, Reasons* (London: Croon Helm, 1985); J. M. Bumsted, *The People's Clearance. Highland Emigration to British North America, 1770–1815* (Edinburgh:

52. The AEMI website can be viewed on http://vip.cybercity.dk/~ccc13652/ info/info.htm. The Ellis Island oral history collection already contains several hundred interviews with immigrants who were processed at Ellis Island.

53. Buckner, *English Canada*, 13, 23.

Americans in Upper Canada, 1791–1812: "Late Loyalists" or Early Immigrants?

Peter Marshall

HISTORIANS OF THE FIRST YEARS OF UPPER CANADA FREQUENTLY, IF briefly, allude to "late Loyalists" but seem reluctant to define the term.[1] Clearly, it represents a mark of distinction from an earlier or original wave of arrivals, but the dividing line is not clear. It is tempting to ignore the question and apply the assertion of James J. Talman in his introduction to *Loyalist Narratives from Upper Canada*, in which, after setting out changes in the official definition of loyalism, he adds, "The subject is further confused by the use of the absurd term 'late Loyalist,' when undoubtedly 'post-Loyalist immigrant' or 'settler' is meant. If a man was 'late' he was not a Loyalist."[2] The unfortunate fact is that this judgment, delivered in 1946, has never before or since gained general acceptance. Historians have found it nearly impossible to make a clear-cut distinction between Loyalist and immigrant, perhaps owing to decades of legal and political argument over its applicability. To this day, the "late Loyalists" can be wished, but not declared, out of existence.[3]

Such is the case despite inroads made in recent years by scholars highly skilled—if that does not sound too ungracious—in scientific guess-work. Facts, figures, and phases relating to the population growth of Upper Canada are neither substantial in quantity nor consistent in detail, but the calculations of J. David Wood and Douglas McCalla appear reconcilable. Wood posits an American influx between 1780 and 1812 that can "be legitimately separated into Loyalists, 1780 to 1787 (by which time approximately 10,000 settlers had entered Upper Canada) and the so-called Late Loyalists"—referring to those who arrived between 1788 and 1812. During this period, the 1787 population had doubled by 1794 and would reach nearly 32,000 by 1800. In the years before the war, the growth rate diminished.[4] McCalla, compiling totals for "Loyalists, 'late-loyalists,' and ordinary pioneers," notes the arrival during 1784 and 1785 of some six thousand Loyalists of European background, and a population that more than doubles by 1791 and increases fourfold between 1785 and 1796. By 1805, it is "probably over 45,000," representing an average annual growth rate of more than 10 per cent, or four times what could be expected by natural increase. By 1811, the population numbered about sixty thousand inhabitants, of whom "a large majority (which included some whose original birth-place was in Britain or Europe) came from the United States."[5]

No attempt to distinguish between the numbers of Loyalists and those who, however described, arrived later from the south has yet been undertaken. As J. K. Johnson stresses in his analysis of the Upper Canadian House of Assembly, "the important distinction has been taken to be not where someone was born, nor even necessarily when, but when, and for what motive, that person came to Upper Canada. The essential point has been to distinguish between those who belong to a Loyalist group and others who belong to a Post-Loyalist American group."[6]

Since land acquisition and ownership depended on national status, which, in turn, determined political rights, recognition of Americans as Loyalists was a matter of major concern. Can the numbers involved be estimated? If it is assumed, arbitrarily, that "late Loyalist" applies to those who arrived between 1791 and 1800, and if we apply McCalla's estimate of an excess population increase over natural growth, it would appear that the population increase of twenty thousand in that decade was fuelled by the arrival of some seventeen thousand immigrants. Their origins were diverse. Some came from elsewhere in British North America, not all from outside the British Empire, and certainly not all from the United States. If the term "Late Loyalist" is applied to some fifteen thousand of these newcomers, an inexact but not wildly improbable total can be posited.

Numbers, however, constitute a relatively simple aspect of a larger, more complex problem. The emergence of the United States disrupted an empire with little experience in defining the means by which its subjects were added or lost. No concept of a nation-state to which inhabitants pledged allegiance yet applied when loyalty was a birthright, when the ownership of property was restricted to those thus qualified, and when only entry into office required the taking of the Oaths of Allegiance, Supremacy, and Abjuration. While it is essential to bear in mind Dr. A. F. Madden's observation that "uniformity was not confused with imperial unity after the 1770s. That was the lesson of American independence,"[7] it remains equally important to remember that lessons are often long in the learning. In Upper Canadian society, the principal problem was not reconciling diversity but accepting past claims.

After coming into being in 1791, Upper Canada had an essential need for population for settlement, quite apart from the creation of a new government. After 1783, peace brought the separation of a population. If those content to inhabit the United States were to be declared Americans, what were those unwilling to accept that allegiance to be called? What case would have to be made for them? How rapid a decision was required? In Canada, put to Haldimand and to Dorchester, these questions failed to obtain answers. Members of Loyalist regiments evacuated at the end of the war did not present a problem, but of many others it had to be asked, How late did you leave? How loyal had you been? The majority could claim to be natural-born British subjects and appeal to the Common Law ruling that nationality could not be shed or lost by the action either of the subject or of the Crown. But after the signing of the Treaty of Paris in September 1783, this would no longer hold good. Henceforth, in law, Americans were aliens and accordingly not entitled to own British land.[8] How would this affect their entry into Upper Canada?

Legally, imperial statute was the only recourse, providing one certain, if restricted, qualification for admission with full rights, and another, arguable. An Act of 1740 allowed the naturalization of aliens provided that they took the oath of allegiance and completed seven years' residence. But it could not have foreseen the situation of the pre-1783 American-born. In any case, land acquired by aliens before those conditions were met did not convey a valid title.[9] The second line of approach, derived from the Acts of 1731 and 1773, appeared more promising though it had not specifically come into being in anticipation of a North American problem. During the eighteenth century, British subjects living abroad, increasingly alarmed at their children's and grandchildren's potential loss of nationality, had secured legislation to prevent such a possibility. Could the same not apply to descendants of native-born subjects who had not left the United States by 1783? It was a question worth asking, but which would remain unanswered until 1824.[10]

This confusion may have resulted from unprecedented circumstances, but it was protracted by the need to populate the colony. The dilemma facing its government was so clear that any official response called for obscurity: how else could a society founded on a rejection of American government admit that its growth demanded the attracting of American immigrants, the only available and compatible source of capital, skills, and labour? If Upper Canada were to be settled, possessing a plough and knowing how to use it was altogether more desirable than was any proof of origins or of loyal activities during the Revolution. Such considerations accounted for the otherwise surprising view of the Tory Americanophobe John Graves Simcoe, the first Lieutenant Governor of Upper Canada.

Simcoe may not have led the way in encouraging recognition of late Loyalists, but he was the first to reward a migration that others had noted but could not direct. By 1788, Lillian Gates has concluded, Dorchester had been forced to prefer an increase in numbers to purity in politics: "In the end, the policy adopted seems to have been to grant land to all whom the term loyalist could be stretched to cover and to encourage the 'speedy settlement of the upper country with profitable subjects.'"[11]

On his arrival in 1792, Simcoe's "enthusiasms"—to borrow S. R. Mealing's term—distinguished him from his contemporaries and colleagues. He had assumed office determined to demonstrate that the British Empire in North America was not collapsing but would, given time and his leadership, outgrow a republican neighbour whose unwarranted aggression deserved humiliation. Mealing's most instructive essay appeared in 1958 and opened with the comment that it had been thirty-odd years since Canadians had written Simcoe's biography. Forty years later, unfortunately, the task still remains undone. Imperial Britain foisted on the world a superfluity of tedious representatives, many of whom later secured the biographers they deserved. Simcoe was not among them: his energies and personality commanded attention, though his judgments were far less assured. If he is seen only as English, it was in a fashion formed entirely in North America. Wartime service had left him with indelible memories, a grudging respect for individual Americans, and a loathing of the new nation's politics. When the Duc de La Rochefoucauld-Liancourt called at Simcoe's Niagara residence in 1795, a dinner led to an invitation to stay and extended conversations that markedly impressed a visitor to whom his qualities, both as a governor and personally, were evident: he was "actif, éclairé, juste, bon, ouvert. . . ." But La Rochefoucauld's praise was not unbounded. Simcoe hated the United States and was still obsessed with the war's failure. His guest experienced real discomfort as Simcoe, incapable of forgetting or forgiving, boasted of the number of houses he had burned before and would burn again if war resumed. Not that he wanted this to happen, of course. He, more than anyone, desired peace. It was just that he so hated the rebels . . .[12]

How did Simcoe envisage a *British* North America? By demonstrating an uncritically favourable disposition to its potential growth while remaining hostile to the land of his enemies. Outward appearances—those observed by La Rochefoucauld—were deceptive: Simcoe was something more than he seemed. As Mealing has put it, "If his Constitutional models for Upper Canada were avowedly British, his models of economic progress were basically American."[13] And, given an American working model, who better to operate it than American settlers? The only other labour force to hand was that of French Canada and, given that option, Americans were a seemingly unavoidable, but still worthwhile, risk. Nineteenth-century solutions had yet to be devised: slaves were inappropriate and too expensive, contract labour remained unknown. The days of Indians and Chinese supplied to order, destinations as required, were decades away. Simcoe really had no choice: if immigrants were required, he could have Americans—or nothing.

This held good for both Upper and Lower Canada. Identical proclamations, issued on 7 February 1792, stated the terms on which land would be made available. Grants were offered without distinction of nationality, and details were circulated through New England and the northern states. How could this be reconciled with an unrelenting mistrust of American intentions?

First, the enemy were reduced in number: this allowed them to be declared an unrepresentative group. The United States was seen to be filled with unwilling citizens desperate to escape a republican captivity and yearning for a return to old ways which, once regained, would never again be cast off. These assertions departed from reality but provided Simcoe with a necessary justification. In October 1792, he assumed responsibility, assisted by the new Council and seven land boards, for granting land certificates to incoming settlers who, taking an oath of allegiance, were advised that "tho' His Majesty's bounty is not restricted solely to his own subjects, yet it is not meant to be extended to such as have willfully resisted his Crown and Government, and who persist in principles and opinions which are hostile to the British Constitution."

How these subversive immigrants would be detected, and by whom, was not indicated. As it was, an opportunity dawned for those willing to follow, modestly, in the path of Henri IV: if Paris was worth a mass, 200 Upper Canadian acres justified an oath, "mumbled through or avoided altogether, if the settler so desired. For most immigrants it was a trivial formality that was performed in order to acquire property." Simcoe persuaded himself that, once started, population growth would come from elsewhere than the United States: he looked for sizeable arrivals from Europe, as well as many Loyalists who would seek refuge from the unbearable climate of New Brunswick.[14]

Simcoe's hopes of achieving increased numbers were partially fulfilled, though his conviction that communal unity would arise out of a mixture of newcomers proved quite unfounded. He had thought it possible to avoid too close an inquiry into the motives for American arrivals since, as Bruce G. Wilson has observed, he "believed in the centralization of political authority and in the vital role of the military in colonial government."[15] In fact, neither factor proved able to control the pattern of Upper Canadian development, a process that demanded practical deviations from conventional constitutional and legal provisions if *any* rapid and necessary growth was to be achieved.

Simcoe's grandiose ambitions, such as his vision of a Montreal that, "with the assistance of a few sluices," might dominate a waterway extending from Hudson Bay to the Gulf of Mexico, were accompanied by more modest aims: Upper Canada would control communications and commerce between the Eastern seaboard and Middle America and so link power and profit. However these prospects might be judged, their pronouncement served to distinguish the early years of Upper Canada from those of other fledgling colonies: gazing back anxiously at a mother-country from which all assistance must come, did not characterize Simcoe's outlook.

Accordingly, from these beginnings until 1812, Upper Canada remained an American community pursuing American ends. If its political structures were largely traditional, they marked an inheritance from the thirteen colonies, not the introduction of a new, imperial imposition. Partition had not transformed British North American institutions.

An estimate in 1812 of the Upper Canadian population's origins declared eight out of ten to be of American birth or descent. That this group comprised a numerical majority seems impossible to deny.[16] It is equally clear that Americans did not exercise any political influence proportionate to their numbers, though that growth served to arouse alarm. Whereas admitting new settlers to politics attracted little concern in the early 1790s, by 1795, the American presence supplied grounds for the House of Assembly to require that all non-British settlers reside seven years in the province before becoming eligible for election. Four years later, additional precautions appeared necessary after the defeat of Attorney-General Peter Russell in a by-election, allegedly by American votes. In consequence, the Assembly determined in 1800 that not only its members but also any electors who had ever lived in or sworn allegiance to the United States must have lived in Upper Canada for seven years. The aftermath of the Revolution continued to shape the government of the province.[17]

To present the major Upper Canadian problem as a conflict between established Loyalists and an encroaching majority American population would both unduly simplify and distort the events of these early years. Certainly, constant care was taken to prevent a Loyalist loss of control: as J. K. Johnson's analysis of the Assembly Members concludes, "Post Loyalist Americans . . . were largely excluded from anything more than the most basic, non-paying public offices."[18] But political power did not provide an economic living. That was seen to depend upon the securing and disposing of land. Yet legal title was not compatible with alien status. Confronted with this dilemma, as Garner concludes, "the economic self-interest of the old settlers had assuaged their misgivings as to the loyalty of the Americans."[19]

These conditions posed problems that proved as weighty for Loyalist proprietors as for recent immigrants. Fashioning a solution that would satisfy both sets of interests was not easily achieved. Development and settlement depended upon an effective use and transfer of land, but the entwined implications of legal title, alien status, and naturalization rendered the process uncertain. To remedy this situation, Loyalist recognition was bestowed long after its official September 1783 termination. This prolongation could enlist the flimsiest of excuses: as late as 1817, William Dickson, legislative councillor and owner of a Grand River township, disposed of his lands after administering, in his capacity as magistrate, the Oath of Allegiance to Americans.[20] This evaded rather than resolved an enduring legal problem. Widespread though the practice may have been, newcomers did not receive an assured property title: it was a situation that would persist and await challenge.

Before the War of 1812, Loyalists had kept a vigilant eye on the politics of American immigrants, "many of whom" were, in the July 1800 opinion of Solicitor-General Gray, "not altogether destitute of the democratical principles which prevail in that country nor is it always known whether their motives for coming into the Province are good or bad." The frequent expression of official fears of American intentions was echoed by similar alarm-raisings: shortly after his arrival, Lieutenant Governor Gore reported in 1806 that although some emigrants from the United States had "proved peaceable and Industrious settlers . . . there are a considerable number from that Country of a different description, who have come here adventurers, and have brought the very worst principles of their own Constitution along with them, and from what I have experienced even during my very short residence here, endeavour to oppose and perplex His Majesty's Government." Such feelings were not extinguished by the outbreak of war. It not only ensured that the residential qualification continued, but raised it to fourteen years for admission both to the House and to the franchise. It would not revert to the seven years' requirement until 1818.[21]

The significance of the War of 1812 in defining Upper Canadian allegiance seems exaggerated: the colony was not so much divided between Loyalists and Americans as trying to cope with the military demands of both sides. George Sheppard makes a convincing case in support of his assertions that "at the best of times Upper Canadians had shown themselves to be unwilling participants" and that "Upper Canadians had no strong attachment to either the United States or Great Britain."[22] It was not that the conflict remained unimportant, but rather that Upper Canadians, irrespective of their origins and attachments, were not impelled to proclaim an allegiance to either an Imperial or an American identity. Their interests were, quite literally, far more down to earth. If Loyalists laid claim to pre-eminence in holding land, such possession was pointless in the absence of settlers. Before 1812, only the United States could furnish a supply, welcome for farming skills, essential for capital resources, and compelling Loyalists to balance economic necessity against political prejudice. If the newcomers were more concerned with the cultivation of land than the promulgation of republican doctrine—and so the great majority proved to be—then an accommodation could be reached. That this did not continue indefinitely owed not to the course or consequences of war, but to changes in the structure and composition of the colony.

After 1815, a non-American minority set to work to convert Upper Canada into a British society to be governed by truly British leaders. In

1821, the victory in a by-election of Barnabas Bidwell, who had left Massachusetts, having played a prominent part in state politics after the Revolution, provided the opportunity for resolving the American issue. Government determined to exclude Bidwell—and subsequently his son—from the political scene: the Bidwells occupied centre stage in a major confrontation, dubbed the Alien Question, that might more accurately have been entitled the American Question.

Paul Romney's excellent analysis offers an essential account of a political struggle that masqueraded as a matter of law.[23] Almost forty years after the partition of North America, it became apparent that the territorial separation, crudely undertaken as it was, had received altogether more attention than had the need to distinguish between American citizens and British subjects. What was the new order? Was residence in the United States before 1783, or subsequent birth there to British-born parents, grounds to claim to be British after a seven-year residence in Canada? If this was not so, those who found themselves in such a situation could not buy or inherit lands, vote, or sit in the Assembly. Examining these questions, Romney finds that historians have "unanimously assumed that the provincial government was correct in its view that the mass of late Loyalists were aliens."[24] Any sense of relief that one point at issue is resolved proves unfounded: this conclusion is held to proceed from excessive reliance on government documents and must be declared erroneous.

In the event, legal status was subordinated to political considerations: the decision could not be left to the courts. Its resolution would require the major step of proclaiming the Britishness of Upper Canada. If Americans were prepared to accept incorporation, ways might be found to bring this about. But if this were done, Late Loyalists would have to become precisely that, in an Upper Canadian colony of British subjects, in which true Loyalists would occupy an honoured place and the rest of the population, pending their legal acceptance, would be classified as alien. Unfortunately, so clear-cut a distinction proved impossible to maintain, even by so vigorous a proponent as John Beverley Robinson, the Attorney General: "Forced to admit that the late Loyalists possessed an equitable claim to political as well as to property rights, Robinson conceded this was so only as a political matter, a subject for legislation not a judicial right. He continued to pronounce them to be aliens, who might be admitted into the Upper Canadian community as an act of grace but could claim no right to membership."[25] As is so often the case, the law, in the absence of imperial statutes, took its stand until the outright incompatibility of contemporary conditions and legal precedents became untenable.

Many years had to pass before the "late Loyalists" were to fade from view. The terms of the Treaty of Paris waited three decades for an examination of their relevance to American rights in Upper Canada and a further ten years elapsed before the legal process was concluded. That a topic as basic as the distinction to be drawn between birthright and admitted subjects, and that the role and rights of yet another category—the Alien—should be so long undetermined, reflects not so much provincial or imperial tardiness and indifference as a situation that, for all involved, was unprecedented.

Before 1783, no body of British subjects had successfully renounced their allegiance; no means of assessing the professions of those claiming to maintain their loyalty existed. Both the emergence of the United States and the formation of British North America after 1783 involved major changes that nevertheless fell far short of revolutionary upheaval. The partition of North America brought death, suffering, and displacement in full measure but was not accompanied by the instant creation of states defined to the last national symbol. The "Americans" of Upper Canada were fortunate in their time of arrival: they did not have to follow the Texan example and experience an Alamo at Niagara. Their loyalty was limited to land and, for the great majority, expressed, in benefit or failure, a far more tangible touchstone of allegiance than would have been displayed in the mere assertion of national bonds.

If Upper Canadians eschewed patriotic commitments during the War of 1812, so too did the Americans in their midst. Who can doubt that it was the best thing to do? The relatively short casualty lists testify to the fledgling nationalisms of two peoples whose connections and similarities were still far more substantial than their rivalries.

Notes

1. For example: "Many of the loyalists . . . had looked with disfavour on grants of land being made to 'late' loyalists," Lillian F. Gates, *Land Policies of Upper Canada* (Toronto: University of Toronto Press, 1968), 154; "One visitor noted that more recent arrivals, the so-called Late Loyalists," . . . George Sheppard, *Plunder, Profit, and Paroles* (Montreal and Kingston: McGill-Queen's University Press, 1994), 19–20.

2. *Loyalist Narratives from Upper Canada,* ed. James J. Talman (Toronto: Champlain Society, 1946), xxix–xxx.
3. Useful comment on this point is to be found in David T. Moorman, "Where are the English and the Americans in the Historiography of Upper Canada?" *Ontario History* 88 (1996): 65–69.
4. J. David Wood, "Population Change on an Agricultural Frontier: Upper Canada, 1796 to 1841," in Roger Hall, William Westfall, and Laurel Sefton MacDowell, eds., *Patterns of the Past* (Toronto: Dundurn Press, 1988), 59–61.
5. Douglas McCalla, *Planting the Province: The Economic History of Upper Canada 1784–1870* (Toronto: University of Toronto Press, 1993), 15–16, 31.
6. J. K. Johnson, *Becoming Prominent: Regional Leadership in Upper Canada, 1791–1841* (Kingston: McGill-Queens University Press, 1989), 6.
7. A. F. Madden, "1066, 1776 and All That: The Relevance of English Medieval Experience of 'Empire' to Later Imperial Constitutional Issues" in John E. Flint and Glyndwr Williams, eds., *Perspectives of Empire* (London: Longman, 1973), 19.
8. John Garner, *The Franchise and Politics in British North America 1755–1867* (Toronto: University of Toronto Press, 1969), 164.
9. Gates, *Land Policies,* 119–20.
10. Garner, *Franchise and Politics,* 164.
11. Gates, *Land Policies,* 19.
12. S. R. Mealing, "The Enthusiasms of John Grave Simcoe," in J. K. Johnson, ed., *Historical Essays on Upper Canada* (Toronto: McClelland and Stewart, 1975), 302–16; La Rochefoucauld-Liancourt, *Voyage dans les Etats-Unis d'Amérique* (Paris, 1797), vol. 2, 58–60.
13. S. R. Mealing, "John Graves Simcoe," in *Dictionary of Canadian Biography,* edited by F. G. Halpenny and J. Hamelin (Toronto: University of Toronto Press, 1983) vol. 5, 755.
14. Gates, *Land Policies,* 28–9; La Rochefoucauld, *Voyage.,* 44; Sheppard, *Plunder,* 17; Garner, *Franchise and Politics,* 165.
15. Bruce G. Wilson, *The Enterprises of Robert Hamilton: A Study of Wealth and Influence in Early Upper Canada, 1776–1812* (Ottawa: Carleton University Press, 1983), 109.
16. Mealing, "Enthusiasms of John Grave Simcoe," 305; Marcus Lee Hansen, *The Mingling of the Canadian and American Peoples* (New Haven: Yale University Press, 1940), 90.
17. Garner, *Franchise and Politics,* 86–8, 165.
18. Johnson, *Becoming Prominent,* 26.

19. Garner, *Franchise and Politics*, 167.
20. Ibid., 166.
21. Ibid., 86–7; Gore to William Windham, 1 October 1806, Canadian Archives *Report*, 1892 (Ottawa, 1893), 38.
22. Sheppard, *Plunder*, 82–3.
23. Paul Romney, "Reinventing Upper Canada: American Immigrants, Upper Canadian History, English Law and the Alien Question" in Hall et al., *Patterns of the Past*, 78–107.
24. Ibid., 99.
25. Patrick Brode, *Sir John Beverley Robinson: Bone and Sinew of the Compact* (Toronto: University of Toronto Press, 1984), 320.

The Myth of the Great Upper Canadian Emigration of 1838

Ronald Stagg

MONG THE MINOR MYTHS OF CANADIAN HISTORY IS THE STORY OF THE thousands of disenchanted inhabitants who fled Upper Canada following the failed rebellion of 1837. While not all of the works dealing with the aftermath of the rebellion address the subject of emigration, one book which describes large-scale emigration is a standard reference for information on the uprisings of 1837.

Early writings on the rebellion tended to take the emigration for granted and to concentrate instead on the border troubles precipitated by those fleeing Upper and Lower Canada. Charles Lindsey's biography of William Lyon Mackenzie, for instance, says merely that "there were refugees scattered all over the Union, from Maine to Florida."[1] The idea that this movement of people into the United States involved a very large number of individuals emerged in the 1930s. It was advanced first by R. S. Longley in 1936, in an article in the *Canadian Historical Review*. He maintained that while the exact number of those who left was impossible to determine, it amounted to at least several thousand.[2] E. C. Guillet, who produced what has become a standard source of information on the rebellion for students and general readers, went even further. In *The Life and Time of the Patriots*, published in 1938, he argued without references that the total was at least twenty-five thousand.[3]

From the time that these works were published until the 1980s, relatively few works focussed on the rebellion period. Where the question of emigration was addressed, as in Greg Keilty's "popular" history of the 1837 rebellions[4] and W.H. Graham's biography of William "Tiger" Dunlop,[5] the tendency was to accept Guillet's estimation. In the 1980s, two works on the post-rebellion period, one on military history by Mary Beacock Fryer[6] and one on William Lyon Mackenzie's life after the rebellion by Lillian F. Gates,[7] were silent on emigration. Only Colin Read, in his work on the rebellion in the London District, devoted a paragraph to examining population statistics for the rebel townships, and he concluded that large-scale emigration was highly unlikely.[8]

Twenty-five thousand refugees seeking the democratic freedom of the United States would have caused tremendous upheaval in Upper Canada, which had a population of about four hundred thousand. Given that large areas of the colony were anti-rebel or at least neutral,[9] these emigrants would likely have represented a small portion of the total. Such a huge exodus from only certain areas of Upper Canada would have left vast tracts of farmland unpopulated.

At first glance, considerable evidence seems to support such a possibility. Many writers of the day commented on the large numbers leaving for the United States. Guillet quotes Elijah Woodman, who wrote in his diary, "Many farmers have sold farms worth three thousand dollars for five hundred or a like proportion. West of the Mississippi there has been a large company formed of Canadians for the purchase of lands and large numbers have been flocking in." The Detroit *Free Press*, Guillet pointed out, mentioned that in one day "'twelve covered wagons, well filled and drawn by fine horses' had crossed the frontier at that point and similar emigrations were reported over many months at various other border localities."[10]

A March 1838 petition by John Van Arman from Lockport, New York, claimed that there were "thousands" in exile "of the most respectable and most loyal" citizens, driven away "by the lawless violence of an excited and unprincipled soldiery."[11] The Reverend John Roaf, of the Zion Congregational Church in Toronto, wrote in 1838,

> Some, too, of our warmest and most efficient friends are irrecoverably gone from the Province—many are leaving,—others have lost their situations; all are suffering from the overthrow of commercial business; while the spirit of the ascendant party and their laws is such as must depress and diminish the classes, within which we might have looked for attention and success.[12]

While this quotation points out that the depression of 1837–38, as well as unhappiness with the political situation, contributed to the desire to leave, it still supports the notion of mass emigration.

William T. Kennedy wrote to William Lyon Mackenzie in April of

1838 from Buffalo claiming, "The Canadians are flying here as thick as pigeons in the fall."[13] William Poole wrote Mackenzie from Lewiston, New York, in May of 1839 to say that most of his (former) neighbours were offering their homes for sale.[14] Another of Mackenzie's correspondents, M. A. Reynolds, wrote from Toronto in July 1838, "The whole system of oppression has been so severe that thousands are . . . flying as if it were a land of pestilence and famine."[15] Even George Arthur, the lieutenant governor, wrote in December of 1838, "The number of persons who have left the Province and gone to the States is astonishing."[16]

These and other similar writings from the period do seem to suggest a mass emigration. Statistical evidence, however, suggests otherwise, and strongly contradicts the estimate of at least twenty-five thousand. Guillet undoubtedly derived this figure from information taken from the writings of Charles Durand, an eccentric lawyer, who played a very peripheral role in the rebellion. In October of 1838, Durand wrote to Mackenzie, "Twenty-five thousand people of the best class have left the country this year."[17] Sixty years later, Durand incorporated this information into his autobiography,[18] no doubt providing the basis for Guillet to claim that at least that number had left.

Population statistics for the rebellion period contradict not only the Durand assertion, but also the assertion of others, such as Longley and writers of the 1838–39 period, that thousands fled. Using population statistics for the period 1836–39, from the Home and London Districts, the two most disaffected areas, and immigration statistics for the port of Quebec, where most immigrants of the period entered, a crude estimate of population shifts is possible. Collection of data at the time was not always carried out with the care used by later generations, and although it is impossible to know what percentage of the arrivals at Quebec moved on to Upper Canada, the evidence is nevertheless very convincing.

In 1836, 27,827 immigrants passed through the port of Quebec. A certain percentage would have gone on to Upper Canada. This immigration, plus natural increase, boosted the population of the Home District from 63,529 in about June 1836, to 68,390 in about June 1837. During 1837, 22,500 passed through Quebec, and the population rose to 69,885 by about June 1838. During the succeeding year, when most of the thousands would have left following the rebellion and during the recession, only 4,992 immigrants arrived at Quebec, yet by about June 1839, the population had increased to 71,109.[19] Population statistics are not available for Norfolk County and Oakland Township for 1838, but examination of the 1838 figures from the remaining counties in the London District, and the two townships in other districts involved in the London rising, together with the figures for 1839, gives a result similar to that in the Home District: an overall increase.

Population decreases in some townships of both districts were offset by increases in others, and decreases in most townships were very small. The largest decrease, save two, occurred in Norwich Township in the London District, which dropped by over 250 between 1836 and 1839. Two anomalies exist. Yarmouth Township in the London District lost almost 400 people in 1838 (down from 3,625 to 3,247), but regained almost all of this population by 1839, and had more adult males than in 1837, in a period when emigration should have been at its peak. York Township in the Home District seems to have lost about 800 inhabitants in 1839 (down to 3,701 from 4,513 in 1838). This figure, however, may have been a statistical error, since York Township had a population of 4,424 in 1837 and a population of 4,732 in 1840. The 800 people lost in 1839 had reappeared, along with a seemingly normal increase of over 200.

Adult males (over sixteen) would logically be among the largest group to go, since single men found it easiest to uproot themselves. Looking at changes in the Home District in the 1836–39 period, fifteen townships had slightly fewer adult males, while twenty, plus the City of Toronto, had more. For the townships which provided rebels in the London District, and for two other rebel townships, the records are incomplete, but six townships had slightly fewer adult males, and six had more males in 1839 than in 1838. The more complete figures for 1837 show that nine townships had fewer adult males in 1839 than in 1837, and seven showed an increase. The differences were mostly very small, with the largest change being an increase of one hundred and seventy in Brantford Township.

These figures strongly suggest that either the thousands of emigrants departed from less disaffected townships or, more likely, that the emigration was much less, more likely in the hundreds. Since the disaffected tended to be concentrated in certain areas, a few hundred leaving would give the impression of a much larger exodus given the small population of the township and a natural tendency to project a strong local movement of people onto the whole colony.

An analysis of what was written at the time also clashes with the idea of thousands leaving. Elijah Woodman, whom Guillet quoted, referred to the creation of the Mississippi Emigration Society by prominent Reformers, which sent agents to investigate possible sites for a colony. However, the plans came to nothing, and there were never "large numbers ... flocking in." The Detroit *Free Press* observation of twelve wagons crossing and Guillet's unsupported assertion that many more crossed later provide no factual basis for a mass migration. William Poole's comment that most of his former neighbours were offering their homes for sale was balanced by several writers who pointed out that, with the recession and so much property for sale, the price commanded was so low as to prevent most who wished to go from leaving.

While more may have wished to go to the United States, it was not economically feasible. William Proudfoot, writing from London in August 1838, noted,

> The discomfort in which the liberals have lived has produced a desire to leave the Country and go to the States. Indeed I scarcely know any one who would not remove if he could get his farm sold—The multitude of farms for sale and the fewness of the purchases has reduced the value of property one half at least.[20]

The editor of the Toronto *Commercial Herald*, in May 1838, made a very telling comment on the many stories of people leaving for the United States. Having received a letter stating that sixty to eighty people were emigrating every day through the port of Toronto, he went to the harbour to check. Upon investigation, he declared the departures to be "insignificant."[21]

Unhappiness with the anti-Reform climate following the uprisings of 1837 and despair over the poor state of the economy may have driven many to contemplate leaving. Numerous departures from very limited areas may have given the impression of a massive shift of population. Population statistics, however, do not support the claim that such a shift took place. While the idea of persecuted multitudes fleeing to freedom and hope in the southern republic is a romantic one and suitable fare for a myth, the reality seems to be more prosaic.

Notes

1. Charles Lindsey, *The Life and Times of Wm. Lyon Mackenzie*, vol. 2 (Toronto, 1862), 242.
2. R. S. Longley, "Emigration and the Crisis of 1837 in Upper Canada," *Canadian Historical Review* 17 (1936): 33–4.
3. E. C. Guillet, *The Lives and Times of the Patriots: An Account of the Rebellion*

in Upper Canada, 1837–1838, and the Patriot Agitation in the United States, 1837–1842 (Toronto: T. Nelson and Sons, 1938), 59.

4. William Lyon Mackenzie, *1837: Revolution in the Canadas*, edited by Greg Keilty (Toronto: NC Press, 1974), 224.
5. W. H. Graham, *The Tiger of Canada West* (Toronto: Clarke, Irwin, 1962), 173.
6. Mary Beacock Fryer, *Volunteers & Redcoats, Rebels and Raiders* (Toronto: Dundurn Press, 1987).
7. Lillian F. Gates, *After the Rebellion. The Later Years of William Lyon Mackenzie* (Toronto: Dundurn Press, 1988).
8. Colin Read, *The Rising in Western Upper Canada 1837-8: the Duncombe Revolt and After* (Toronto: University of Toronto Press, 1982), 160–1.
9. See Colin Read and Ronald J. Stagg, eds., *The Rebellion of 1837 in Upper Canada* (Toronto: Champlain Society and Ontario Heritage Foundation, 1985), for a discussion of the reaction to the rebellion in the various districts of Upper Canada.
10. E. C. Guillet, *Lives and Times*, 59.
11. National Archives of Canada, RG5 A1 Upper Canada Sundries. V. 189, pp. 105267–68. Petition for pardon of John Van Arnam, Lockport, New York, 22 March 1838.
12. Colonial Missionary Society Report, 1838 (London, 1838), 13.
13. Archives of Ontario, F37 (MS516) Series A-1-1, Mackenzie-Lindsey Papers, Mackenzie Correspondence, William T. Kennedy, Buffalo, to William Lyon Mackenzie, 10 April 1838.
14. Ibid., William Poole, Lewiston, to Mackenzie, 29 May 1839.
15. Ibid, M. A. Reynolds, Toronto, to Mackenzie, 24 July, 1838.
16. Sir George Arthur, *The Arthur Papers*, vol. 1, edited by C. R. Sanderson (Toronto: Toronto Public Libraries, 1957), 430.
17. Mackenzie Correspondence, Charles Durand, Buffalo, to Mackenzie, 10 October 1838.
18. Charles Durand, *Reminiscences of Charles Durand* (Toronto, 1897), 381.
19. Population statistics are found in the National Archives of Canada, RG5 B26. Vols. 2, 4: Journals of the Legislative Assembly of Upper Canada, 13th Parliament; 1st Session, Appendix; 3rd Session, Appendix, V. 1; 4th Session, Appendix, V. 1; 5th Session, Appendix V.1; C. P. Lucas (ed.) *Lord Durham's Report on the Affairs of British North America*, vol. 2, (Oxford, 1912), 243.
20. Archives of Ontario, F974 (MS54), Proudfoot Papers, Section 1, William Proudfoot, London, U.C., to an unidentified member of the Missionary Committee of the United Secession Church in Scotland, 18 August 1838.
21. *Commercial Herald*, Toronto, 17 May 1838.

Regional Patterns of English Immigration and Settlement in Upper Canada

Bruce S. Elliott*

IN 1958, THE DISTINGUISHED CANADIAN HISTORIAN ARTHUR R. M. LOWER, in discussing the national origins of nineteenth-century immigrants to Canada, contrasted the English with the Scots and the Irish. He described the English as "almost without feature and untraceable" and "hav[ing] little clan sense."[1] In characterizing them as invisible, he was referring to the kind of impressionistic literature that then typified the comparatively voluminous writing on the Scots in Canada[2] and the then mere handful of works on the Irish. The status of invisibility was nonetheless plausible enough. The English emigrant experience seemed not to have been punctuated with episodes of historical high drama, no *grands dérangements* to compare with the Acadian expulsions, the Highland Clearances, or the Great Potato Famine, or to give rise to an exile mythology.[3] This circumstance in turn encouraged assumptions of easy assimilation, or the mistaken idea that the English were the numerical majority with which other groups had to assimilate, and the English have continued to occupy little place in a growing literature on Canadian immigration and ethnic history that has tended to focus on more exotic groups.[4]

The resolution of this historical visibility problem lies as much in method as in attitude. The patterns of immigration and settlement and something of the economic and religious behaviour, if not experience, of the English need not remain a matter for conjecture. They can be

* The author wishes to thank the Social Sciences and Humanities Research Council of Canada and Carleton University for financial assistance during the research for his larger project on English emigration to British North America, of which this paper forms a part.

extrapolated by exploring the collective patterns encoded in routine documentation by the thousands of obscure individuals who left a momentary trace of their lives in emigration lists and port statistics, census returns, obituaries, gravestones, and land petitions. The materials were there all along, but the methods of the historical geographers and cliometricians were little employed by Canadian historians in 1958. Indeed, Lower's inclusion of a graph that he termed a "cowgram" in his *Canadians in the Making* that year was something of a novelty. This paper will make use of these sources and methods to trace the chronology and geography of English emigration to Upper Canada, now Ontario, the destination of the greatest numbers of nineteenth-century English immigrants to British North America.

We must first define what we mean by "English"—a term easily prone to misinterpretation, especially to confusion with the term "British," which seems to mean something more inclusive. By English, we mean those immigrants who were born in England, not elsewhere in Great Britain or the British Isles, nor in the United States or the antecedent American colonies, though of ultimate English descent. We therefore exclude the minority of American Loyalists of English ancestry, and the planters of eighteenth-century Nova Scotia, also of old New England descent. We exclude those born in Wales; though the published aggregates of the Canadian census in some contexts combined these two categories, the numbers of Welsh in Canada have always been very small and little affect the general patterns. For the purposes of this paper, the English will be those who were born in England and emigrated directly to Canada, or came after only a short sojourn elsewhere, along with their descendants. That understood, this paper will delineate the major areas of England from which emigrants came to Upper Canada before Confederation, explore how these patterns changed over time, and make an initial attempt to explain the changing regions of origin and the changing social composition of English immigration.

Why must we determine regional origins first, before probing the reasons for emigration? In studying emigration from old France to New France, Peter Moogk noted that push and pull factors—things that made life uncomfortable in the old country and preferable in the new— are insufficient to explain who emigrates and who does not. In the case of Irish emigration to Canada, for example, it has been established that those with the most reason could not afford to emigrate. Factors such as trade cycles, the impact of war, industrialization, and the agrarian revolution affected different localities and regions of the old world in different ways, to differing extents, and with varying chronologies, and impacted upon social classes differently. Hence the importance of discovering *where* emigrants came from and *when* before attempting to explain *why* they came.

The exploration of push and pull factors assumes that emigration was always an option, and a naturally occurring idea. Moogk points out that this was not so, and that of equal or even greater importance were *facilitating* factors: an event that kick-started emigration from an area, for example, or an emigrant-recruitment system, favourable publicity or information, and a physical means of reaching the new land and even of reaching a port of embarkation.[5] These last points might seem self-evident, but securing transport across the Atlantic from certain parts of the old world was not as easy as from others. Sometimes, as frequently for Scots in the eighteenth and early nineteenth centuries, the will to emigrate required banding together to hire a vessel to come and collect a group of emigrants from an obscure harbour in the Highlands or Islands.[6] For the English, it more commonly meant taking passage on mercantile carriers making regular cargo runs, hence the importance of pre-existing trade links for directing the flow of emigrant settlers.[7]

The immigration and settlement patterns of the English and Irish[8] in Upper Canada differed markedly in both chronological and spatial terms. Let us start with the numbers. Nearly two-thirds of the English who came to Canada before 1950 landed between the turn of the twentieth century and the onset of the Great Depression of the 1930s, arriving in Canada's great era of industrialization and settling mostly in urban areas, though some took up lands in the Prairie West. Half the Irish, by contrast, came during the 1830s and 1840s, and fully two-thirds of them before Confederation. Irish immigration was mostly a pre-Famine movement, whereas the English influx was mostly twentieth-century. English numbers before Confederation were much smaller than the Irish numbers, though the proportions reversed dramatically thereafter. About 300,000 English arrived before 1867, against some 850,000 Irish. Between 1900 and 1930, however, 1.6 million English arrived, but only 175,000 Irish.[9]

Of course, these are national figures, and many counties of rural Ontario received their English populations during the pre-Confederation period. In Ontario, the great increases in English numbers took place in two periods: the 1840s–50s (somewhat later than the main Irish influx) and the Laurier urban-industrial boom at the turn of the century. The focus here is on the neglected pre-Confederation period, when settlement was mostly rural and when the English constituted a minority in the Upper Canadian population. It is seldom appreciated that while the number of Irish-born in the province doubled during the 1840s, the number of English did also. Irish immigration began to drop off markedly by the mid-1850s. In the 1860s, the English registered a net increase of 10,000, while Irish numbers declined by nearly 40,000 due to emigration, reduced immigration, and the deaths of earlier immigrants. During the 1860s and 1870s, the numbers of people leaving Canada, mostly for the United States, exceeded the numbers arriving, but the English continued to make up a growing proportion of those who did come. Natives of Ireland and Scotland in the province declined by half between 1881 and 1901, whereas English numbers diminished only by one-seventh, with immigration accounting for much of the difference. The numbers of English-born equaled the Irish-born by 1881, and by the end of the century, the proportions had reversed, with the English clearly in the lead.

Let us now look at the geographical patterns of English settlement in the Confederation generation and contrast them with the patterns of Irish settlement already known.[10] The Irish (especially the Irish Protestants, who were by no means all from the north of Ireland), as the largest ethnic group in the province until very late in the nineteenth century, were almost everywhere, but most concentrated in eastern Upper Canada. East of Peterborough, the population was better than 60 per cent Irish, and around Ottawa many townships were more than 80 per cent Irish. The Irish accounted for a fifth to a half of the population in most of southwestern Ontario as well, though to a lesser extent along Lake Erie and in a few central counties (see map 1 in the appendix).

The English accounted for 60 per cent of the population almost nowhere, and, aside from a few shopkeepers and tradespeople scattered through the towns and villages, they were seldom encountered in eastern Upper Canada. Generally speaking, the proportion of English in the population increased as one headed west, with most counties of southwestern Upper Canada being 20 to 30 per cent English, but with the greatest concentration in the rural areas around Toronto (see map 2 in the appendix). Mapped at the township level,[11] the pattern becomes more complex, but there were no heavily English townships east of Kingston and, interestingly, few English in the new frontier townships in Bruce-Grey and Renfrew. The greatest concentrations were in the city

Table 1. Numbers of Foreign-born, 1842–1901

	English	Irish	Scottish	American	English %	Irish %	Scottish %	American %
1842	40,685	78,255	39,781	32,732	21	41	21	17
1852	82,699	175,963	75,811	43,732	22	47	20	10
1861	114,290	191,231	98,792	50,758	25	42	22	11
1871	124,062	153,000	90,807	43,406	30	37	22	10
1881	139,031	130,094	82,173	45,454	35	33	21	11
1901	120,600	68,094	49,881	44,175	43	24	18	16

Source: *Census of Canada.*

of London and in a band of rural townships east of Toronto in York, Ontario, and Durham counties, along the western half of the Lake Ontario shore from Cobourg and Port Hope to Toronto. Here, the English accounted in 1852 for 30 to 50 per cent of the foreign-born. Like the Irish, they lived mostly in rural areas, for they had arrived in a period when Upper Canada was an agricultural colony with its great period of industrialization still in the future.[12]

From where specifically did the English come? What social and economic niches had the immigrants occupied in the land from which they came? What impact might this have had upon where they settled? These questions are not easily answered. Virtually no passenger lists or records of immigrant arrivals in Canada survive for this period of the kind that have been analyzed so fruitfully by Charlotte Erickson and William Van Vugt in their studies of the English in the United States.[13] A number of sources do yield information about immigrant origins, though seldom do they include every immigrant, and all have limitations. Nonetheless, quantifying information about large numbers of immigrants found in different types of documents yields patterns that are comfortingly similar. This gives the historian some confidence that the patterns they trace were real. Three such sources will be discussed here: petitions for grants of land, obituaries in the province's Methodist press, and statistics on immigration collected at the port of Quebec and published in official reports and in the newspaper shipping columns.

Petitions for grants of land submitted by immigrant settlers tended more often than not to specify at least the county in England, Ireland, or Scotland from which the immigrant came. Stating at least the country was necessitated by official attempts to exclude American aliens after the War of 1812, and when asked for place of birth or origin, many immigrants tended to be more rather than less specific. This tendency was enhanced by the presence in Toronto of a number of private land agents who made a living from immigrants' lack of familiarity with governmental procedures. Some of these agents had standard forms of petitions printed up, including a space for place of origin, and simply filled in the blanks to fit the occasion. Petitions are a useful source especially for the pre-1826 period, when free land grants, subject only to the payment of certain administrative fees, were available to ordinary adult male settlers. After 1826, policies of Crown land sales generated documentation that is less useful for our purposes. This is the first limitation of this source that must be recognized.

There is also a marked geographical bias. Because of administrative decentralization, land petitions markedly over-represent settlers who located in the central parts of the province. Fortunately, our census analysis has revealed that it was here that most of the English took up residence. Much of the western part of the province was under Colonel Thomas Talbot's eccentric personal superintendence, which left a less substantial paper trail than did direct government supervision.[14] Much of eastern Upper Canada in the late 1810s and early 1820s was under military superintendence, which did leave records but few land petitions, most often just long lists of settlers who had completed their settlement duties, seldom specifying from where in England the few English came. As well, a number of new townships were the responsibility of District Land Boards from 1819 to 1825; this process, too, generated records, but again left no surviving land petitions.[15]

Nor do the limitations of the sources end here. Many settlers wanted to live in more settled areas, often near their friends, rather than in the frontier townships where land grants were available, and so they bought their farms from speculators or existing residents in the older townships. The geographical patterns of settlement already examined suggest that the English were more prone to this tendency than were the Irish. Fortunately, many of these settlers applied for land grants anyway, hoping to hold their granted lands as a speculation against the day when the inland push of settlement made them attractive to latecomers.

Reading through the hundreds of microfilm reels of land petitions at the National Archives of Canada is a daunting task that heretofore has deterred historians and geographers from the effort. Fortunately, a knowledge of the administrative records enables us to take a couple of short-cuts. In some years, the minute books which recorded the decisions of the Executive Council Land Committee (the so-called Upper Canada Land Books) noted the immigrants' counties of origin as stated in the petitions.[16] Warrant registers summarize the same information in more convenient tabular form for some additional years.[17] Finally, the Crown Lands Office preserved a register of oaths of allegiance sworn by visitors to the office, which again in some years recorded counties of origin.[18] The oaths registers are especially useful for 1817–18, when no handy summary of the petitions exists that notes origins. The results are displayed in table 2.

Of the nearly three-quarters of English applicants who stated a county of origin, nearly a third were from Yorkshire and nearly half from Yorkshire and the four counties lying between it and the Scottish

Table 2. Origins of English Immigrants to Upper Canada from Oaths of Allegiance and Land Grants

	Oaths 1817–18	Land grants 1819–22
Number of English	233	581
Of these, stating county	104 (44.6%)	424 (73%)
Of these, from Yorkshire	31 (29.8%)	130 (30.7%)
From Yorkshire and four other northern counties	42 (40.7%)	200 (47%)

Source: Oaths of allegiance sworn in the Executive Council Office 17 March 1817 to 9 October 1818; land petitions 1819–22. See notes to text.

border, a strongly northern preponderance, which will be discussed at greater length below.

Another source that customarily notes at least the county of emigrants' birth within England is the obituary columns of the province's Methodist newspapers. Many of these have been abstracted and indexed by the Reverend Donald McKenzie of Ottawa. An analysis of the origins of pious laymen and laywomen contained in the *Christian Guardian*, the weekly published by the Wesleyans, the province's largest Methodist denomination, and the *Canada Christian Advocate*, the paper of the Episcopal Methodists,[19] evidences a pattern similar to that revealed by the land petitions and oaths of allegiance (see map 3 in the appendix). Over one-third of the Methodists commemorated came from Yorkshire and adjoining Lincolnshire, and 10 per cent from other northern counties (Northumberland, Cumberland and Lancashire). Another fifth originated in distant Devon and Cornwall in the extreme southwest. In all, the majority came from highland areas of the far north and west. The West Country had not been especially prominent as an origin amongst the pre-1826 land petitioners, but the obituaries carry our pool of immigrants into the Confederation years and, as we shall see, West Country immigration largely postdated the government's switch to a land sales policy.

There are, of course, biases in this data source, too, for these are Methodist obituaries and the northern and southwestern English counties were hotbeds of Methodism. One might suspect that the data reflect the English distribution of Methodism more than the Canadian distribution of the English, but other strongly Methodist counties are barely represented, and I have omitted from my statistics the newspapers of

**Table 3. Origins of English Immigrants in
Ontario Methodist Obituaries, 1836–70**

Yorkshire	214	29%
Cornwall	75	10%
Devon	54	7%
Lincolnshire	47	6%
London	35	5%
Lancashire	29	4%
Northumberland	28	4%
Cumberland	21	3%
Kent	20	3%
Fewer than 20	223	30%
TOTAL	746	

Source: *Christian Guardian*, 1836–70, and
Canada Christian Advocate, 1845–57, from
abstracts edited by Donald A. McKenzie.

the Methodist denominations that were most strongly regional: the Bible Christians who originated in Devon and were represented most strongly in the south west, and the Primitives, who were over-represented in the north.[20] Had they been included, however, they would merely have strengthened the already evident pattern.

Though departure and arrival statistics did not specify the local or county origins of immigrants, we know the numbers who arrived at Quebec on each vessel, and their ports of sailing are at least suggestive of the parts of England whence the immigrants came. Passenger lists, unfortunately, do not survive for the port of Quebec until 1865, too late to be of use in this study. Statistics were compiled by customs officials at the ports of departure from 1825 onward, however, for publication in Parliamentary papers, and the *Quebec Gazette* always recorded the names of cabin passengers and the numbers in steerage arriving on each inbound vessel, specifying the port whence the vessel had come. I compiled my tables from data in the newspaper directly before 1825; thereafter, I drew upon the figures compiled for the British Parliament by the official emigrant agent at Quebec who used the same source as the press, the now-vanished harbour master's books.[21]

This material is more comprehensive of immigrant numbers than is either of the sources considered heretofore, but the port statistics, too, are not without their problems. Until 1863, cabin passengers were omitted from the official statistics since many were merchants making periodic buying trips, or government officials, clergy, and army officers and their families coming out to the colonies temporarily.[22] Some in these categories were emigrants nonetheless: half-pay officers bringing out their families to take up military land grants, or prosperous gentlemen and manufacturers venturing their capital in British North America. Local historians can pick out specific examples of these amongst the cabin passengers' names recorded in the newspaper shipping columns, but at a general level, we cannot distinguish the immigrant from the transient. The consequence is that the statistics considered here relate to steerage passengers, who were presumed to have been emigrants; indeed, the newspapers frequently referred to them as "settlers."

A second problem is that while these statistics may approximate the number of immigrants who landed at Quebec (or Montreal after reporting at Quebec), this number is not the same as the number of immigrants who *settled* in Upper Canada. Some, though a minority, took up residence in the Lower province, and a very small number proceeded eastward to the Maritime colonies. Others no doubt went on to the United States. We know that before the late 1840s, more Irish emigrated to Boston via New Brunswick than arrived there directly from Ireland, and it was estimated that (in some years) up to 60 per cent of the Irish landing at Quebec went on to the United States.[23]

Contemporary commentary, however, remarked little about English arriving at Quebec en route to the American states. Rather, the literature from the period suggests that many English who possessed any kind of means tended to sail to New York City and then travel north to Upper Canada via the Hudson River and the Erie Canal, and across Lake Ontario. Given that the English concentration within Upper Canada was westward, this route made more sense for the English than it did for many of the Irish who were emigrating to join relatives and friends in the eastern counties of the province. The Quebec route was cheaper, but the New York route was accounted more comfortable. Such were the numbers of British immigrants coming in off the street to seek directions to Upper Canada by the early 1830s that James Buchanan, the British trade representative in New York City, wrote home repeatedly asking for an assistant to relieve him of the burden.[24]

The use of the New York route plays havoc with the immigration statistics, as only broad estimates are available of the numbers crossing into Upper Canada from the States, and these do not distinguish the ethnic groups. For more closely detailed study, however, the New York route has an advantage in the survival of the American arrivals lists.

Charlotte Erickson has pointed out the inadequacies of ethnic reporting in the statistics derived contemporaneously from the New York lists;[25] the original manuscripts themselves, moreover, underestimate those bound for Canada. The more carefully compiled lists state "Canada" or "Upper Canada" or a town therein in the column for destination, but many harried officials simply wrote "U. States" at the top of the column and ran a line down to the bottom of the page. Many of the passengers were bound for Canada nonetheless, as detailed searches for specific settlers reveal.[26]

A third problem with the port statistics is that they become less useful for regionalizing origins by the 1840s, when the proliferation of railways and coastal steamers in the United Kingdom made it easier for emigrants to travel to the larger ports (especially Liverpool) while the ever-larger ocean-going vessels that could not negotiate the smaller harbours and estuaries concentrated sailings in these larger ports. Before the 1840s, however, we can assume with a fair degree of confidence that people sailing from ports at the extremities of the country came from their local or regional hinterlands. Even after that, those sailing from minor ports such as Fowey or Truro are unlikely to have been other than local people.

In sum, the statistics are far from exact and reveal general trends rather than absolute conclusions. Nonetheless, the general patterns of origin emerging from the Quebec arrival data accord well with the evidence gleaned from land records and obituaries.[27] They have the added advantage of allowing a more precise dating of shifts in regional patterns of origin. What do these statistics tell us?

In the ten years following the Napoleonic Wars (1815–24), some 10,000 settlers from English ports arrived at the port of Quebec, but their numbers were overshadowed by twice as many Scots and four-and-a-half times as many Irish. The Scots dominated at first, accounting for one-third to one-half of immigrants up to 1821, continuing the eighteenth-century tradition of settlement in Glengarry County, supplemented by some government-assisted schemes and chain migration.[28] But by 1822, 80 per cent of those arriving at Quebec had sailed from Irish ports. The English accounted for one-fifth to one-quarter of arrivals before 1820, but thereafter their numbers fell below 10 per cent, accounting for a few hundred arrivals a year compared to an Irish influx of 5,000 to 10,000. Evidently, a flurry of English interest was sparked in the years of economic disruption immediately following the wars, but by 1820 this interest declined, while Irish interest remained

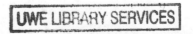

Table 4. Quebec arrivals by Country of Departure, 1815–24

	Quebec arrivals	Irish arrivals	%	English arrivals	%	Other, mostly Scottish	%
1815		25		68			
1816	1,250	238	19.0	277	22.2	735	58.8
1817	6,796	2,218	32.6	1,614	23.7	2,964	43.6
1818	8,543	4,599	53.8	1,616	18.9	2,328	27.3
1819	12,809	5,971	46.6	2,438	19.0	4,400	34.4
1820	11,239	5,580	49.6	1,002	8.9	4,657	41.4
1821	9,591	4,041	42.1	971	10.1	4,579	47.7
1822	10,468	8,374	80.0	521	5.0	1,573	15.0
1823	10,258	8,413	82.0	1,005	9.8	840	8.2
1824	6,515	5,168	79.3	317	4.9	1,030	15.8
Total	77,469	44,627	57.6	9,829	12.7	23,013	29.7

Sources: Totals by A.C. Buchanan from harbour-master's registers; Irish calculated by W. F. Adams from *Quebec Mercury*; English calculated from *Quebec Gazette*; Scottish and other approximated by subtraction.

strong. English interest waned as the postwar depression eased, to be reawakened as the English economy deteriorated again at the beginning of the 1830s.

In this first decade, moreover, an important regional concentration is clear: more than half the English passengers sailed from northern ports (see table 5), with a quarter of all steerage passengers embarking at Kingston-upon-Hull, in Yorkshire. During the period 1825–29, when English interest in general declined, 71 per cent sailed from northern ports, with Hull accounting for nearly half the total departures, three times as many as from Liverpool. Cumbrian ports accounted for another 16 per cent.

In terms of regional origins, a dual pattern of emigration seems clear, with the larger proportion of emigrants coming from northern districts within England that had an established tradition of transatlantic migration. The last period of heavy emigration from England had occurred before the American and French Wars, in the early 1770s. Bernard Bailyn's study of emigration to the old British North American empire just prior to the American Revolution, using an unusual Customs register dating from that period, traced what he termed provincial and metropolitan streams, the emigrants being of two types. Young single males took passage on merchant vessels out of London for economic opportunities, mostly in the shipyards and frontier iron industry of the old middle colonies (New Jersey, Pennsylvania, and Maryland). These emigrants, sailing primarily from London if not always originating there, constituted the metropolitan stream. The parties sailing from provincial ports were mostly farming families from the north of England or Scotland who banded together and hired vessels to take them to frontier lands at the northern and southern extremities of the pre-revolutionary colonies: the Carolinas, the Mohawk Valley of New York, and the Maritimes.[29] In the latter, at a distance from the more numerous Scots, a large emigration from rural Yorkshire took root in the Chignecto region at the head of the Bay of Fundy, around Amherst, Sackville, and Dorchester, where New Brunswick and Nova Scotia now meet.[30] They had been recruited by the governor himself, Michael Francklin, to settle speculative holdings that he had acquired there, though many took up land elsewhere in the region rather than on his estate.[31] Some families maintained contact with relatives in their home area over the ensuing years, and this proved more important in reviving emigration to Chignecto after the wars than emigration promotion, which bounded onto the bandwagon after large-scale emigration had recommenced.[32]

Table 5. Emigration to Quebec and Montreal from English Ports, 1815–54

	1815–19	1820–24	1825–29	1830–34	1835–39	1840–44	1845–49	1850–54	TOTAL
North	3,218 54.2%	2,012 52.7%	2,961 70.9%	16,569 38.0%	2,681 10.1%	3,177 9.7%	2,775 4.4%	4,964 9.1%	38,357 16.0%
West	334 5.6%	216 5.7%	40 1.0%	5,580 12.8%	1,275 4.8%	5,979 18.2%	10,134 16.2%	11,604 21.3%	35,162 15.0%
London/ Home	1,004 16.9%	491 12.9%	474 11.4%	7,952 18.2%	3,692 13.9%	3,711 11.3%	4,765 7.6%	2,841 5.2%	24,930 11.0%
Liverpool	1,195 20.1%	722 18.9%	651 15.6%	6,730 15.4%	7,970 30.0%	16,933 51.5%	42,768 68.4%	32,150 59.0%	109,119 47.0%
Welsh Borders	92 1.5%	220 5.8%	45 1.1%	3,047 7.0%	3,913 14.7%	1,386 4.2%	549 0.9%	1,213 2.2%	10,465 4.5%
East Anglia	8 0.1%	0	0	2,119 4.9%	5,657 21.3%	171 0.5%	0	0	7,955 3.4%
South-east	88 1.5%	155 4.1%	5 0.1%	1,660 3.8%	1,353 5.1%	1,545 4.7%	1,579 2.5%	1,763 3.2%	8,148 3.5%
TOTAL	5,939 99.9%	3,816 100%	4,176 100%	43,657 100%	26,541 99.9%	32,902 100%	62,570 100%	54,535 100%	234,136 100%

Sources: *Quebec Gazette*, 1815–30, 1841–43; Colonial Land & Emigration Commissioners, *Reports*, Irish University Press British Parliamentary Sessional Papers, *Emigration* 19: 295, 20: 203 (1831–40); 21: 400–1 (1844–54). Bristol 1836 corrected from IUP *Colonies Canada*, 1836: 7; Lynn corrected from *Quebec Gazette*.

The 1810s and 1820s saw a revival of Yorkshire emigration to this traditional region of Yorkshire settlement on either side of the New Brunswick–Nova Scotia border, and an extension of the receiving area from the traditional Bay of Fundy heartland, briefly, to nearby Prince Edward Island as it became clear that little land was available for new settlers in Chignecto.[33] Hull had been heavily involved in the Baltic timber trade and had become a major carrier of North American wood after Napoleon's wartime blockade cut off Britain's Baltic supplies. By the end of the war, significant numbers of Hull vessels were therefore bound for Quebec as well as for Saint John and Dorchester. Yet after 1822, Yorkshire emigration to the Maritimes virtually ceased.[34] The Quebec voyages had facilitated the diversion of the northern emigration stream to greater opportunities in Upper Canada.

Where specifically did these north-of-England emigrants settle? The first two Hull vessels to carry emigrants to the port of Quebec after the wars, in 1816, were the *Fame* and the *Nancy*. Thanks to the survival of a detailed register of settlers kept by a military administrator, we know that half these ships' passengers located initially in the Perth Military Settlement, but most stayed only a year or two and then moved on, and few of the north of England settlers arriving in later years went to Perth.[35] Where did they go? Nothing in the press or in the government agent's reports suggests that many located in Lower Canada. However, a York (Toronto) newspaper of 1830 stated that though four-sevenths of immigrants at Quebec were Irish, nine-tenths of those reaching York were English, "from Yorkshire chiefly . . . farmers or farming labourers of the better class. . . . Some proceeded to the head of the Lake, and some to the Canada Company's tract, but far the greater proportion remained in this town . . . while some have proceeded to join friends previously settled in the country—towards Newmarket, Whitby, Toronto [Township], Esquesing, Yonge St. &c."[36] The Yorkshire settlers had found a new York, the one that is now Toronto.

This impressionistic account is confirmed by other sources. Yorkshire accounts for about a third (33.4%) of all English places of origin noted on gravestones in Halton, Peel, and York counties, while the other northern counties account for another fifth (see map 4 in the appendix).[37] Yorkshire is also far and away the most common place of origin given in individual biographies in the second biographical volume of C. Blackett Robinson's *History of Toronto and County of York Ontario* (Toronto, 1885). Moreover, 1832 was the most common year of arrival for these settlers. Because the free grant period was by then over, many worked in the city for several years before buying farms in the county, as the biographies recount. We can also trace the movement in the genealogical sections of more recent local histories for the counties and townships around and north of Toronto, as many families from Yorkshire migrated further north from their original locations over the next couple of generations.[38]

The second major contributor to the early English population of the province was the West Country. Several firms of Devon shipowners and timber importers brought growing numbers of West Country settlers to Quebec and also to Prince Edward Island, where they had shipyards as well as timber contracts. Most of the West Country immigrants arrived after 1830, though emigration from Devon and Cornwall began immediately following the wars, mostly out of Plymouth, with some 400 passengers landing at Quebec in the first ten years and 200 in Prince Edward Island. In the late 1820s, only 69 West Country settlers landed at Quebec and 94 in Prince Edward Island, but the early 1830s saw a surge in English immigration, with 4,600 West Country settlers disembarking at Quebec and another 800 on the Island. By then, Bideford interests had overtaken Plymouth by a two-to-one margin in the Island trade, but at Quebec, only 2 per cent of the West Country immigrants in this period sailed from there. Plymouth remained the port of choice for central Canada, though some small West Country havens like Padstow and Truro, and the packetship port of Falmouth, contributed a quarter of the numbers from 1830 to 1834. Small ports accounted for half the West Country movement of the late 1840s and a quarter of that of the early 1850s, when Bideford finally assumed some minor significance in the Quebec trade.[39] The 4,600 who landed at Quebec in the early 1830s pales beside the 20,000 who landed in the 1845–54 period, bucking a general trend by emigrating from small harbours as well as from Plymouth in an era when passenger traffic was centralizing in the largest English ports. In part, this was because local shipping concerns with interests in British North America provided ready conveyance from nearby ports, and in part because the railway arrived late in the West Country, as Cornwall was not connected to the national network until 1859.

Why were so many emigrants from Devon and Cornwall? The stereotype of West Country emigrants created by authors writing on American immigration, such as A.L. Rowse and John Rowe,[40] is of unemployed Cornish tin miners emigrating to hard-rock mining opportunities in the new world. Though some Cornish miners found work at Bruce Mines in the 1850s and at Silver Islet near Thunder Bay in the 1870s, their numbers were small and their very presence owed much to the larger communities of Cornish hard-rock men in the mineral areas of Michigan and Wisconsin.[41]

The vast majority of West Country settlers in Upper Canada did not come from mining areas, nor were they miners. They were mostly farmers and farm labourers from north Devon and northeastern Cornwall,[42] the part of Cornwall where the place names are Anglo-Saxon rather than Cornish.[43] Whether the emigrants themselves can be considered Cornish in any real ethnic sense, I shall argue in another work.[44] Assistant Poor Law Commissioner C. P. Villiers informed Parliament that the availability of ports close at hand and the opportunity provided by local timber importers' vessels from 1829 onward made it easy to go out, and because the farmers went, the labourers and poorer people were not as suspicious of the motivations of those encouraging emigration as they were elsewhere.[45]

The West Country immigrants were important. They accounted for the greatest regional concentration of English in Upper Canada, the preponderance along the western half of the Lake Ontario shore between Port Hope and Toronto. Nine townships in the area were each home to more than 1,000 English-born in 1852, with only Brantford Township and four of the five urban areas (Toronto, Kingston, Hamilton, and London) accommodating more. The foreign-born were 56 per cent English in Darlington, 47 per cent in Whitby, 41 per cent in Hope, and 34 per cent in Clarke, the majority in each case West Country people. Their settlement area overlapped the Yorkshire heartland, which was generally closer to Toronto since many from the north of England had arrived earlier.

How did West Country people manage to settle on the Lake Ontario front in such numbers as late as the 1830s and 1840s? Robert Gourlay, in his 1822 *Statistical Account of Upper Canada,* recounted that "this district [Newcastle] has, like the last [Home], been made the spoil of power, and large blocks of unoccupied land everywhere hem in and distress the industrious settlers. It contains excellent land, finely watered."[46] The land between Cobourg and Toronto had largely been granted away to army officers, Toronto Compact families, and Loyalists in the 1790s, and had since been held for speculation. The area therefore became attractive once free grants were abolished in 1826. Not only were the townships well-watered, but the climate was mild enough to allow the

cultivation of fall wheat, with fields planted in fall and spring har-
vested in succession with the same scarce labour resources.[47] By 1852,
the English settlers here were faring better economically than were the
Irish who had settled a decade or two earlier, for reasons of government
encouragement and proximity to the port of entry, on poorer lands in
eastern Ontario.

By the early 1830s, West Country people were also settling in the
Huron Tract around the later village of Exeter (named for the county
town of Devon), where a Devon emigrant was made the Canada
Company's agent for Usborne Township in 1835.[48] Until the late 1840s,
larger numbers settled, at least temporarily, in the more familiar and
accessible Lake Ontario townships around Darlington. In the 1850s,
however, farmland in the newer townships of Huron and Perth counties became the bigger draw. West Country settlers also located outside
these major concentrations, and did not cluster to the same degree as
the Tipperary Protestants from southern Ireland, whom I studied a
decade ago.[49]

The 1830s saw the opening of the floodgates to English immigration, and the West Country exodus was only a part of this increase. In
England, prolonged commercial and agricultural depression and the
attendant social and political strife, especially underemployment of
farm labour in grain-growing counties, led to a widening of the emigration net to parts of England previously untouched and the arrival of
much poorer emigrants than before. The year 1831 saw a great increase
in immigration generally, and arrivals from England exceeded the numbers that had sailed thence during the entire previous decade. The
government's newly appointed agent at Quebec, A. C. Buchanan, reported that "a large proportion were possessed of considerable property, particularly those from Yorkshire and Cumberland," and estimated
that £250,000 in capital had been brought into the colony that year. One
Quebec shopkeeper was reported to have taken in 18,000 gold sover-
eigns. But emigration was increasing from all parts of the kingdom
with "vast numbers . . . from counties that hitherto were not in the habit
of sending any." Arrivals from the north dropped from 71 to 25 per cent
of the total, and the proportion departing London and the Home Counties doubled to a quarter of the sum, with another third coming from
the southeast, the West Country and Bristol, which hitherto had sent
negligible numbers. Over 1,000 arrived from East Anglian ports whence
none had sailed in the previous five years.

The influx, which caught Canadian authorities unprepared, was partly the result of efforts by landowners and parish vestries to reduce the poor rates that fell heavily on local proprietors by providing their paupers with a passage to North America. During the 1830s, assisted pauper emigration was more significant amongst English emigrants than amongst the much larger numbers of Irish arrivals, because until 1838, England had a Poor Law and Ireland did not.[50] The population of Toronto experienced considerable difficulty caring for these poor people and finding them employment or lands, especially in 1831–33. By the end of the decade, emigration societies, private charities, and a Toronto House of Industry were in place to cope with the continuing influx. In 1836, the heaviest year for pauper immigration, Governor Sir Francis Bond Head (who the year before had been the Assistant Poor Law Commissioner in Kent[51]) lamented that "instead of the English yeoman arriving with his capital, its mechanics in groups are escaping in every direction."[52]

It has been assumed that assisted pauper emigration began with the provisions of the Poor Law Amendment Act of 1834 that permitted parishes to borrow against the security of the rates for emigration purposes. In fact, the utilitarians in government were attempting to facilitate and regulate a practice that was already widespread. The advantage to the historian of the bureaucratic controls put in place by the Poor Law Commissioners is that they generated lists and statistics that enable us to quantify and regionally identify the movement with more precision after 1834 than before. Unfortunately, the statistics are incomplete, for the Commissioners were not interested in parishes that raised their emigration funds by private subscription, as many continued to do.

From the Commissioners' statistics and from the more impressionistic earlier evidence contained in government reports, newspaper accounts, and publications of emigrant letters by interested parties, we can identify the three major areas from which the assisted emigrants came. A first notable concentration was in deteriorating industrial areas in west Wiltshire and the adjoining cloth-making town of Frome in Somerset, marginalized by the mechanization of the industry in other parts of the country. Central to organizing this emigration was the Reverend Joseph Silcox, who had founded a Congregational church in Southwold Township on Lake Erie after his arrival in 1818. He had gone back to England and encouraged an assisted party from Corsley in Wiltshire that was much publicized.[53] Wiltshire accounted for 6.6 per cent of emigrants assisted to Canada from 1835 to 1847, but substantial numbers left earlier. A second group, accounting for 12.9 per cent of those assisted during the same period, came from the Sussex area, recruited by Thomas Sockett, the rector at Petworth, and was largely funded by the Earl of Egremont.[54] However, fully half of the 1836–47 pauper emigrants were farm labourers from the corn-growing counties of Norfolk and Suffolk in East Anglia. The adjacent county of Kent accounted for another 12.0 per cent, but two-thirds of them arrived during the 1840s rather than the 1830s.[55]

Let us examine the most statistically significant movement: the newly awakened emigration from Norfolk and Suffolk, which was to prove largely a phenomenon of the 1830s. Only eight emigrants had taken ship directly from East Anglian ports before the 1830s, when 7,742 embarked there, though some emigrants from the region took ship in London. The major East Anglian port was Great Yarmouth, which entered the Canadian emigration trade for the first time in 1830 and soon assumed significant proportions, accounting for a quarter of all English sailings in 1836.

Some East Anglian parishes sent paupers to the United States during the 1820s, although generally this movement is poorly documented.[56] In April 1830, a Bury newspaper reported, "Seventy-eight men, women and children from Diss, Palgrave and Wortham, and fifty-eight from Winfarthing and Shelfanger, passed through Bury in stage waggons on the way to London to take shipping for America." The Shelfanger emigrants at least went to New York and the parties appear to have been unassisted,[57] but Shelfanger and Winfarthing would figure prominently among the parishes sending paupers to Canada later in the decade.

By 1830, the destination of choice was British North America, though initially not the Canadas. The first vessel to embark emigrants locally, at Great Yarmouth, was the *Minerva*, which landed 12 passengers in Charlottetown in 1829. The first local vessels carried settlers to Quebec only in the autumn of 1830 and passengers to Prince Edward Island outnumbered those to the Canadas that year. By 1831, Yarmouth vessels were landing at Prince Edward Island en route to Quebec rather than making the island a primary destination, however. The island received bad press in England; its late growing season was disparaged in letters published in the newspapers and by the Canada Company. After 1833, Yarmouth vessels bypassed the island entirely, and in 1836, the Agent General for Emigration denied knowledge of Prince Edward Island and directed the poor to Upper Canada. The East Anglians, like the Yorkshire emigrants a decade earlier, abandoned the island as a destination in favour of Upper Canada.[58]

Some of this early movement was assisted by parishes or landowners. Census enumerators in 1831 attributed declining populations in the Suffolk parishes of Benhall, Cratfield, Frostenden, and St. James and St. Margaret South Elmham to emigration.[59] The Benhall party at least was assisted out to Prince Edward Island, and some of the South Elmham residents appear to have been among the *Minerva's* first party to the island.[60] The parish of Uggeshall claimed in 1837 to have sent out upwards of 30 paupers "about seven years ago," though their destination is uncertain.[61]

From the winter of 1830–31, emigration to Upper Canada was actively promoted by a number of entrepreneurs, the most prominent of whom was William Cattermole, an East Anglian returned from three years in the province and acting on commission for the Canada Company. In 1831 alone, he superintended the embarkation of more than 1,000 emigrants, mostly labourers but also some small farmers with capital. Cattermole, who was most active in Suffolk, as well as in Kent and Essex, lamented the tendency of his recruits not to locate on Canada Company lands, though most did settle in Upper Canada. He also deplored the efforts of the government agent in Quebec to promote the competing British American Land Company's properties in the Eastern Townships of Lower Canada.[62]

The lists of emigrants submitted to the Poor Law Commissioners under the 1834 legislation permit us to regionalize the origins of the East Anglian emigrants. We see from map 5 in the appendix that the movement had two major foci, in north Norfolk and in north Suffolk (the latter spilling over the county boundary into south-central Norfolk). In Norfolk, the emigration centred both numerically and geographically on the rural parishes of Briston and Edgefield, and in Suffolk, on Stradbroke.

The record in both areas demonstrates that the movement authorized by the Poor Law Commissioners was merely a continuation of existing practice. Many of the fertile wheat-producing parishes of north Suffolk were held in small farms of 30 to 100 acres, the farmers, thanks to low corn prices, little better off themselves than the paupers and staggered by the soaring poor rates. The rector of Wilby reported that "in many of the parishes round me, I find they are now adopting the *ruinous* system of classing out the Labourers to the different Farmers, & making up their wages out of the *rate*."[63] This practice had been adopted in the populous agricultural parish of Stradbroke as early as 1825, where the vestry also experimented in employing the labourers at spinning hemp. However, in 1830, the parishioners decided to sub-scribe funds to send 43 of their poor, mostly families, to Canada. An-other 41 followed in 1832, the paupers themselves having petitioned to go.[64] The allocation of labourers was readopted in 1834, but the poor rates continued to climb: "The princaple [sic] part of the Corn being trashed with a Machine has caused the Labourers to be unemploye [sic] also a great deal of the Drawing of land is done by Machinery when the labourers is standing still and paid by the Parish—which cause so much Money to be paid for Unemployed Labour."[65] In 1836, another 93 paupers departed Stradbroke.[66]

The problem of controlling the poor rates was exacerbated in north Suffolk by the dearth of resident gentlemen.[67] Many of the farmers were illiterate, the magistracy was dominated by lenient clergy, and the parish overseers of the poor were in many instances shopkeepers who turned a tidy profit supplying small, ill-regulated parish poorhouses where the labourers came and went virtually at will.[68] The new Hoxne Poor Law Union organized the numerous 1836 departures from the area, and to encourage emigration forbade outdoor relief to the able-bodied before the policy was generally adopted throughout England. The end of subsidized wages and the application of the "workhouse test" of indigence were greeted by protests and riots in 1835, one provoked by shoemakers who were disciples of William Cobbett.[69] The embarkation of labourers from Stradbroke at Ipswich in 1836 provoked a riot as a mob from the town attempted to dissuade the families from leaving. Most were persuaded by the parish officers to return to the vessel, and several men from the crowd were jailed for using "inflam-matory and profane language."[70]

Though many of the Suffolk paupers of 1836 were carried directly to Port St. Francis on the south shore of the St. Lawrence and encour-aged to acquire land from the British American Land Company in the Sherbrooke area of Lower Canada (notably in Bury Township), the lack of employment opportunities, the poor quality of the land, and the difficulty of overland transportation encouraged many of these emi-grants to depart quickly for the upper province.[71]

In northern Norfolk, the roots of the movement similarly went back to the beginning of the decade and likewise drew most heavily upon parishes where it was difficult for small landowners (some of them non-resident) to support the burgeoning rates and reach a consensus on how to provide the poor with employment.[72] At the movement's centre was Briston, divided among numerous proprietors, with a population of 1,037 in 1831, up from 750 in 1801, and a long, straggling village encroaching on common land. Sir Jacob Astley had attempted to provide for the poor by letting six acres to 24 families at low rents, but he assisted the other landowners in sending 79 parishioners to Upper Canada from 1831–34. In 1834, the proprietors subscribed for two-thirds of the cost of sending another 54 on the *Venus* out of Yarmouth (the passage of 10 paid by neighbouring parishes), with the other third of the cost taken from the rates. In 1836, another 84 followed. Most of the 1834 party found work and later land west of the head of Lake Ontario, following Dundas Street inland from Hamilton.[73]

In 1836, George Baker Ballachey, a lawyer residing in the neighbouring and heavily pauperized parish of Edgefield, seized the reins. Ballachey had tried everything he could think of to employ the labourers and reduce the rates, including a short-lived bombazine factory employing the paupers to weave cloth for mourning garb. Now resolved to try assisted emigration as a *"dernier ressort,"* he organized an emigration committee involving at least 16 parishes, prior to the organization of poor law unions in the county, and chartered two ships at Yarmouth. No fewer than 123 emigrants were assisted out of Edgefield itself in 1836 (1831 population 774), and at least two other parties followed in later years. Most of the Edgefield emigrants followed Briston's 1834 party to Oxford and Waterloo Counties, and many of the Norfolk emigrants seem to have located in southwestern Ontario.[74]

It is well to emphasize that most English emigration continued to be unassisted, but its origins become harder to define regionally as land sales policies adopted in the colonies undercut land petitions as a source of origin information, and as emigrants traveled farther to reach larger ports of embarkation, diminishing the utility of port statistics. Most movement out of the two East Anglian counties was assisted, and largely confined to the 1830s, but even here, assisted emigration moved in tandem with self-financed departures. In Blenheim Township, Oxford County, the Edgefield and Briston emigrants lived side by side with several dozen other Norfolk families whose names do not appear on the pauper lists. Perhaps the most amusing evidence of the extent of the Canada mania during the decade was the quixotic venture of Beeston Wright, a farmer and miller in Langham, Norfolk. Wright auctioned his property and embarked a small party of emigrants for Quebec on a river hoy from the tiny, silted-in medieval port of Cley-next-the-Sea. By autumn, the party had turned back from Scilly to overwinter in the Channel Islands, where they were derided by the local inhabitants for their inexperienced seamanship.[75] The fate of the party awaits discovery, but in the late 1860s, Wright's son finally arrived in Canada, taking employment as a factory worker in London, Ontario, following sojourns in north London (England) and Australia.[76]

In the 1850s, most emigration to Canada continued to be British, and the English proportion rose as the Irish turned increasingly toward the United States and, to a much lesser extent, Australasia. In the latter half of the nineteenth century, however, an incongruity of demand and supply arose. Though Ontario's arable lands had mostly been taken up by the 1860s, the growth of commercial agriculture in well-established areas continued to absorb large numbers of farm labourers, and the increasingly prosperous population also generated an insatiable demand for female domestics that immigration was slow to supply. Increasingly, however, those unable to make a satisfactory living in England were neither farm nor service workers but people leading a troubled existence in the industrial cities. Some arrived in Canada with neither farming experience nor appreciable skills; others came with training in specialized industries that had no Canadian counterparts. Canada was still an agricultural colony, with large-scale and mostly heavy manufacturing in only a few large centres like Montreal and Hamilton.

Both the Yorkshire and West Country migrations continued into the 1850s and beyond. Hull remained an important port for emigration to Canada, still controlling 10 per cent of English passenger traffic, though by then also becoming a re-embarkation point for Germans bound for Canada and the United States via the St. Lawrence.[77] English passengers on Hull ships continued to catch the eye of Buchanan, the government agent at Quebec, who reported them for the most part "farmers and agriculturalists, possessing capital": "The emigrants from Hull . . . are generally respectable farmers, proceeding to friends in different sections of western Canada" (1857).

West Country emigrants proceeding to the Lake Ontario shore or Huron and Perth counties attracted similar comment. In May 1856, two-thirds of arrivals at Quebec were farmers and farm labourers from England and Scotland: "Many of the former have brought out a considerable amount of capital with them and with a very few exceptions have all proceeded to settle in Western Canada [Canada West] where all appear to have friends or relations already settled. . . . Those from

Plymouth and Truro have chiefly proceeded to friends in the Newcastle and Home Districts." In 1857, Buchanan characterized eight shiploads of immigrants from Plymouth as "a fine healthy body of west of England farmers and agricultural labourers, many of whom appear to possess good means; a large proportion have emigrated to join their friends in the Newcastle, Home, and Gore, Brock and London Districts, and a few to the western States." He contrasted them with "those by the *Montezuma* from London who are chiefly mechanics and labourers seeking employment; there were a number of young men who had acted in the capacity of clerks or store porters, who aspire to a position above that of ordinary labourers: to persons of this class Canada offers but little inducements at present."[78]

Thus, in a modified form, Bailyn's provincial and metropolitan streams were with us still. Farming families from the north and now the west of England emigrated in large numbers to join those who had made the move before, and growing numbers of young men displaced from London's labour market still came out to British North America in search of work. Most remarkable was the continuing exodus of Yorkshire farming families, still directing toward the newer colony the stream that in 1772 was first but not for long directed toward Nova Scotia. The young urbanites were the wave of the future, at first unwanted, but harbingers nonetheless of the second, and much greater, wave of English immigration between the turn of the century and the Great Depression that would provide much of the labour force for Canada's great era of industrialization.

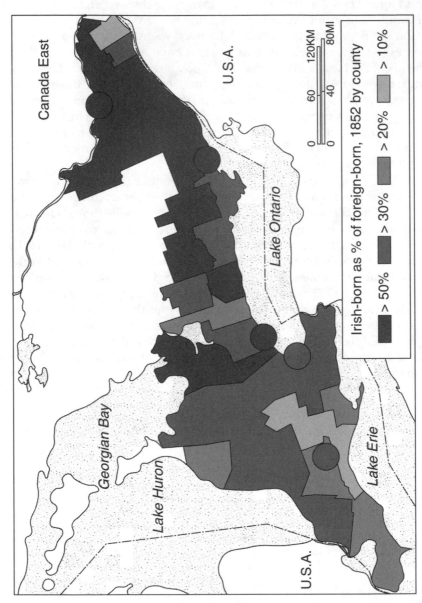

Appendix 1. Irish-born as a % of Foreign-born by County, 1852.

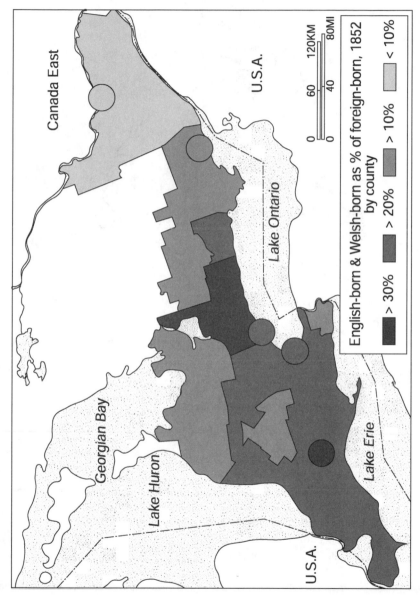

Appendix 2. English & Welsh as % of Foreign-born by County, 1852.

Appendix 3. County Origins recorded in Ontario Methodist Obituaries, 1836–1870. (See Table 3, p. 59)

Source: *Christain Guardian*, 1836–1870; Canadian Christian Advocate, 1845–1857 from abstracts edited by Donald A. McKenzie.

Map by Peter D. Béla Mérey / Pro Familia Publishing

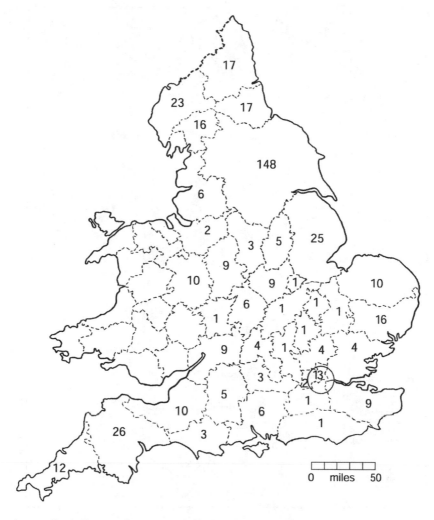

Appendix 4. County Origins recorded on Gravestones in Peel, Halton and York Counties.
Source: Inscription collected by B. Gilchrist & W. Britnell.
Map by Peter D. Béla Mérey / Pro Familia Publishing

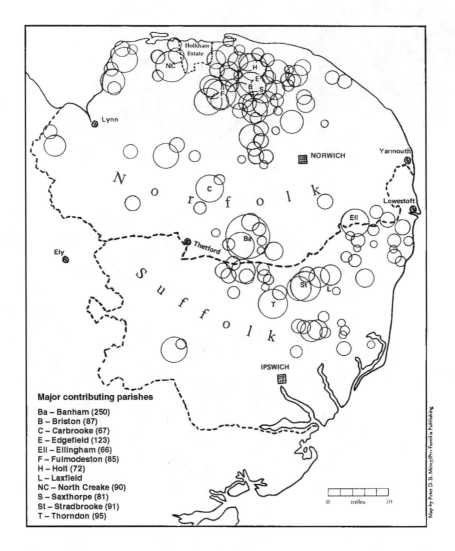

Major contributing parishes

Ba – Banham (250)
B – Briston (87)
C – Carbrooke (67)
E – Edgefield (123)
Ell – Ellingham (66)
F – Fulmodeston (85)
H – Holt (72)
L – Laxfield
NC – North Creake (90)
S – Saxthorpe (81)
St – Stradbrooke (91)
T – Thorndon (95)

Appendix 5. Parochially-assisted Emigration to B.N.A. 1835–July 1837 Norfolk and Suffolk.

Map by Peter D. Béla Mérey / Pro Familia Publishing

Notes

1. Arthur R. M. Lower, *Canadians in the Making: A Social History of Canada* (Toronto: Longmans, Green and Company, 1958), 196.
2. See Donald Whyte, *The Scots Overseas: A Selected Bibliography* (Aberdeen: Scottish Association of Family History Societies, 1995).
3. Of course, historical revisionism since Lower's day has reversed the former emphasis on these dramatic episodes as causal of migration history. See J.M. Bumsted, *The People's Clearance* (Edinburgh: Edinburgh University Press, 1982) on clearance from below, and D.H. Akenson, *The Irish in Ontario: A Study in Rural History* (Kingston and Montreal: McGill-Queen's University Press, 1984), and Cecil Houston and William J. Smyth, *Irish Emigration and Canadian Settlement: Patterns, Links, and Letters* (Toronto: University of Toronto Press, 1990), on the largely pre-famine nature of Irish immigration and settlement.
4. With the exception of Gordon Handcock, *Soe Longe as There Comes Noe Women* (St. John's: Breakwater Books, 1989), on English settlement in New-foundland, and Alan G. Brunger, "The Distribution of English in Upper Canada 1851–1871," *The Canadian Geographer* 30, no. 4 (1986): 337–43, what little there is on the English tends to deal with the twentieth century, though general overviews are still lacking: Pauline Greenhill, *Ethnicity in the Mainstream* (Kingston and Montreal: McGill-Queen's University Press, 1994); Ross McCormack, "Cloth Caps and Jobs: the Ethnicity of the English Immigrants in Canada 1900–1914," in Jorgen Dahlie and Tissa Fernando, eds., *Ethnicity, Power and Politics in Canada* (Toronto: Methuen, 1981), 38–55; Richard Harris, "A Working Class Suburb for Immigrants, Toronto 1909–1913," *Geographical Review* 81, no. 3 (1991): 318–32. Much deals with specific categories of immigrants: W. J. C. Cherwinski, "'Misfits', 'Malingerers,' and 'Malcontents': The British Harvester Movement of 1928," in J. E. Foster, ed., *The Developing West* (Edmonton: University of Alberta Press, 1983), 273–302; Joy Parr, *Labouring Children* (London: Croom Helm, 1978), and *The Gender of Breadwinners* (Toronto: University of Toronto Press, 1990); Geoffrey Bilson, *Guest Children* (Saskatoon: Fifth House, 1988); Ben Wicks, *Promise You'll Take Care of My Daughter: The Remarkable War Brides of World War II* (London: Stoddart, 1992).
5. Peter N. Moogk, "Reluctant Exiles: Emigrants from France in Canada Before 1760," in Gerald Tulchinsky, ed., *Immigration in Canada: Historical Perspectives* (Mississauga: Copp Clark Longman, 1994), 8–47.
6. Bernard Bailyn, *Voyagers to the West: A Passage in the Peopling of America on the Eve of the Revolution* (New York: Alfred A. Knopf, 1986).

7. The most dramatic example of the importance of commerce in shaping immigration patterns is Newfoundland, with its vast majority of immigrants from the hinterlands of England's West Country ports of Dartmouth, Teignmouth, and Poole, whence the offshore fishery was organized, and from the hinterland of Waterford in Ireland, where the English vessels took on provisions and servants before heading west across the Atlantic. Gordon Handcock, *Soe Longe;* John J. Mannion, ed., *The Peopling of Newfoundland: Essays in Historical Geography* (St. John's: Institute of Social and Economic Research, Memorial University, 1977); R. L. Gentilcore, ed., *Historical Atlas of Canada* (Toronto: University of Toronto Press, 1993), vol. 2, plate 8.

8. Bruce S. Elliott, "Regionalized Migration and Settlement Patterns of the Irish in Upper Canada," in Robert O'Driscoll, ed., *The Untold Story: The Irish in Canada* (Toronto: Celtic Arts, 1988), vol. 1, 308–18; Houston and Smyth, *Irish Immigration and Canadian Settlement*.

9. *Census of Canada.*

10. See the accompanying maps compiled from 1852 census ethnicity data at the county level.

11. Brunger, "Distribution of English in Upper Canada."

12. It is a mistake, however, to think that all who were enumerated in rural townships by the census-takers lived on farms as farmers or agricultural labourers. Within 20 years of initial settlement, it was not uncommon for township populations to include populous, unincorporated villages full of late-arriving immigrants. By 1848, a large proportion of the West Country immigrants in Darlington and Clarke were working at trades or general labour in the villages of Bowmanville, Orono, Solina, and Newcastle, though some later moved to farms nearby or in western Ontario. The retreating frontier, the increase in land prices in established communities, and employment opportunities in the developing villages made this a growing option if not a necessity. I have argued elsewhere that the development of the railway town of Lucan in Biddulph Township provided the opportunity for members of the second generation of Tipperary Irish families to keep store or practise a trade without leaving the neighbourhood. Bruce S. Elliott, *Irish Migrants in the Canadas* (Kingston and Montreal: McGill-Queen's University Press, 1988), 177–81.

13. Charlotte Erickson, "Emigration from the British Isles to the U.S.A. in 1831," *Population Studies* 35 (1981): 175–97; idem, "Emigration from the British Isles to the U.S.A. in 1841: Part. I. Emigration from the British Isles," *Population Studies* 43 (1989): 347–67; idem, "Part II. Who Were the English Emigrants?" 44 (1990): 21–40; idem, "Who Were the English and

Scots Emigrants to the United States in the Late Nineteenth Century?" in D.V. Glass and Roger Revelle, eds., *Population and Social Change* (London: Edward Arnold, 1976), 345–81; William Van Vugt, "Running from Ruin? The Emigration of British Farmers to the U.S.A. in the Wake of the Repeal of the Corn Laws," *Economic History Review*, 2nd ser., 41 (1988): 411–28; idem, "Prosperity and Industrial Emigration from Britain During the Early 1850s," *Journal of Social History* 22 (1988): 339–54; idem, "Who Were the Women Immigrants from Britain in the Mid-Nineteenth Century?" in M. D'Innocenzo and J.P. Sirefman, eds., *Immigration and Ethnicity: American Society, "Melting Pot" or "Salad Bowl"?* (Westport, Conn.: Greenwood Press, 1992), 163–75; idem, "Welsh Emigration to the U.S.A. During the Mid-Nineteenth Century," *Welsh Historical Review* 15 (1991): 545–61. Erickson's articles are reprinted in her *Leaving England: Essays on British Emigration in the Nineteenth Century* (Ithaca: Cornell University Press, 1994). Each of these articles analyzes passenger lists for a single year. Passenger lists for the port of Quebec survive only from 1865 onward.

14. Talbot refused to report locations to central authorities, arguing that it would complicate the processing of new applications for abandoned claims. He entered names on maps in pencil and then erased them if a location was abandoned, destroying the record of numerous transient occupations. Once settlement duties had been completed, he forwarded lists of names of eligible patentees to the Executive Council, obviating the need for land petitions (except to complain of Talbot's actions!). National Archives of Canada (NA), Upper Canada Sundries, RG5, A1, pp. 24316-9, Talbot to Hillier, 6 October 1820, reel C-4605.

15. Fawne Stratford-Devai and Bruce S. Elliott, "Upper Canada Land Settlement Records: the Second District Land Board, 1819–1825," *Families* 34, no. 3 (August 1995): 132–7. Some of the returns made to central government by the Land Boards did specify the county of origin within the British Isles, though most did not. Stratford-Devai and I have in progress a publication of the surviving returns, which will permit an analysis of origins as recorded therein.

16. This was the case in 1825–26. I analyzed Irish regional origins using this source in my article in O'Driscoll, *The Untold Story*. However, English immigration at Quebec dipped to a low of 238 in 1826, and so the numbers of English land petitioners that season are very small. There were 68 English petitioners, of whom 20 stated no county of origin. Of those who did, Yorkshire accounted for 9, Cumberland for 6, and London for 3. Other counties accounted for 1 or 2 each. Even so, a third were from the

north, lending support to the pattern traced by the larger numbers from earlier in the decade analyzed below.

17. NA, RG1, I6b, vol. 17.

18. It is well known by students of Upper Canada, including the genealogical community, that British subjects did not need to become naturalized in order to hold property or vote in elections. It is, however, often assumed that swearing the oath of allegiance was tantamount to naturalization. They were quite distinct procedures, however, and applicants for grants of land were required to swear an oath of allegiance regardless of their birthplace or national origin. These were often sworn before local magistrates, whose hand-written certificates were appended to the land petitions, or filed later with the warrants by government bureaucrats. Some of the private land agents who wrote up and submitted petitions for settlers were also authorized to swear such oaths, for example, Benjamin Geale: NA, U.C. Sundries, RG5, A1, pp. 22033-5, 22040, 11 November 1819. John Small, the Clerk of the Executive Council, also swore in visitors to the Executive Council Office and his register is the one analyzed here: NA, RG1, E11, vol. 13. Some of these applicants did not complete the land granting process, and so the statistics derived from Small's register are not quite the same as the ones taken from the petitions would be.

19. Donald A. McKenzie, *Death Notices from the Christian Guardian 1836–1850* (Lambertville, N.J.: Hunterdon House, 1982); idem, *Death Notices from the Christian Guardian, 1851–1860* (Lambertville, N.J.: Hunterdon House, 1984); idem, *Obituaries from Ontario's Christian Guardian, 1861–1870* (Lambertville, N.J.: Hunterdon House, 1988); idem, *More Notices from Methodist Papers, 1830–1857* (Lambertville, N.J.: Hunterdon House, 1986).

20. Obituaries from the Primitives' *Christian Journal* and the *Bible Christian Observer* are abstracted in Donald A. McKenzie, *More Notices from Ontario's Methodist Papers 1858–1872* (Ottawa: the author, 1993).

21. *Quebec Gazette*, 18 May 1832, p. 1, col. 4.

22. N. H. Carrier and J. R. Jeffery, *External Migration: A Study of the Available Statistics, 1815–1950* (London: HMSO, 1953), 138–9.

23. Marie E. Daly, New England Historic Genealogical Society, Boston; analysis of western Massachusetts naturalization petitions by Edward J. O'Day of the University of Southern Illinois, Carbondale. An analysis of "Missing Friends" advertisements in the Irish-American Boston *Pilot*, 1831–50, indicates that "more 'missing friends' first came to St. John [sic], Quebec City and Montreal than to all reported American ports": Ruth-Ann Harris and Donald M. Jacobs, *The Search for Missing Friends* (Boston: New England Historic Genealogical Society, 1989), vol. 1, xxi, xliv.

24. NA, "Q" Series, vol. 211, part 1, pp. 13–17, A. Buchanan to R. W. Hay, Quebec, n.d., reel C-11948; pp. 34–6, James Buchanan to R. W. Hay, 24 May 1833; vol. 220, part 1, pp. 37–8, James Buchanan to R. W. Hay, 15 April 1834, reel C-11952.

25. New York officials assumed a constant ratio of 70 per cent Irish amongst British arrivals between 1825 and 1846 in all but two years, creating artificial ethnicity statistics. Charlotte Erickson has recalculated the proportions for some years from the actual lists: "Emigration from the British Isles to the U.S.A. in 1841," *Population Studies* 43 (1989): 352–3; idem, "Emigration from the British Isles to the U.S.A. in 1831," *Population Studies* 35 (1981): 180–1. British official returns distinguished only ports of sailing, rather than ethnicity, until 1853 (Carrier and Jeffery, *External Migration,* 139), and one might reasonably assume that vast numbers of Irish sailing before then from English ports would contaminate port statistics as a data source on English emigration. Erickson has shown that the percentage of Irish arriving at New York has been much exaggerated, but the problem is less serious in any case for Canadian statistics. Liverpool did not become a major port of embarkation for the Irish heading to British North America until comparatively late; only 9,725 passengers departed thence in the 1825–35 decade, a mere 3.2% of the total British traffic. Though we cannot say what proportion of these were Irish, the present paper shows that early movement out of England was concentrated in ports from which there is no suggestion that the Irish ever took ship in significant numbers; if we could eliminate the Irish from the Liverpool statistics, the exercise would merely increase the proportion of English sailing from the north and southwest. In any case, as late as 1850, only 20% of Irish-born emigrants sailing for Quebec embarked from English and Scottish ports. Liverpool came to dominate traffic to British North America only from 1853 onward, by which time Canada's major Irish influx was subsiding. Colonial Land and Emigration Commissioners' *Reports.*

26. Genealogical study of the passenger list of the bark *Cosmopolite's* 1835 voyage from Plymouth (Devon) to New York (US National Archives microfilm M237-26, list no. 269), for example, reveals that the 150 passengers aboard were bound for expatriate Devonshire colonies in New York, Pennsylvania, and Ohio as well as Hamilton and Darlington, Upper Canada. All were stated in the list, wrongly, to be intending settlement in the States.

27. In his attempts to determine the numbers of Irish landing at Quebec, Donald Akenson took into account yet another problem: that passenger

numbers sometimes represented individuals or "souls," and at other
times "statute adults"—that is, the number of persons for victualling
purposes, children prior to 1833 being accounted half or a third of a
"statute adult." As my intention is to determine proportional regional
origins rather than the numbers actually arriving, I am using the statistics
as the government emigrant agents reported them. Akenson, *The Irish in
Ontario*, 14, citing W. F. Adams, *Ireland and Irish Emigration to the New
World from 1815 to the Famine* (New Haven: Yale University Press, 1932),
411–13.

28. Marianne McLean, "Achd an Rhigh: A Highland Response to the Assisted
Emigration of 1815," *Canadian Papers in Rural History* 5 (1986): 181–97;
idem, "Peopling Glengarry County: the Scottish Origins of a Canadian
County," Canadian Historical Association *Historical Papers* (1982): 156–71;
idem, *The People of Glengarry: Highlanders in Transition 1745–1820* (Montreal and Kingston: McGill-Queen's University Press, 1991).

29. Bailyn, *Voyagers to the West*, passim.

30. I tell my students, only half in jest, of what I term Elliott's Iron Law of
Local History, which states that any group in which one is interested
settles so that the group straddles as many administrative boundaries as
possible, simply so that one has to research in a greater number of archives. There is a corollary to this law: that they will also settle where
four map sheets meet, so that one has to purchase all four. Even where
a settlement appears initially to defy this natural law, as did the Nova
Scotia Yorkshire settlement of the 1770s, it will later be brought into line.
In this instance the administrative setting-off of New Brunswick from
Nova Scotia after the American Revolution resolved the question.

31. Bailyn, *Voyagers to the West*, 361–429; John Robinson and Thomas Rispin,
Journey Through Nova-Scotia (York: C. Etherington, 1774), 11, 15, 16, 18.

32. NA, MG24, I 123, Robert & Ann King, Sledmere, Yorkshire, to Thomas
King, Sackville, NB, 19 August 1810; Howard Trueman, *The Chignecto
Isthmus and its First Settlers* (Toronto: William Briggs, 1902), 115–19.

33. Bruce S. Elliott, "English Immigration to Prince Edward Island," *The
Island Magazine* 40 (Fall/Winter 1996): 6–9.

34. This is made clear by an examination of the dates of immigration of the
English-born recorded in the 1851 New Brunswick census, especially for
the County of Westmorland where the Yorkshire settlers of the 1770s had
concentrated. The county volumes have been published by the provincial
archives in Fredericton.

35. Perth settlement register, NA, MG9, D8-27. Six of 18 families were still in
the Perth area in 1822.

36. *York Courier* quoted in *Quebec Gazette*, 15 July 1830, p. 2, col. 2.

37. Only a small minority of English stated even their country of origin on their gravestones; the tendency to do so was most pronounced amongst the Scots. The data used here come from inscriptions transcribed by William Britnell and J. Brian Gilchrist and made available to me by the latter.

38. See, for example, Allan McGillivray, *Decades of Harvest: A History of Scott Township 1807–1973* (Uxbridge, Ontario: Scott History Committee, 1986), 11–12, 18–20, 31–32, where arrivals are noted by decade. The most commonly identified places of origin were Yorkshire and Cumberland.

39. Others bound from Devon and Cornwall for Upper Canada came from Bideford or Bristol via New York. On West Country emigration, see Philip Payton, *The Cornish Overseas* (Fowey: Alexander Associates, 1999); Basil Greenhill and Ann Gifford, *West Countrymen in Prince Edward's Isle* (Toronto: University of Toronto Press, 1967); B. Elliott, "English Emigration to Prince Edward Island," *The Island Magazine* 40 (Fall/Winter 1996): 3–11, 41, (Spring/Summer 1997): 3–9; Margaret James-Korany, "Blue Books as Sources for Cornish Emigration History" in Philip Payton, ed., *Cornish Studies: One* (Exeter: University of Exeter Press, 1993): 31–45; Mark Brayshay, "The Emigration Trade in Nineteenth-Century Devon," in Michael Duffy et al., *The New Maritime History of Devon* (London: Conway Maritime Press, 1994), vol. 2, 108–18.

40. A. L. Rowse, *The Cousin Jacks: The Cornish in America* (NY: Scribner's, 1969); John Rowe, *The Hard-Rock Men: Cornish Immigrants and the North American Mining Frontier* (Harper & Row, 1974); A. C. Todd, *The Cornish Miner in America* (Glendale, CA: The Arthur H. Clark Co.).

41. On Bruce Mines, see John Tyacke's clever analysis of the Bruce Mines post office money letter books for 1857–61, which record the addressees of money letters sent from the mines, *Cornwall Family History Society Journal* 83 (March 1997). On Silver Islet, see Elinor Barr, *Silver Islet: Striking it Rich in Lake Superior* (Toronto: Natural Heritage/Natural History, 1988), 38, 55, 57, 91; Thunder Bay Museum, B 25/6/1, Silver Islet Mining Company Records, contract book, 1872-74.

42. Here is Elliott's Iron Law in operation again.

43. K. J. Melhuish, "Migration from the South-West," in James Jupp, ed., *The Australian People: An Encyclopaedia of the Nation, its People and their Origins* (North Ryde, NSW: Angus & Robertson, 1988), p. 405.

44. For a discussion of the evolving nature of Cornish identity, see Bernard Deacon and Philip Payton, "Re-Inventing Cornwall: Culture Change on the European Periphery" and Caroline Vink, "Be Forever Cornish! Some

Observations on the Ethno-regional Movement in Contemporary Cornwall" in Payton, *Cornish Studies*, 62–79 and 109–19.

45. Appendix (A) to the First Report from the Commissioners of the Poor Laws, British Parliamentary Sessional Papers (1834) 44, Pt. II, no. 23, p. 68a.

46. Robert Gourlay, *Statistical Account of Upper Canada* (London: Simpkin & Marshall, 1822), 468–9.

47. R. M. McInnis, "The Early Ontario Wheat Staple Reconsidered," in D. H. Akenson, ed., *Canadian Papers in Rural History* (Gananoque: Langdale Press, 1992), vol. 8, 17–48, esp. map p. 43.

48. *Illustrated Historical Atlas of the County of Huron, Ont.* (Toronto: H. Belden & Co., 1879), p. xx, col. 2; James Scott, *The Settlement of Huron County* (Toronto: Ryerson Press, 1966), 167.

49. Elliott, *Irish Migrants in the Canadas.*

50. Liz Young, "Paupers, Property, and Place: A Geographical Analysis of the English, Irish, and Scottish Poor Laws in the Mid-19th Century," *Environment and Planning D: Society and Space* 12 (1994): 325–40.

51. British Parliamentary Sessional Papers, (1835) XXXV, pp. 104–5.

52. Rainer Baehre, "Pauper Emigration to Upper Canada in the 1830s," *Histoire sociale/Social History* 14, no. 28 (November 1981): 349–67.

53. This movement is the focus of another paper in this collection: Terry McDonald, "'A Door of Escape': Letters Home from Wiltshire and Somerset Emigrants to Upper Canada, 1830 –1832."

54. See Wendy Cameron, "English Immigrants in 1830s Upper Canada: The Petworth Emigration Scheme" in this collection.

55. The Norfolk movement in 1836 is the subject of a study by Gary Howells; the East Anglian movement has also been a substantial focus of my own research. The adjoining county of Kent accounted for another 12.0% of assisted emigrants. Norfolk, Suffolk, Kent, Sussex, and Wiltshire accounted for 80 per cent of the paupers assisted to Canada under the terms of the Poor Law Amendment Act (1834). Statistics from British Parliamentary Sessional Papers (1835) XXXV, p. 24; (1836) XXIX, pp. 571–4; (1847–48) XLVII, pp. 694–703.

56. The evidence must be sought in parish financial accounts, which have survived spottily and are not yet all in the record offices.

57. "The 1830 Wagon Train for Diss Emigrants," in Eric Pursehouse, *Waveney Valley Studies: Gleanings from Local History* (Diss: Diss Publishing Co., 1966), 233–6.

58. Bruce S. Elliott, "English Immigration to Prince Edward Island: Part Two," *The Island Magazine* 41 (Spring/Summer 1997): 4–6.

59. Census of Great Britain, 1851 (with retrospect to 1801), *British Parliamentary Papers: Population* (Irish University Press), vol. 6, 653.
60. Elliott, "Prince Edward Island: Part Two," 5–6.
61. MH12/11731, 12 February 1837.
62. William Cattermole, *Emigration, the Advantages of Emigration to Canada* (London, 1831); John Weaver, "Cattermole, William" in T. M. Bailey, ed., *Dictionary of Hamilton Biography* (Hamilton, 1981), vol. 1, 46.
63. MH12/11728, Blything Union, Henry Owen, Wilby Rectory, Eye, Suffolk, 18 April 1835.
64. Eric Pursehouse, *Waveney Valley Studies*, pp. 237–9; Peter Rose, *Stradbroke: Scenes from Village History* (Ipswich: Suffolk Books, 1992), p. 29.
65. PRO, MH12/11837, William Dowser to Poor Law Commissioners, Stradbroke, 13 December 1834.
66. Similarly, Kettleburgh (in Plomesgate Union), which had drawn on the rates to send out 42 paupers to Etobicoke, near Toronto, in 1831, in 1836 borrowed from the government to send out 52 more. PRO, MH12/11932, Rev. Geo. Turner, Kettleburgh, Suffolk, 22 April, 30 June 1836.
67. MH12/11837, Augustus Cooper, Syleham Hall nr Harleston, 30 November 1835.
68. MH12/11837, Charles Mott, 4 May, 1 July 1835.
69. MH12/11837, Henry Owen, Wilby Rectory, 26 May 1835, and late 1835, passim.
70. *Bury & Norwich Post*, 21 September 1836, NA, MG55/25 #5.
71. The story of the Eastern Townships settlement is told in part in the Chief Emigrant Agent's report for 1836, IUP *Colonies Canada*, vol. 8, and in J. I. Little, *Nationalism, Capitalism, and Colonization: The Upper St Francis District* (Kingston: McGill-Queen's University Press, 1989).
72. Unlike Hoxne Union in Suffolk, numerous gentry proprietors lived in north Norfolk, some of them "gentlemanly capitalists" or solicitors such as Ballachey and his compatriot on the emigration committee, William Hardy Cozens-Hardy of Letheringsett, but the ownership of the larger parishes was much broken up. The estates of the larger and more aristocratic landowners tended to form "closed" parishes that, by restricting settlement, were less likely to resort to assisting emigration. On the Cozens-Hardys, see David Cannadine, "Landowners, Lawyers and Litterateurs: the Cozens-Hardys of Letheringsett" in his *Aspects of Aristocracy* (New Haven and London: Yale University Press, 1994), 184–209.
73. William White, *History, Gazetteer, and Directory of Norfolk* (Sheffield: Robt Leader, 1836), p. 584; William White, *History, Gazetteer, and Directory of Norfolk* (Sheffield: Robert Leader, 1845), 736; PRO, MH12/8293, Robert

Bond, Briston, 21 March 1835; *Norwich Mercury,* 6 February 1836, p. 4, cols. 2–3; MH12/8293, Robert Bond, Briston, 17 March 1836 and G. Ballachey, 5 Apr. 1836. The list of prospective emigrants from Briston in 1836 contained 87 names, but the Robert Riches family, and possibly others, did not go.

74 *Norwich Mercury,* 18 May 1833, p. 3, col. 5; Norfolk Record Office, Marcon Papers, NRS 507 9D.4, misc. bundle 1821–63, G. B. Ballachey to W. P. Pillans, Holt, 14 June 1834; to Mrs Marcon Junr., Holt, 18 September 1834; PRO, MH12/8293, G. B. Ballachey, Edgefield, 8 April 1833, 7 October 1834, 12 June 1835, 21 January, 26 February, 1, 12, 21, 23 March, 5, 7 April, 3 June 1836; MH12/8185, G. B. Ballachey, Edgefield, 23 March 1836; MH12/8294, John Crowe, 18 December 1838; MH12/8295, G. B. Ballachey, Edgefield Mount, 1, 8 April 1840; MH12/8296, Hewitt O'Bryen, Edgefield, 24 March 1845.

75. *Norwich Mercury,* 23 April 1836, p. 2, col. 5; 30 May 1836, p. 3, col. 2; 3 September 1836, p. 3, col. 3.

76. NA, 1871 census, London, Ontario, 010 E, p. 97.

77. In 1854, 295 of the 1,073 passengers from Hull were German. Canada Sessional Papers, Chief Agent's report, 1854.

78. Chief Agent's reports for 1856 and 1857.

English Immigrants in 1830s Upper Canada: The Petworth Emigration Scheme*

Wendy Cameron

IN EARLY SEPTEMBER 1832, WILLIAM UPTON WROTE FROM UPPER CANADA to his mother, "I dare say you have heard bad accounts of Canada, from the Petworth party, for I know that they wrote home in the midst of their trouble in travelling, before they knew what it was, or had time to get situations." His own troubles ended when he got a good job in a sawmill. In the rest of the letter he enthused about the country, re-counted success stories, and urged his brothers and sisters, "if they cannot get a living in England, to come to Canada, where they may soon get an independency."[1]

Upton was one of some 1,800 men, women, and children sent by the Petworth Emigration Committee from the south of England to Upper Canada between 1832 and 1837. As his letter implies, they travelled as individuals and in groups, leaving from a total of over a hundred parishes. If they are to be described as pauper emigrants, these people were paupers in the sense of the old poor law. Very few came from a workhouse. They were members of the working poor who turned to the parish on occasion for outdoor relief to supplement the low wages of an agricultural labourer. Families with a number of young children had received a child allowance; others had had help during the winter. They also looked to the parish for assistance with extra or unusual expenses such as emigration.[2]

The Petworth Emigration Committee was initiated and organized

---

*   This article was written as part of a study of the Petworth Emigration Scheme undertaken by Wendy Cameron and Mary McDougall Maude and sponsored by Father Edward Jackman. The project is supported by the Jackman Foundation and located at the Northrop Frye Centre, Victoria University, University of Toronto.

by Thomas Sockett, the rector of Petworth, and it sent emigrants under the protection of Sockett's patron, the eighty-one-year-old Earl of Egremont. This committee was unusual for its sustained effort over six years and for the comparative generosity of its assistance. In other respects, it was quite typical of large parish emigrations in representing financing drawn from a mix of prominent sponsors and parish contributions. Although certainly not the case for all parish-aided emigration, this particular scheme was in part a humanitarian attempt to better the lives of the people sent.[3]

Most Petworth emigrants were rural people, even if their sponsors lived in a town. The largest contingent came from parishes in West Sussex, and especially from the Petworth area. Other emigrants were sent by East Sussex parishes centred on Brighton and Lewes, from the Dorking area of Surrey, from the Isle of Wight, and, in less concentrated numbers, from parishes scattered through other southern counties. They travelled from Portsmouth to Quebec and Montreal on chartered ships. From Montreal, the great majority travelled on to Toronto in the charge of the superintendents who had brought them from Portsmouth. The emigrants of 1832, 1833, and 1836 made the difficult journey from Montreal to Prescott up the St. Lawrence rapids crowded together in Durham boats and bateaux. Although the Atlantic crossing looms largest in the story of emigration, Upton's fellow emigrants from Petworth ships had most "trouble in travelling" and many more casualties on this inland route. The emigrants of 1834, 1835, and 1837 had an easier journey over the Ottawa River and the Rideau Canal. From Prescott on the St. Lawrence route, or from the Kingston terminus of the Rideau Canal, regularly scheduled steamboats took immigrants up Lake Ontario to York (Toronto).

In Upper Canada, some of the committee's emigrants settled in the Home District around Toronto. Larger numbers went to the Gore District, to the hinterland of Hamilton. They travelled both by water and by land to Burlington Bay, where they settled initially in Hamilton itself, as well as in Dundas and Ancaster or on farms and in still smaller villages nearby. Hamilton was also the entry point for many Petworth emigrants to inland townships along the Grand River, where rapid development in several new communities created a demand for their labour. Another large group of Petworth emigrants went farther west to the London and Western districts, particularly to communities based on the modern towns of Woodstock in Blandford Township and Strathroy in Adelaide Township. In addition to the assistance they received through the Petworth committee, many Petworth emigrants had help from the Upper Canadian government to travel beyond Toronto within the province, and some received help from agents of the Crown Lands Department in getting settled.

The Petworth emigrants sailed in an era when the vast majority of immigrants arriving at Quebec were Irish, and Irish immigrants have had the most attention from historians. Contemporaries noted in the early 1830s that a higher proportion of English immigrants were choosing Canada over the United States. Yet parish-aided emigration to Upper Canada in the 1830s is just beginning to be fully investigated.[4] Parish emigrants during these years came from England or Wales. Ireland did not have a poor law until 1838, and the Scottish poor laws of the time did not support emigration. English parishes did send some emigrants before 1831, mainly to the United States. In that year, however, parish emigration increased significantly, and the principal initial destination became Upper Canada.

The best overall guide to the ups and downs of parish emigration during the years of the Petworth emigrations is provided by emigration agents at Quebec, starting in 1831.[5] In 1831 and 1832, more immigrants of all classes arrived at Quebec than at any time before the famine of 1847. Of these, the agent tallied just under five thousand emigrants aided by parish or landlord in each of these years, close to one in ten of all arrivals. In 1833, the numbers and proportion of assisted emigrants dropped sharply. A second peak of well over four thousand parish emigrants occurred in 1836 after the introduction of the new poor law. All immigration to the Canadas had slowed to a trickle by the Rebellions of 1837. After this date, parish emigration to Upper Canada never regained the same vitality and importance. The assisted emigration from England that received the most support in the next two decades was to Australia and New Zealand.

The parish emigration of the 1830s began under the Whig government of Earl Grey. Grey's administration took office in November 1830 at the height of the Swing disturbances, named for the mythical Captain Swing. During the autumn and winter of 1830–31, Sussex was one of a number of counties in the south and southeast where normally unnoticed agricultural labourers set fires, broke up the threshing machines that took their winter work, and combined in strikes or riots to back demands for better wages and working conditions.[6] In this region, the value of assisted emigration as a social safety valve had never seemed greater. Sponsors such as those organized by the Petworth

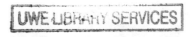

committee acted without waiting for government to provide a financial incentive.

In government circles, the Swing disturbances brought the rural labourers of the affected counties under intense scrutiny. The eventual outcome of this review was the passing of the Poor Law Amendment Act in 1834 and the introduction of the new poor law. As an interim step, parish emigration was also closely scrutinized in 1831–32. The strongest argument for direct government assistance to parish-aided emigration was as a measure of pacification which would smooth the way for reform.[7] This option was dismissed once the government became committed to reform of the poor laws and started the process.

Reformers who introduced the new poor law in England did so by discrediting the old one. They were particularly critical of parish allowances such as many Petworth emigrants had received. Under the new law, able-bodied applicants and their families were to receive relief only if they took the drastic step of entering a workhouse.[8] By association, the aid given under previous administrations in assisting settlement in Upper Canada was also discredited. Assisted settlers had received help with shelter and food, and sometimes tools and clothing, and they were employed at public expense on the roads. Petworth emigrants travelled to Upper Canada during the transition from the guiding paternalism of the old system to a free market in labour under the new. For them, the process was slowed because until 1836, Upper Canada had in Sir John Colborne a governor of the old school.[9]

Instructions from the Colonial Office to Colborne in 1832 called for aid to able-bodied immigrants to be phased out as rapidly as possible. If there were to be an exception, the least objectionable aid was help in travelling to where work was available—the assistance that Upton received to get from Toronto to Hamilton. Otherwise, immigrants should appeal to local charities. These charities were expected to sort out the worthy cases and bear the cost of the relief they gave.[10]

As was typical of most Petworth immigrants, William Upton had previous work experience, which gave him an advantage in finding employment. Most of the men were trained farmhands or had worked as artisans.[11] Nonetheless, such immigrants arrived anxious and restless with good reason. Their experience at home had taught them all about seasonal unemployment, and they did not bring enough money to see them through their first Canadian winter. Colborne's two initiatives in assistance that involved Petworth emigrants indicated the circumstances under which he believed that such immigrants should be helped to establish themselves. He made assistance available to all immigrants during the emergency of the cholera epidemic of 1832 and gave limited help in the lesser epidemic of 1834. When the job market began to shrink in 1834 and recession set in in 1835, his concern was for families.

In 1832, cholera killed hundreds of people in towns and along migration routes through the Canadas.[12] Agents of the Crown Lands Department believed that Colborne's vigorous policy of quickly dispersing immigrants away from ports and crowded shanty towns saved hundreds more. The agents pushed immigrants on with little thought for the last agent in a line that led westward from Quebec. This agent was Roswell Mount. Over the summer, he reported the arrival of about four hundred Petworth immigrants and total numbers in the range of thirty-five hundred. His district was thinly settled, and employment was correspondingly limited.

Mount located close to two thousand of these people in a government-sponsored settlement in the newly opened townships of Adelaide and Warwick. We have been able to track one cluster of Petworth immigrants on the fourth and fifth concessions of Adelaide near the modern town of Strathroy. Providing land and assistance to these people confirmed the experience of earlier assisted settlements founded on similar plans. As Colborne predicted, the immigrants who stayed created a settled community. They attracted chain migrants, families intermarried, and this community has the most developed memory of its roots in Egremont's emigrations of any we have found. This achievement was won at a cost totally unacceptable to the Colonial Office.

Letters sent by Petworth emigrants in the Adelaide settlement show that some of these people were determined to surmount the hardships and loneliness that were the price of independence as a poor frontier farmer. Other Petworth emigrants who wrote from established communities gave a different perspective. Some of them questioned whether the benefits of beginning life in Upper Canada as a backwoods settler justified the difficulties and gave as their own the opinion that new immigrants were best to start out as wage-earners. As a group, Petworth emigrants were not necessarily single-minded about becoming landowners in America.[13]

The Petworth emigrants whom we can trace seem to have arrived in Upper Canada ready to take the first good opportunity available, whatever it might be. The 1833 emigrants demonstrated this flexibility. The majority arrived hoping to be given lots near the Adelaide settlement on similar terms. But Colborne had overspent in 1832. All he could offer was land and transportation to the even more remote township of Plympton on Lake Huron. Toronto's labour market was flourishing in 1833, and most Petworth emigrants took the agent's advice and found work there. The forty or so emigrants who made the journey to Plympton probably included some who were difficult to employ, and a couple of families did become well established, but minimal assistance achieved minimal results.

At the beginning of the decade, the Upper Canadian economy was buoyant, despite the ravages of cholera in 1832. By 1834, accounts reaching England from the province were less favourable than they had been.[14] Sockett reported that he was having trouble attracting the best potential emigrants. What he thought would be a solution, although he was never able to implement it, was to have Egremont buy a Canadian estate. He did not expect all his emigrants to go there. His object was to provide at least one secure option for emigrants who did not have connections in Canada. Since his purchase did not go through, he remained dependent on the goodwill of the Upper Canadian government for assistance to his people beyond Toronto.

Colborne's second strategy to help parish emigrants involved families only and temporary possession of lots of five acres rather than the hundred acres assigned in the Adelaide settlement. The idea was to make not instant farmers, but artisans and labourers with enough resources in land to save from their wages and better themselves over the next three to five years. Although modest in scope and in numbers, this plan is interesting to us because it was pioneered by Petworth emigrants and rooted in the recent experience of parish emigrants who found their own opportunities.

At the beginning of the 1830s, an influx of half-pay officers had brought rapid, if temporary, prosperity to the Canadian communities where they were allowed to draw land for their military service. Canadian farmers traditionally hired single men to avoid the cost of supporting a family. Officer settlers, and others with the means, were prepared to take on a family for the sake of the farming skills and background of Petworth immigrants. In 1834, Anthony Hawke, Colborne's chief emigration agent, launched the five-acre plan in response to a flurry of demands for labour, which identified areas where rapid growth still obtained.[15]

Hawke sent most of the Petworth emigrants of 1834 to the future town of Woodstock in the township of Blandford. Single men found work, and eleven families were placed on a government reserve surveyed to give each family a five-acre plot where a log house was built for them. In Woodstock, some immigrants stayed to purchase their lots and others settled nearby. Petworth emigrants here, as in Adelaide, attracted chain migrants and established enough of a presence to be remembered in local history.

Upper Canada slid into a recession in 1835 and 1836. Hawke reported pessimistically that the immigration of 1835 barely balanced the outflow of new and recent immigrants across the border to the United States. Although he made a qualified exception for those with useful skills, he recommended that labouring emigrants should not be encouraged unless they had family in the province. He also expanded his five-acre lot plan to two new communities. The scanty information available on Petworth families sent to Brantford suggests that they benefited from this temporary refuge even if they travelled on within a relatively short time. In 1837, Petworth families were again directed to Woodstock. Hawke later stated that under this plan he had settled rather more than sixty families, of whom perhaps half were sent by the Petworth committee.

In England, Sockett's conclusions are interesting because they were based on the reports of James Marr Brydone, his superintendent from 1834 to 1837, and on the news shared with him by families and friends of Petworth immigrants—sources different from those of Colborne and Hawke and closer to those available to potential emigrants. His project to have Egremont buy an estate was in part an attempt to re-create for his immigrants the alternative offered by Colborne in the Adelaide settlement in 1832. During the period of the five-acre lot plan, Sockett sent families that were larger and had more young children than was usual for emigrants arriving at Quebec.

Sockett had sought Egremont's patronage in 1832 in order to smooth the way for his people as much as he could. He had no illusions that he could eliminate hardships and individual failures, but he took greatest comfort from letters which affirmed his belief that those he sent to Upper Canada had a better prospect of improving their standard of living than if they had remained at home. Between 1832 and 1837, Sockett and his Petworth Emigration Committee chartered and organized seven emigrant ships and were closely involved in sending an eighth. The immigrants from these ships had the support in Upper Canada of a Petworth superintendent, and received more than usual attention from the local administration. After Egremont died in the autumn of 1837, these advantages were not available to Petworth immigrants.

In 1838, and until at least 1845, a scaled-back Petworth Emigration
Committee continued to send a few emigrants to Upper Canada as
individuals on ships sailing from London. They sent the largest numbers in 1843 and 1844, but available records suggest no more than one
hundred in all. In these years, Sockett wrote, his committee assisted
mainly people who approached them for assistance to join immigrants
already settled in Upper Canada. He took his cue from the experience
of the Uptons and other families of chain migrants.

Relatives and friends settled in Upper Canada offered the security
of a destination where immigrants could find temporary shelter. Some
Petworth immigrants offered to share land with family members or to
take them when they themselves went to pioneer in a new area; more
often, they promised help in finding work. In the case of the Uptons,
William Upton and his young brother, Clifford, were the first members
of his family to emigrate from Petworth in 1832. By 1834, when three
more of William's brothers came to Upper Canada on a Petworth ship,
he and Clifford were established in Hamilton. The three newcomers
joined them and found work there. A year later, their mother followed
on the Petworth ship for 1835, accompanied by her youngest son and
Frederick's fiancée. Although his mother did not learn of it until after
she arrived, William died in March 1835. She did not see him, but she
did find her family re-established in Upper Canada.

The nature of the Petworth scheme as the project of private sponsors limited access to it. Before 1837, these emigrations were effectively
restricted to those who had sponsors and parishes willing to take part
and pay the extra costs associated with this scheme. After 1837, the pool
of potential emigrants who could persuade their parishes and the
Petworth committee to assist them shrank to a smaller geographic area
and to fewer people within that area. For the people who did go to
Upper Canada with aid from the Petworth Emigration Committee,
assistance from parish and sponsors, and from emigrants of earlier
years, mitigated the risks of emigrating in poverty.

Notes

1. [Thomas Sockett], *Emigration: Letters from Sussex Emigrants who Sailed from
   Portsmouth, in April 1832* (Petworth: John Phillips, 1833), 22–3.
2. G. E. Mingay, ed., *The Agrarian History of England and Wales: 1750–1850,*

vol 6, gen. ed. Joan Thirsk (Cambridge: Cambridge University Press, 1989); Michael E. Rose, *The English Poor Law 1780–1930* (Newton Abbot, England: David and Charles, 1971); K. D. M. Snell, *Annals of the Labouring Poor: Social Change and Agrarian England 1660–1900*, Cambridge Studies in Population, Economy and Society in Past Time (Cambridge: University Press, 1985).

3. Francis W. Steer and Noel H. Osborne, ed., *The Petworth House Archives*, vol. 1 (Chichester: West Sussex County Council, 1968); Timothy J. McCann, ed., *The Goodwood Estate Archives: A Catalogue*, vol. 3 (Chichester: West Sussex County Council, 1984). Useful government records are in the Public Record Office, London, in Colonial Office series relating to Upper Canada, and in the volumes of the Ministry of Health containing the correspondence of the Poor Law Commissioners. Canadian sources include the National Archives of Canada, Upper Canada Sundries, and the Archives of Ontario, RG 1, Ministry of National Resources, records of the Crown Lands Department.

4. Helen Cowan, *British Emigration to British North America: The First Hundred Years*, rev. ed. (Toronto: University of Toronto Press, 1961). Donald Harman Akenson, *The Irish Diaspora* (Toronto: P. D. Meany, 1993), surveys recent work on Irish emigration to North America and to Australia and New Zealand. Charlotte Erickson, *Leaving England: Essays on British Emigration in the Nineteenth Century* (Cornell: Cornell University Press, 1994), includes essays on English emigrants to the United States in the 1830s and 1840s.

5. A. C. Buchanan's annual reports for 1831–32 and for 1834 on were published in the British Sessional Papers; his report for 1833 is in PRO, CO 384/35, fo.23 v.

6. E. J. Hobsbawm and George Rudé, *Captain Swing* (London: Lawrence and Wishart, 1969); Andrew Charlesworth, ed., *An Atlas of Rural Protest in Britain 1545–1900* (London and Canberra: Croom Helm, 1983); John Stevenson, *Popular Disturbances in England, 1700–1832*, rev. ed. (London and New York: Longman, 1992).

7. Nassau Senior, *Remarks on Emigration with a Draft of a Bill* (London, 1831).

8. S. G. and E. O. A. Checkland, *The Poor Law Report of 1834* (Harmondsworth, Middlesex: Penguin Books, 1974); Peter Dunkley, "Whigs and Paupers: The Reform of the English Poor Laws, 1830–1834," *Journal of British Studies* 20, no 2 (1981): 124–49; Anthony Brundage, *The Making of the New Poor Law* (New Brunswick, N.J.: Rutgers University Press, 1978).

9. "John Colborne," in Francess G. Halpenny and Jean Hamelin, eds., *Dictionary of Canadian Biography*, (Toronto: University of Toronto Press, 1976), vol. 9, 137–44.

10. Rainer Baehre, "Paupers and Poor Relief in Upper Canada," Canadian Historical Association, *Historical Papers* (1981), 57–80.

11. Terry Crowley, "Rural Labour," in Paul Craven, ed., *Labouring Lives: Work and Workers in Nineteenth-Century Ontario*, Ontario Historical Studies Series (Toronto: University of Toronto Press, 1995), 10–103.

12. Geoffrey Bilson, *A Darkened House: Cholera in Nineteenth-Century Canada* (Toronto: University of Toronto Press, 1980).

13. Wendy Cameron, "'Till they get tidings from those who are gone . . .': Thomas Sockett and Letters from Petworth Emigrants, 1832–37," *Ontario History* 85, no. 1 (March, 1993): 1–16.

14. Douglas McCalla, *Planting the Province: The Economic History of Upper Canada 1784–1870*, Ontario Studies Series (Toronto: University of Toronto Press, 1993).

15. British Parliamentary Papers, 1841 (298), XV, 429-35, Sydenham to Russell, enclosure no. 4, Hawke to Harrison, 17 December 1840.

"A Door of Escape": Letters Home from Wiltshire and Somerset Emigrants to Upper Canada, 1830–1832

Terry McDonald

THE TITLE OF THIS ARTICLE COMES FROM A PHRASE USED IN JOHN Buckmaster's autobiography, *A Village Politician*. Around 1830, he mentioned a letter arriving in his Buckinghamshire village from a farmer who "had emigrated some years ago to America [and] wrote a glowing account of the country and its prospects, urging all who could to come over to Iowa. The letter was read in almost every cottage. It was read at the village inn and at the Methodist chapel every Sunday until it was nearly worn out. The Lord had opened a door of escape."[1] Although Buckmaster's farmer had gone to the United States and of his own accord, the impact that his letter had on those at home was being repeated in other villages and towns across the country. Large-scale emigration, especially to Canada and often backed by the community and with the half-hearted support of the government, became commonplace in the 1820s and early 1830s. This paper investigates this phenomenon from the point of view of those who went, rather than those administering. It also suggests a certain "sleight of hand" by the supporters of emigration as a solution to poverty and unemployment by manipulating information about those planning to go or already living in Canada.

Letters home, as Buckmaster revealed, had an enormous impact not just on the recipients, but on a wider readership in the community and even within the educated classes in the country. The letters from Wiltshire and Somerset emigrants which form the basis of this paper attracted a great deal of attention when published in printed collections, and they were discussed in the earnest journals of the day, such as the *Quarterly Review* and *Gentleman's Magazine*. Perhaps they were simply among the first to be brought to a wider audience, but they were certainly celebrated. Yet suspicion always dogged them: were they simply propaganda rather than a true record of emigrant experiences and feelings? Possibly—there are marked similarities in the content and style of each individual letter and with those in other collections, especially on the prices of goods and the general conditions in Canada. There were people who thought so; witness Thomas Sockett's evidence to the Select Committee on the Post when he said that there was a general opinion among the poor in 1832 that the Corsley letters (those published in 1831 by G. Poulett Scrope from Corsley, Wiltshire emigrants)[2] "were got up and published for the sake of getting rid of them and that when other emigrants were sent out. . . . They hit upon a variety of devices to ascertain the genuineness of the letters that were returned."[3]

In 1836, James Inches published an anti-emigration pamphlet maintaining that

> . . . letters . . . from emigrants are almost together of the same strain. They are written in the style of other advertisements of that kind. . . . The substance of the whole is exactly similar—condolence with their friends in Europe for the starvation and other miseries to which they are doomed to submit in England, as well as Ireland, from want of food and want of money—fullness of everything in Canada—from 3s to 8s per day for wages, besides board and lodging—plenty of beef, butter, poultry, turkeys, and every thing that is good—well stocked farms of their own in a few years—no taxes—lots of invitations to come out—directions to starving Emigrants at home to take a great many things out with them—long list of articles which will be useful in Canada—weather pleasant, and flour three farthings per pound![4]

Inches set out to prove that the content of the letters was "pure invention and completely at variance with the truth," citing letters from the Corsley emigrants and from Frome, in neighbouring Somerset, to support his arguments. The Frome letters, along with the Corsley ones are central to this article.

The published letters were always presented as being "Copied from the originals, with exception of occasional corrections of spelling and omission of Private Affairs,"[5] but an idea of what the letters looked like when received in England is given by one from William Clements of Corsley, which appeared in its original form in at least two publications and in corrected form in another. The *Bath Chronicle* of 4 August

1831, for example, published parts of it with uncorrected spelling, and Clements's phrasing and grammar are similar to those in other manuscript letters held by the Wiltshire County Record Office.[6] Clements's letter, addressed to his father, proudly told him,

> Now I am goun to Work on My One frme of 50 Eakers wich I bot at 55£ and I have 5 years to pay it in. I have bot Me a Cow and 5 pigs. . . . If I had staid at Corsley I never should had nothing.—I like the Contry very Much—I am at librty to shout terky, Quill, Pigons, Phesents, Dear, and all kind of Geam wch I have on My Back Wood.

The publication of Clements's letter had the desired effect, for the *Bath Chronicle* marvelled at his situation: "Think of a mere labourer talking of working his own farm of 50 acres, buying cows and pigs—sowing wheat, building a house etc. When shall we see a labourer in England in one year at such prosperity?"

A longer version of this letter was also used by an advocate of emigration, William Cattermole, who published the texts of two lectures that he gave at Mechanics' Institutes in Ipswich and Colchester in May 1831. He, too, kept Clements's idiosyncratic spelling but published a longer version in which other Corsley emigrants were mentioned. Clements's letter also appeared in its corrected form in the *Quarterly Review.*[7]

Although there were many other collections of letters published, including those of emigrants from Petworth in Sussex, who went to Canada between 1832 and 1837 with the support of the Earl of Egremont, those from the Wiltshire and Somerset emigrants attracted particular attention at the time. Thus, versions of the letters appear not only in Scrope's publication and, for the Frome emigrants of 1831 and 1832, in Lewis's collection,[8] but also in journals and pamphlets whose authors supported emigration as a means of solving or alleviating the problems of rural poverty. As Inches had said, they tended to be formulaic and were clearly published to encourage others to follow them.

But, propaganda or not, the letters have one great advantage. The people whose names appeared as the authors were real, settled in real places, and these letters are full of clues as to what happened to them once they reached Canada. Thus, they are a legitimate source and can be used to find out how particular individuals survived in the years after their arrival, and what they and their children achieved. Letters from the people listed below entered the public domain and form the basis of this research. There are two main collections:

> The Corsley emigration of 1830, published by G. Poulett Scrope contained letters from:

> William Clements (longer version in Cattermole, also in the *Bath Chronicle* and the *Quarterly Review.*)
> James Treasure (longer version in Doyle,[9] and also in *Gentleman's Magazine* and the *Quarterly Review.*)
> Philip Annett
> Joseph Silcox
> Thomas Lister-Axford
> John Down (also in *Gentleman's Magazine*)
> C. Henitage
> James Watts (two letters—probably two parts of one letter. Also in the *Quarterly Review.*)
> Thomas Hunt (two letters, also appearing in Doyle but signed "J. and J. Hunt." Also in the *Quarterly Review.*)
> Esau Prangley (longer version appears in Doyle but with different date and signed "Esau and Elizabeth." Also cited in Inches.)
> George Lewis
> William Snelgrove (slightly different version in Doyle, also in the *Quarterly Review.*)
> William Singer (longer version in Doyle)
> John West

> The Frome emigrations of 1831 and 1832, published c. 1833:[10]

> The 1831 emigration:

> William Harding
> Richard and Mary Barter
> John and Sophia Hill (cited in the *Quarterly Review*)
> William and Jane Grant
> Robert Slade (also appearing in Bunn, along with a different one in *Gentleman's Magazine.*)
> William and Jane Rawlings (also in *Gentleman's Magazine*)
> James Carpenter
> Joseph Lansdown
> Levi Payne
> Thomas and Sarah Dredge
> Mary Ann Cuzner

The 1832 emigration:

William Jeanes (three letters, which were also included in Bunn)
John Thomas (also in Bunn)
Sylvia Lawrence (also in Bunn)
William Moore (also in Bunn with excerpts from two of his later
    letters)
William Thracher (also in Bunn)
Edward Moon (also in Bunn)

Bunn also has letters from two people, John Balch and Hannah Sutton, which do not appear in the Lewis collection. Many of the letters refer to other emigrants, including letter-writers, thus providing a reasonable sample of the hundreds of people who left Somerset and Wiltshire around the year 1830.

The towns and villages that these emigrants left were from the part of the West Country where Somerset becomes Wiltshire—Frome, Warminster, Corsley, Westbury, Chapmanslade, Maiden Bradley, Longbridge Deverill, and Horningsham. In all of these, the parish authorities helped people to emigrate and the marked increase in numbers from this area in the late 1820s prompted the *Quebec Mercury* to note in April 1831, "Nearly 600 settlers have already arrived in the port of Quebec, principally in the *Airthy Castle* from Bristol and the *Euphrosyne* from Bridgewater which brought out between them 510 souls, almost entirely families from Wiltshire and Somerset, counties the population of which have hitherto been little prone to emigrate."[11]

In Frome and other towns in the area, the state of the woollen-cloth industry has long been seen as the major factor in convincing people to pack up and leave England for the uncertainties of British North America, although there may have been other motives.[12] Elsewhere, the depressed state of agriculture provided the spur. However, in all cases there was also the active encouragement of those charged with maintaining the unemployed poor who saw emigration as a solution to their problems. And there were problems—the *Bath Chronicle* in 1831 described the unemployed weavers of Frome as "a wretched and almost famishing mass,"[13] while Cobbett, five years earlier, noted that "[the] poor creatures at Frome have pawned all their things, or nearly all. All their best clothes, their blankets and sheets; their looms, any little piece of furniture that they had."[14] The letters from the Corsley and Frome emigrants, though, include evidence that may refute the idea that they were paupers with few possessions.

In 1831 and 1832, the Select Vestry of Frome, like other parishes across the land, agreed to pay the passage and expenses of those who wished to emigrate to Upper Canada. Overall, the cost per person was about £6 which included £3.17.0d adult passage to Montreal (28/6d for youths) plus allowances for provisions, clothing, tools, and so on, plus £1.0.0d per adult and 10/- per child to help them when they arrived. In March 1831, 85 people left Frome for Bristol on the first stage of their journey to Quebec and Montreal.

The Frome emigrations have been described as inspired by the success of that of the previous year from the nearby village of Corsley. There, the parish "shipped off at its own cost sixty-six of the least desirable of its inhabitants, about half being adults and half children."[15] The origin of this belief that they were "undesirables" lies in a memo from the Marquess of Bath's steward, who told his master that the emigrants were "several poachers and other such characters . . . of the very class we would wish to remove—men of suspected bad habits and bringing up their children to wickedness."[16] Secondary sources such as nineteenth-century histories of the Ontario townships tend to credit the Marquess of Bath with the financing of the Corsley and Frome emigrations but, unlike Petworth, where the Earl of Egremont underwrote the cost, he simply provided £100 toward the costs of the 1831 party. A neighbouring peer, the Earl of Cork, gave £50, and the town's leading employer, George Sheppard, gave £30. The community parties emigrating typically numbered between 50 and 200, usually family based, although there were always a number of men on their own, both married and unmarried. The 85 Frome emigrants were among 254 people who sailed from Bristol on the *Airthry Castle* in March 1831 and arrived in Quebec five weeks later. Their arrival was noted by William Lyon Mackenzie, who went on board and described the new settlers as "all English, from about Bristol, Bath, Frome, Warminster, Maiden Bradley etc. . . . and poor, but in general . . . fine looking people and such as I was glad to see come to America."[17] Once in Canada, some emigrants went no farther than Montreal,[18] but the majority pressed on toward the new settlements being established along the shores of Lake Ontario and Lake Erie. Some, but not many, went to the United States. From their new homes, letters were sent to their relatives in England and, as already noted, like the earlier letters from the Corsley emigrants, these were circulated and published. Three examples serve to illustrate how the emigrants fared in Canada.

One letter was from a teen-age girl, Mary Ann Cuzner, and it began

"Dear Gentleman and Ladies." It has the usual catalogue of prices and a good description of the Atlantic crossing, but it also has an intriguing human touch: "I am glad to say my father's wicked heart is turned, and he is getting quite sober, he behaves better to my mother, he is in a good business, he has left Montreal and gone to Bytown. . . ." Mary Ann's father was James Cuzner, "the Barber of Bytown" as she referred to him in her letter, and he had left England with his wife Hannah and six children, including Mary Ann and a son named Luke. The Cuzners stayed in Ottawa (as Bytown is now known), and James died there in July 1858. He was still married to Hannah.[19] James Cuzner did apply for a grant of land, but more on this later.

The Cuzner children did well in Ottawa; Luke, who was seven when the family left England, became a successful boot and shoemaker. He appears in various directories as a "Manufacturer and Dealer in Boots and Shoes, leather findings etc.," and by 1861, the capital invested in the business was $4,400 and he employed six people.[20] Another of James's children, John, became a clerk, but then went into business with a partner as a hardware merchant.[21] A third Cuzner, William, who was probably a grandson to James, became a reporter for the *Ottawa Citizen*.[22]

The only examples of "serial" letters in the collection published in Frome in 1833 were three from a man who was apparently part of the 1832 emigration, William Jeanes. He was one of those who, although married, went on his own, expecting to be able to bring his wife and family out later but found this extremely difficult to do. In three lengthy letters, Jeanes describes how, as an ex-soldier, he was given 200 acres of land at Tilbury, near the shores of Lake Erie. He says how well he is doing, but in the second letter he worries that he has not heard from his wife. In the third (August 1833), he is becoming desperate, despite having cleared six of his 200 acres and built "a snug little house." "What," he asked, "is 200 acres of land to me if you cannot come to me? I would not be cut off from you and the poor children for all America." He then goes on to tell of a dream that he has had in which one of his children (Betsy) is ill and another (Henry) is dying. There is a comment at the end of the letter from Thomas Bunn, the Frome gentleman who played a leading role in organising the emigrations:

It is an unhappy circumstance that this man has separated himself from his family. His wife has written to him by no means to return from Canada, and that she hopes to be enabled to join him there, with her children. Possibly every person who reads the above letter . . . will contribute something to pay the expense of their voyage.

Someone obviously did, for the Jeanes family appear in the 1861 census for Tilbury East, albeit with the name now spelt "Janes." William was 80 years old and a farmer, while Elizabeth was 82. His premonition about Henry was not fulfilled because he, too, appears as a 40 year-old farmer. There are, however, other references to William Jeanes in the Ontario Archives which will be discussed at a later stage of this article.

The third example is that of Richard and Mary Barter. Their letter, dated 9 July 1831, says all the usual things—they have a farm of 100 acres, they would like their relatives to join them—but its most distinctive feature is that it gives their address as "St. Stephen's." According to all the gazetteers of Canada, the only town of that name is not in Ontario or Quebec, but in New Brunswick, where it is actually "St Stephen." Given that all the other letters are from locations in Upper Canada, Montreal, or the United States (usually New York state), the Barters' letter suggests that they had travelled in a very different direction than the other Frome emigrants. Indeed they had, for the 1851 Census for Charlotte County, New Brunswick (which includes the town of St. Stephen), records the presence of English-born Richard Barter, a 52-year-old farmer living with his wife Mary, age 51.[23] The census lists several other people with the same surname, including Thomas Barter, who was also born in England and was now 39 years old. Thomas would therefore have been about 20 when the first Frome emigration took place, and someone of that name is mentioned in William and Jane Rawlings' letter from "Auguste, Upper Canada." This township (actually Augusta) is near Prescott, at the eastern end of Lake Ontario and a long way from St. Stephen. The 1861 census[24] has Mary Barter, widow, as head of family. The St. Stephen Rural Cemetery includes several Barter graves, with Richard's recording him as being from "Somersetshire, G.B."

The life histories of most of the other Frome and Corsley emigrants can be traced through documents in the Ontario Archives, especially those who settled at Dummer, part of modern Peterborough. The Dummer Township papers of 1831 list the names of over 30 men and describe them as "Wilts settlers."[25] Later documents record their success or failure in clearing and farming the land allocated to them when they first arrived.[26] The majority stayed on their land, but some sold it or passed it on to other settlers.

Another Frome emigrant whose letter home was published, Levi Payne, successfully settled in Dummer and founded what was almost a Payne dynasty in that area. He and his wife Sarah, and several of his brothers, successfully farmed their lands, and the censuses and assessment rolls give an indication of how they lived and worked. The Dummer Assessment Roll of 1839 records their property in great detail and shows that it included several buildings plus a grist mill "wrought by water," sawmills, merchant shops, and storehouses, as well as stallions, horses, oxen, milch cows and young cattle, and several carriages or wagons. One of Levi's daughters, Charlotte, married a Corsley emigrant, Isaac Snelgrove, whilst another, Elizabeth, married a William Harding.[27]

Levi and Sarah are mentioned in Guillet's *The Valley of the Trent*, complete with a photograph of them and their original log house. They are described as "prominent early settlers."[28] However, Levi also crops up in Susanna Moodie's classic, middle-class view of settler life, *Roughing it in the Bush*, in which he is described as "the little wiry, witty poacher."[29] Susanna's sister, Catherine, was also involved with people like the Paynes for, as she wrote, "I have a very good girl, the daughter of a Wiltshire emigrant, who is neat and clever, and respectful and industrious, to whom I give three dollars only: she is a happy specimen of the lower order of English emigrants and her family are quite acquisitions to the township in which they live."[30] This "very good girl" may have been Levi's daughter Mary, for he wrote that she and her brother David "is at service under one roof . . . [with] English people." What is known is that Mary was later in service with Susanna Moodie.[31]

Not all emigrants became farmers. The Cuzners, as noted above, stayed in Ottawa, whilst John and Sophia Hill lived in York, where John was able to pursue his trade as a stone mason. One of the Corsley emigrants, James Treasure, worked as a shoemaker in that city.[32] Several of the letter writers seem to have gone no farther than Montreal, and evidence in the trade directories for that city suggests that they settled there.[33]

One emigrant mentioned in the letters—although he did not write any of them—appears in correspondence in 1859 between his daughter and the office of the Hon. Peter Robinson regarding ownership of a piece of land. Mary Ann Saunders maintained that her father, "James Saunders, emigrant from England sometime in the year 1831 was located by the Agent in this place."[34] As the only heir, Mary Ann wanted to know how to get her hands on the deed. She added that she had been informed that her father "served in the Military Service in Britain and was entitled to a free grant of land for his service."[35] It was discovered that Saunders had been located at Dummer and had occupied the land for four years "when he left the township and never returned. His wife [Susan] did not accompany him but remained in the neighbourhood with her own family,"[36] eventually signing it over to the current occupant for $80. The township papers record that James (who could not write) was awarded the southern half (100 acres) of lot 17 in the second concession of Dummer on 26 December 1831, but a note on the bottom of the page states, "Inspected 1840 when old James Saunders took away."[37]

So far so good—almost all of those who wrote or are mentioned in the letters can be traced in Canadian archives, and the great majority of these Somerset and Wiltshire emigrants did indeed benefit from their sudden uprooting and subsequent resettlement on the other side of the Atlantic. They prospered, and so did their children. But, was it really a sudden uprooting prompted by local worthies trying to resolve the problem of ever increasing poor-rates? Archival evidence in Canada reveals that many of the emigrants whose letters were published as if they were all part of the parish-sponsored emigrations between 1830 and 1832 were already in Canada (or had been there) before those dates.

Among the examples mentioned so far, reference was made to some who had served in the army and were therefore entitled to extra land. This characteristic of the Frome and Corsley emigrants crops up so many times that it appears to be more than a coincidence. Mann maintains that "Above 800 from Frome had entered the army by 1795"[38] making it likely that some of the emigrants would have served in the armed forces. Those whose military service has been established are listed below:

William Jeanes, Sergeant in the First Garrison Battalion, discharged
    1814
James Saunders, Military Service in Britain
James Hunt, Sergeant in the 50th Regiment
John Thomas, Petty Officer in the Royal Navy
James Carpenter, Acting Sailing Master
John Hill, 9th Regiment of Foot
James Cuzner, Royal Marines
John Singer, Private 66th Company of Royal Marines. Discharged
    1816

James Long, 51st Company of Royal Marines
William Grant, First or Grenadier Regiment of Foot Guards

Quite likely, some of them had served in Canada in the War of 1812. James Carpenter, for instance, petitioning for land in 1832, used his experience as "acting sailing master on board his majesty's fleet during the late American War"[39] and was able to produce documents from 1829 confirming that "James Carpenter served as Acting Sailing Master on board his Majesty's Fleet on Lake Ontario during the late War with America."[40] James Cuzner, despite his urban occupation, petitioned for land in 1832, and the report of the Justice of the Peace has "total service of thirteen years and thirty four days, served seven on board the *Belle Poule* and the remaining period in the Merican [*sic*] War."[41] John Thomas, who wrote from Montreal in October 1832, "earned a livelihood as a seaman on the Lakes . . . as a discharged Petty Officer of his Majesty's Royal Navy."[42] John Hill served in the 9th Regiment of Foot, which, the records show, was in Canada between 1813 and 1815.[43] Thus, to many Frome men, North America was not some mythical place but somewhere they already knew and with which they may even have had connections.

Certainly, one leading figure in the district around Frome knew southern Ontario well and encouraged others to go. This was Joseph Silcox, who went to Canada in 1817, along with, it would seem, his brother Daniel and Thomas Orchard. However, Alan Brunger says that Daniel emigrated in 1816 and was joined by Joseph a year later.[44] They were certainly together in New York in April 1817, when the British Consul General, James Buchanan, signed their passes allowing them to go on to Upper Canada.[45] Joseph is described as a native of Wiltshire and a painter by trade; Daniel is said to be a farmer and had "produced evidence of good character at home and also of recent arrival"; Thomas Orchard was from Somerset and a wheelwright. All three men's passes were dated 29 April. Daniel could, of course, have travelled from Canada to New York to meet his brother.

Joseph Silcox's role in encouraging emigration from Corsley and Frome is well documented. Scrope's introduction to the published Corsley letters states,

> . . . a certain Joseph Silcox, the brother of a respectable farmer of that parish, had lately returned from Canada, after a residence there of two or three years; and being a dissenting preacher, he had frequent op-

portunities of holding forth to his neighbours on the vast difference between the condition of industrious labourers in this country and in America and the advantages they would derive from emigrating there. He declared his own intention of returning immediately; and a considerable number of his neighbours became desirous of following his example.

On his original arrival in Upper Canada, Silcox was located on a lot of 200 acres in the North Branch of Talbot Road in the township of Southwold by Colonel Thomas Talbot. He returned to England in 1821 and stayed for seven years "to arrange his business affairs." Silcox became an important figure in Nonconformist circles in southwestern Ontario, but it is the reference to Colonel Thomas Talbot that is significant.

Talbot is something of a "folk-hero" in the history of pre-Confederation Canada, renowned for his "entrepreneurial" approach to land settlement. He would, for instance, give settlers only 50 of their allotted 200 acres, deeding the balance to himself. In 1817, Talbot held the title to 20,000 acres and controlled, in total, 139,000 acres of surveyed lands. From the outset, he had the backing of those in authority in York, for witness a letter from the Lieutenant-Governor's office dated 12 February 1811 to Thomas Ridout, Surveyor-General: "The Lieutenant-Governor has commanded me to desire you will furnish Colonel Talbot with a list of vacant lots in Yarmouth, which are to be reserved for Persons recommended by the Colonel."[46] He had not, though, made a return of his locations for three years and when, in October 1816, he submitted a list containing about 350 names, only 77 were found to have deposited warrants for land with the Surveyor-General's Office. Talbot's return for August 1817 listed the names of 805 settlers, but six months later, 545 of them had not paid any fees. Talbot excused the ambiguities in his return by pointing out that he

cannot consider the foregoing return as conclusive, it being liable to daily alterations occasioned by frequent casualties, arising from the following causes:

1st Tardiness in commencing to perform settlement duties,
2nd A manifest disposition to impose by offering the land for sale,
3rd Change of sentiment and notifying inability to settle the land.[47]

Talbot's seeming sleight of hand with the terms of his original powers to grant land led one frustrated member of the Executive Council to write to the Lieutenant-Governor and complain, "It is apparent . . . that the province is now at the disposal of Colonel Talbot."[48]

Given the uncertainty about just who was settled on Talbot's lands—he would use pencil on his maps so that the names could be easily changed—it is tempting to ask whether they actually existed. Did Talbot simply allocate land to people whose names came into his possession from other emigrants, or even the army lists? The evidence is circumstantial, but Talbot did return to England early in 1818, managing to win for himself the support of the then Colonial Secretary and the right to claim another 65,000 acres, and returned to Canada in April or May of that year. He came back to England again in 1822, at a time when Silcox had also returned.

The Ontario Archives contain several documents relating to the Frome and Wiltshire emigrants, such as land petitions which state that they had been settled in Canada much earlier than the years that they were supposed to have arrived—and indeed *did* arrive. These include William Jeanes of "Lot no. 11 on the North Side of the Talbot Middle Road in the said township of East Tilbury for which he was located by Colonel Talbot in the year 1820."[49] This was the man whose three letters, showing him to be desperate for his wife and children to join him, were published after the 1832 Frome emigration. Esau Prangley (not a John Smith– or William Jones–type name), who was part of the Corsley emigration of 1830, was, according to his petition, located by Talbot in 1818. Another 1830 Corsley emigrant, Robert Annett, was also located in 1818. There are others. William Singer, another soldier, located by Colonel Talbot in 1819, is an example. Edward Moon, apparently an 1832 emigrant, settled in August 1819 and was granted 100 acres.

There are three explanations for these mysteries. The first is the obvious one that the wrong documents have been used or that people with similar names are being confused. This can be rejected, for the dates are clear and all the evidence shows that the right people have been traced. Witness William Jeanes's discharge certificate which shows him as a native of Frome and a cloth dresser by trade.[50]

The second explanation is that of a wonderful conspiracy between Talbot and those who could provide him with the names of potential, but not actually present, immigrants to whom he could allocate land, with three-quarters of it going to himself. Talbot did, after all, come home in 1818. He produced his list of names at about this time and could have drawn upon Silcox's knowledge and connections in Corsley and Frome. There is, however, nothing but circumstantial evidence to support this hypothesis.

The third is the most mundane but most likely explanation that the letters are "dishonest." As noted earlier, they were from real people in real places and refer to other real people and places. But are the dates attributed to them genuine? Some of them are, for they contain information supported by other sources. Both William Harding and Mary Ann Cuzner refer to the *Airthry Castle* picking up seven sailors shipwrecked five days earlier off Anticosti Island. This is confirmed by the *Quebec Mercury* of 23 April 1831, which reported, "The *Airthy Castle* has brought up Captain Doyle, Mate and four seamen who were wrecked this spring on Anticost on a sealing mission from the Magdelene [sic] islands." However, the Frome letters do contain some curious contradictions. John and Sophia Hill, for example, seem to have been eagerly awaited in Canada by their Carpenter relatives. A letter in the Frome collection from James Carpenter dated 5 November 1831 from Edwardsburgh (Grenville County, near Prescott) says that he had delayed replying to his daughter's letter "in expectation of seeing John Hill here." Further on he says, "If John Hill were to come out, he may depend on plenty of work at his trade." There is, however, another "Carpenter" letter, published in Martin Doyle's *Hints on Emigration*, from George and Anne Carpenter in York dated 29 January 1831. This includes the information that "John Hill is coming" and (later) that "John Hill, his wife and family, are coming out." Yet, according to the various accounts of the 1831 emigration, it was a sudden decision by the Frome Vestry in February to organise and pay for the venture and to seek volunteers. The Hills may simply have taken advantage of this offer, but it does appear that they had decided long before the February meeting that they would emigrate and could afford the cost of the passages. George and Anne address their letter "Dear Brothers and Sisters," and also refer to "my poor father and mother," adding, "I hope my dear brother James will not let them want." Yet the James Carpenter referred to above is clearly well established in Edwardsburgh with his own farm and "another lot of land close by, consisting of one hundred acres, with ten acres cleared, and a house on it" which he was "reserving for you and your husband." It was, as mentioned above, a James Carpenter who had served as an acting sailing master in the war of

1812. Carpenter also said that he was living near to "William Clements of Corsley." In Scrope's collection of Corsley letters, Clements was at Port Talbot, several hundred miles to the west. As has been shown, Richard and Mary Barter did settle in St. Stephen, New Brunswick, but the 1851 census states that they had been there for 31 years.[51] This means that they had left England in 1820, not 1831. Their published letter mentions that they had "a Farm, containing one hundred acres of land, with a decent framed House, and Log Barn" plus "three cows, and cut hay enough to winter them." They also mentioned that their circumstances allowed them "to engage and pay [their parents' and five other family members'] passage in the ship *Heroine* ... to this country." Yet the readers of the letter were meant to believe that they had only been in Canada for two or three months.

Almost every letter can be queried against the archival evidence in Canada. That by Levi Payne is part of the Frome collection, thereby implying that he was from that town and sent out by the parish, yet documents in Ontario show him to have been a Warminster man.[52] A slight difference perhaps, but still a difference. Another letter purporting to be from an 1831 Frome emigrant is that from Joseph Lansdown sent from New York on 26 September of that year. He tells his mother that his two brothers and their families have arrived safely and that he has furnished them with all they needed to establish themselves in America. He also adds a postscript to "Mr. Sheppard"[53] thanking him for his "kind favours to them when they were about to come to America." Once again, the writer is already well established in the new world.

This brings us back to the comments made at the beginning about letters as propaganda rather than as forgeries. It would seem that genuine letters received earlier, perhaps even a few years earlier, were added to those received immediately after the Corsley and Frome emigrations in order to increase their impact and persuade others to go. They were also useful in helping convince the many middle-class sceptics that emigration was a worthwhile and practical policy at a time when there was considerable debate about it.

The phrase normally associated with these parish-sponsored emigrations is "shovelling out paupers."[54] The circumstantial evidence is that Frome emigrants were not paupers in the literal sense of the word. Many of them were connected to some of Frome's better-off citizens, if inclusion in Pigot's Directory and other evidence can be trusted. References in the letters to particular friends at home again suggest that the majority of emigrants were at least artisans or shop-keepers, and instructions from husbands to wives or from children to parents about what to bring with them when they came suggest a surprisingly comfortable home life. There is still considerable work to be done on this aspect of these emigrations, including a search for motivation. The emigrations took place at a time when and in a part of England where there was considerable unrest, both political and social. It needs to be established whether the Somerset and Wiltshire emigrants were leaving because of the uncertain situation that they perceived in their own communities rather than financial hardship, as was popularly supposed.

This article is entitled "A Door of Escape" not just as a literary conceit but because it conveys an emotive message. A door is often the only way out of an enclosed space, and escape usually means achieving freedom from captivity. For the emigrants from Somerset and Wiltshire, the evidence points to the door being open much wider and for a longer period than was suggested by people like Buckmaster. It further shows that Upper Canada began receiving the sort of people that it urgently needed—independent, well-travelled, and possessing the practical skills so necessary in their new homes. That there were some in England who were prepared to amend and enhance the evidence of their success does not invalidate it, but it does reveal a little about how persons in authority achieved their goal of reducing the cost to the parish of maintaining the poor.

Notes

1. J. Buckmaster, *A Village Politician* (Horsham: Caliban Books, 1982), 47–8. Buckmaster rose from agricultural labourer to schools inspector. His son Stanley's rise was more spectacular, for he became Lord Chancellor in 1915.
2. G. Poulett Scrope, *Extracts of Letters from Poor Persons who Emigrated Last Year to Canada and the United States* (London, 1831).
3. Minutes of Evidence Taken before the Select Committee on Postage. Reverend T. Sockett, 23 May 1838. Parliamentary Papers.
4. J. Inches, *Letters on Emigration to Canada, addressed to the Very Rev. Principal Baird* (Perth, Printed for the author, 1836), 166–72 (Toronto Metropolitan Reference Library).
5. Or similar phrasing.
6. A typical one is that to the Overseers of the Poor of Bristol from two

women in Bristol seeking to join their husbands in America. Its spelling and grammar are similar to those of Clements. Document 77/117/1, Wiltshire C.R.O.

7. *Quarterly Review* 46 (November 1831–January 1832): 367.

8. J. O. Lewis, ed. *Letters from Poor Persons who Emigrated to Canada from the Parish of Frome in the County of Somerset* (Frome, 1945). Although no editor is given for the original 1834 publication, it was almost certainly Thomas Bunn, a leading proponent of the Frome emigrations.

9. "Martin Doyle" (William Hickey), *Hints on Emigration to Upper Canada: Especially addressed to the Middle and Lower Classes* (Dublin, London, Edinburgh, 1831) (Toronto Metropolitan Reference Library).

10. The collection in circulation today is the 1945 reprint edited by J. O. Lewis. However, Thomas Bunn's *A Letter Relative to the Affairs of the Poor of the Parish of Frome Selwood, in Somersetshire* of 1834 (which includes several of the letters) makes it clear that the original collection was published around 1833.

11. *Quebec Mercury*, 30 April 1831. The names of the two ships and of the town of Bridgewater are as printed in the *Mercury*.

12. That the emigrations took place at a time of social and political unrest in England may have some significance, and I am currently researching this aspect of the topic.

13. *Bath Chronicle*, 17 March 1831.

14. William Cobbett, *Rural Rides* (Harmondsworth: Penguin, 1967), 340.

15. M. F. Davies, *Life in an English Village—An Economic and Historical Survey of the Parish of Corsley in Wiltshire* (London, 1909), 80.

16. Copy letter in the Longleat collection, ref. WMR Corsley 556.5, 3/4/1830.

17. W. L. Mackenzie, *Sketches of Canada and the United States* (Toronto [York], 1833), 179. Also cited in E. C. Guillet, ed., *The Valley of the Trent* (Toronto: Champlain Society, 1957), 68.

18. This 1831 emigration was among the last not required to call in at the quarantine station at Grosse Isle.

19. Hannah Cuzner's petition for administration of James' Goods and Chattles, etc., following his death, dated 17 July 1858. Ref: GS2 reel 19, entry A150 (Archives of Ontario).

20. Ottawa Trades Directory, 1863. Ref: B70 D4, reel 1. Also, Ref: C1099, 1861 Census for Ottawa (Archives of Ontario).

21. Woodburn's Directory of Ottawa, 1879.

22. City of Ottawa and Central Canada Directory, 1876. Published by A. S. Woodburn (Archives of Ontario).

23. Ref. F1589-90, Archives of New Brunswick, Fredericton.

24. Ref. F1596, Archives of New Brunswick.
25. Ref. MS400 reel 13, vol. 55, p. 4, Archives of Ontario.
26. Ref. MS658, reel 112. Township Papers, Archives of Ontario.
27. This *could* be the William Harding whose letter from Montreal, dated 1 May 1831, is the first one in the Frome collection, for in it he refers to Charlotte Payne, although the inference is that she is still in England.
28. E Guillet, *The Valley of the Trent*.
29. Susanna Moodie, *Roughing It in the Bush* (Ottawa: Carleton University Press, 1988), 338.
30. Catherine Parr Traill, *The Backwoods of Canada* (Toronto: McClelland & Stewart, 1989), 156.
31. Moodie, *Roughing It*, 587.
32. James Treasure is listed as a Boot and Shoemaker at "King Street 190 Cross Bay Street" and as a shoemaker in York Street in George Walton's Directories of 1834 and 1837, respectively. John Hill appears as a Mason in Newgate Street in 1834, but the 1837 version has "Mrs. Hill, Widow" living in Newgate Street.
33. Ref. B70 Series D, reel 1, Archives of Ontario. Thomas and Sarah Dredge, for example, wrote from Montreal in December 1831, and among those they mentioned was their son Thomas. Someone by that name is included in the 1868 Directory, whilst John Thomas, writing in October 1832, mentions George Oborne [*sic*], and there are people of that name with that spelling in the 1863 Directory. Of the five Frome people who appear to have stayed in Montreal, there is no record of anyone with their surnames in the 1819 Directory, but all five appear in post-1830 ones.
34. Dummer Township Records, MS658, reel 112, p. 309, Archives of Ontario.
35. Ibid.
36. Ibid., 316.
37. Ref. MS627, vol. 301, Archives of Ontario.
38. J. de L. Mann, *The Cloth Industry in the West of England, from 1640 to 1880* (Gloucester: Sutton, 1987), 228. Mann cites Sir F. M. Eden's 1797 work *The State of the Poor* as his source.
39. Upper Canada Land Petitions, C Bundle, 17, Archives of Ontario.
40. Ibid.
41. Ibid.
42. Upper Canada Land Books, C105, Archives of Ontario.
43. C. Series, Reel C3267, RG8, Vol. 836, Archives of Ontario.
44. Alan Brunger, "Geographical Aspects of English Emigration to Canada in the 1830s: Settlement and Community Transfer" presented at *Mirrors of the Old World: Europe and its reproduction Overseas*, Oxford, 17–23 July 1983.

45. Upper Canada Sundries, RG5, A1, vol. 37, pp. 17227–17578, Archives of Ontario.
46. Ref. MS892, reel 11, RG-1 series, A-1-7, vol. 18, Archives of Ontario.
47. Ref: Upper Canada Sundries, C4600, Doc. 16232, Archives of Ontario.
48. Letter from William Dummer Powell, dated 5 June 1817, Upper Canada Sundries, C4549, Archives of Ontario.
49. Upper Canada Landbooks, Vol. D, p. 157. Ref. C108.
50. Ref. Ms563/24 and 25, Archives of Ontario.
51. Ref. F1589-90, Archives of New Brunswick.
52. Ref. MS871 reel 17, Archives of Ontario.
53. The Sheppards were Frome's major employer, with several woollen-cloth factories in the town.
54. H. J. M. Johnston, *British Emigration Policy, 1815–1830: "Shovelling out Paupers."* (Oxford: Clarendon Press, 1972).

Migration as a Trans-generational Affair: The Pilkington and Smith Descendants Return to Canada

Kathleen Burke

AT THE END OF THE EIGHTEENTH CENTURY, TWO YOUNG MILITARY officers, David William Smith and Robert Pilkington, arrived in Upper Canada to take up positions which would contribute to the early building of the province. Neither of the men became permanent settlers, but their experiences in the colony were to have a lasting effect on their lives and the lives of their families, for their claims to fame (if not fortune) centred on their interests in Canada long after they left the colony. This paper traces the activities of these two early sojourners in Canada and their continuing links with the country on their return to England, and contends that the connections with Canada and Canadians established during the early period not only endured, but were of central importance to the subsequent permanent and successful migration to Canada of a later generation. In fact, it could be argued that their descendants began a migration process that has never entirely ceased.

This paper differs in several respects from the majority of migration studies. It is a micro-study of two families rather than a study that concentrates on large numbers of people as members of a group migration. Moreover, while members of the first generation were ultimately sojourners, they were not "faceless guest-workers" or men who fit the more familiar profile of the late-nineteenth- and early-twentieth-century Italian migrant workers described by the late Robert Harney.[1] Rather, they were members of an early Upper Canadian elite who viewed "colonial society as an extension of English society."[2] Their descendants who ultimately settled in Canada also subscribed to those beliefs. Thus, none of the characters in this study can be counted among those for whom migration signalled a rejection of traditional values or parental influence.[3]

To some degree, the process described here forms part of the phenomenon of chain migration, since there was a network, "a series of
individuals and institutions,"[4] which facilitated the transition to the
new land. However, the migration process can be approached more
fruitfully from another perspective—that which Stanley Johannesen, in
his work on Norwegian migrants, has referred to as "trans-generational
migration." Johannesen's use of the term refers to a process of slow
alienation from one's place of birth by a series of small migrations,
spread out over more than one generation—what he terms a "long . . .
affair with many starts, reversals and offshoots."[5] Here the term has
been appropriated to refer to the activities of migrants who continue a
settlement process begun, but not completed, by an earlier generation.
Migration was nurtured and made possible by first-generation memories of the past, as well as by continuing links with the country of
resettlement. Eventual success in the new land depended to a significant degree on mentors in Canada who had not only remained in close
contact with those early sojourners, but who continued to uphold and
maintain an elite society based on British customs and values.

It is unclear whether Robert Pilkington, the first of the sojourners
described in this paper, ever seriously considered permanent residence
in Canada. In his capacity as a Royal Engineer, he was instrumental in
overseeing the construction of several of the province's defensive works,
and he designed and constructed York's first Government House.[6] He
was a leader of the expedition from York to Lake Simcoe in 1793, and
his first attempt to perpetuate his name in Canada appears on early
maps that show a Pilkington Island in Cook's Bay.[7] A member of
General Simcoe's staff, he was accepted into the young province's elite
circles, and became Elizabeth Simcoe's friend and riding companion.
Several of Elizabeth Simcoe's sketches are based on Pilkington's work.[8]

But as a young bachelor, "Pilky" also engaged in wilder pursuits.
He spent much of his time dining and drinking with fellow officers in
the towns of Niagara and York, and on one occasion at least, provoked
local farmers into a brawl and ended up with a broken nose.[9] In short,
Upper Canada would remain in his memory as the site of elevated
social status, frontier adventure, and wild bachelor days.

There was no likelihood of Pilkington resigning his military commission in the early nineteenth century in order to settle in the province, but there are indications that he may have had plans to return to
Canada once his term of service was over. He secured a stake in the
province by acquiring land in Niagara-on-the Lake and in nearby

Grantham, but his most ambitious venture was the purchase of 29,000 acres in Wellington County, close to the town of Elora, where he is reputed to have selected a choice site for a palatial home, surrounded, so it seems, by settlers in a village he planned to establish on the land. According to Grand Valley historian Mabel Dunham, Pilkington began to work on plans for his settlement in 1815, when he sent a party of workers out from England to build mills and a church, to start operation of a lime kiln and stone quarry, and to have roads cut through the bush.[10] However, he was not on hand to supervise the peopling of a township in a sparsely settled area of the province, and the land price was set too high.[11] The church was not completed, the bush grew back over the roads, and many disappointed colonists moved away. Nevertheless, it was this large acreage that immortalized Pilkington's name in Upper Canada and provided him with a link to the province that would remain until his death. Indeed, his papers indicate that his family's inflated idea of his wealth may have been based on his ownership of the Upper Canadian "estate."[12] Unfortunately, Pilkington died in reduced circumstances; as one earlier chronicler reports rather delicately, "his affairs were much embarrassed."[13] Settlement of Pilkington township ceased for several years while his affairs were put into Chancery, and the area continues to be sparsely settled today.

Pilkington's name was perpetuated in this Ontario township, but there is no evidence that he ever returned to Canada. His days in the colony ended in 1803 when he returned to Britain, where—tired of a bachelor existence—he started to look around for a "fair girl to decorate [his] habitation,"[14] and it was through this search that he became intimately involved with the second instigator in the migration process, David William Smith.

Smith had been a rising star in the early days of Upper Canada. He, too, had arrived in the colony as a young military officer and had been a favourite of John Graves Simcoe. Unlike Pilkington, Smith had accumulated an impressive number of civil appointments, and had resigned his army commission after receiving confirmation of his post as the province's first Surveyor-General. Smith also took an active part in the political life of the new province; he sat on the Executive Council, was elected to the first three Houses of Assembly, and served as Speaker for the second Parliament and two sessions of the third.[15]

During this early period of prominence, it seemed that Smith was thinking seriously of permanent settlement. A number of circumstances led, though, to his return to England: his wife and four of his children died, leaving him the sole guardian of four surviving young children; he lost favour under the administration of Peter Russell; he—like most Upper Canadians of the time—suffered from a variety of feverish illnesses. Finally, his indiscreet gossiping led to a fatal duel between the Attorney-General John White and the Clerk of the Executive Council, John Small, and, temporarily, at least, Smith was barred from further advancement. Faced with this combination of circumstances and the object of gossip about his own "amour" with a servant, Smith left Canada in 1802, "disgusted" with attempts to impede his progress and complaining of "the treatment I received, formally, in return for my life, health and fortune."[16]

Despite his disappointment, Smith believed that he might use his Canadian experience and status to attain a suitably impressive and lucrative position in Britain. He hoped, too, to find a new wife and mother for his children, and in this he was successful. In 1803, he married Mary Tylee, a daughter of a brewer and banker who has been described as the wealthiest man in Devizes, Wiltshire.[17] Smith's attempts to find a position were not so immediately gratified. He appealed to all his acquaintances from Canada; former Lieutenant-Governor John Graves Simcoe, Chief Justice Osgoode, and Major Henry Darling were all sympathetic but unable to assist Smith. One of the people who constantly sent him advice about possible openings was Robert Pilkington, although it was through the Duke of Northumberland that Smith managed to secure a post as steward for the Alnwick Castle estates in Northumberland.[18]

Although correspondence concerning employment opportunities ceased, Pilkington remained in constant touch with the Smiths and, in 1810, he became Smith's brother-in-law, when he married Hannah Tylee. When two of Smith's daughters also married members of the Tylee family, the connection among all three families became stronger.

Members of the Tylee family had never been to Canada, but they joined the Pilkingtons and the Smiths as part of a group of Canadian visitors and expatriates in Britain who had shared experiences in the early days of the province and who congregated to celebrate colonial life. Convivial meetings of the Canada Club held in the Freemasons' Tavern in London might feature "Canadian boat songs and Indian speeches,"[19] as merchants, traders and members of the governing clique shared nostalgic memories of the colony. Robert Dickson, Alexander Auldjo, and John Beverley Robinson visited the club while in London, and Pilkington and his wife extended invitations to many of these visiting dignitaries. By 1812, carried away with the good feelings of meeting these old friends, Pilkington declared that he was keen to return to Canada, for it was "the finest country he ever saw."[20]

Smith's correspondence, too, indicates that he remained in touch with former military comrades residing in Britain, and that he received a continual flow of visitors from Canada—many of them passing through Northumberland on their way to family homes and business interests in Scotland. Chief Justice Alexander Campbell, banker and entrepreneur William Allan, and, possibly, John Strachan stayed at the Smith home. Montreal merchant Alexander Auldjo was also a frequent visitor. In fact, when he visited Britain in 1804 to marry his Scottish bride, he was, with Pilkington, one of the men who attested officially to the poor state of Smith's health.[21] In 1817, John Beverley Robinson wrote to his fiancée, Emma Walker, describing his visit to Alnwick to call on "Mrs. Pilkington's sister" and her husband, Mr. Smith, who "was formerly our Surveyor General in Upper Canada."[22] Between them, then, Smith and Pilkington retained close connections with many Upper Canadians, and in essence, became expatriate members of the group of men commonly referred to as the Family Compact.

Pilkington's and Smith's land transactions in Canada also required constant attention, and resulted in frequent communication with agents and government officials in the colony. As Pilkington moved from one military posting to another, he continually attempted to recruit colonists for his settlement. From 1810 to 1815, he was in command of construction of the ordnance depot at Weedon, Northamptonshire, a site which, because of its location in the very heart of England, was also designated as the emergency headquarters for the monarchy in case of attack by Napoleon.[23] Several migrants to Pilkington Township in Ontario were born in Northamptonshire, among them Thomas Lepard, who acted as a Clerk of the Works at Weedon.[24] Pilkington moved next to Woolwich, from which place artificers were sent out to prepare the township for settlement. In 1818, Pilkington was sent to Gibraltar, where at least one Pilkington Township settler was born.[25] From this posting, too, came one of the more fascinating migrants to Upper Canada, George Matthews, who served under Pilkington, and who claimed that he was the son of George IV and Mrs. Maria Fitzherbert. His bride, Mary Summers, "had accompanied Mrs. Pilkington [to Gibraltar] from England," possibly as a servant.[26] Mrs. Pilkington's involvement in the Matthews case was just one instance of continuing links among the Pilkington, Tylee, and Smith families as they sup-

ported attempts to capitalize on Robert Pilkington's Canadian real-
estate investment. The birthplaces of other settlers in Pilkington Township reveal, for example, that two settler families came from Wiltshire,
the Tylees' home county, and one from Alnmouth in Northumberland,
close to David Smith's residence.[27]

Pilkington took every opportunity to bring his proposed settlement
to official notice, too. In 1811, affecting to be concerned about the
unstable nature of Canadian-United States relations, he wrote to British
Prime Minister Spencer Perceval, offering to raise a corps of Highlanders to send to the colony. Men who would not ordinarily "be influenced
by money to inlist [sic]," Pilkington wrote, "might be induced to serve
for a donation of land." His "extensive landed property" in Upper
Canada might serve admirably as a reward for the proposed period of
"military servitude."[28] This offer failed to attract interest at the Colonial
Office, but Pilkington continued his attempts to bring his proposed
settlement to official notice. In 1817, for example, he sent unsolicited
plans of the "settled parts of Upper Canada" to Under-Secretary of
State Henry Goulburn. The township of Woolwich, in which Pilkington's
settlement was located, was marked clearly on the map, but again, a
polite note of thanks was his only reward.[29]

Colonization efforts also required that Pilkington keep in constant
contact with his land agents in Upper Canada, James Crooks and Christopher Hagerman, as well as with William Allan, who administered his
financial affairs within the colony. Indeed, the connection with Hagerman
was so strong that when he was on leave in Britain in 1834 he acted as a
witness to Pilkington's will.[30] These Upper Canadian connections continued after Pilkington's death; Hagerman continued as one of the
Upper Canadian agents appointed to administer Pilkington's estates,
and John Beverley Robinson and John Strachan caused further confusion over land sales by going into the township and taking over the sale
of lands without the authority of Pilkington's estate executor.[31]

Land may have been the major concern that continued to tie
Pilkington and Smith to Canada, but it was not the only one. Fifteen
years after leaving the province, Pilkington was still claiming reim-
bursement for extra expenses incurred in building accommodation for
General Hunter in 1800.[32] Missives from Smith abound in Colonial
Office records; from 1804 to shortly before his death, he faced problems
securing his pension payments, relentlessly pushed claims for additional financial recognition of his services to Canada, sent requests to
purchase Crown lands, and submitted memorials on behalf of former
colleagues.[33]

In 1832, at the age of 67, Pilkington was still dallying with the idea that he might return to Canada. "I really am desirous it may be my lot to go there again," he wrote to a friend, and "Mrs Pilkington seems well inclined to emigrate."[34] However, this seems to have been a mere dream, and he died in 1834, (Canadian) land rich but cash poor. One of the executors named in his will was John Simcoe Macaulay, a fellow Royal Engineer and another temporary migrant to Canada. Macaulay had received his early education at John Strachan's school, returned to the colony while on half-pay between 1819 and 1821, became Elmsley's son-in-law, and himself made a short-lived attempt to retire to Upper Canada after Pilkington's death.[35]

William Allan administered Pilkington's financial affairs within the colony, and also acted as financial agent for Smith, who continued to try to sell *his* considerable land holdings in the province. Allan became a trusted friend of the extended Smith and Tylee family, relaying news of people and Canadian events into the 1830s, when Smith died.

Over time, Smith, too, changed his opinion of the province. For some years after his return to Britain, he complained of the treatment he had received in Canada, but this changed after he received a baronetcy, claimed on his service to the colony. In 1821, he became Sir David William Smith of Pickering, Ontario, and Preston, Northumberland, with a coat of arms that included a beaver and was headed by the word "Canada."[36] By 1825, Smith's memory of his colonial days had been altered. Asking William Allan to remember him to friends in the province he said, "I still love them, and Canada, better than others, and other places; but fate has placed me here, probably till I die."[37] His memorial plaque in St. Michael's Church in Alnwick commemorates his service to Canada, and an additional stone inscribed by the three children of his first marriage commemorates Anne Smith, who had died in Canada forty years earlier.

Thus, while Pilkington and Smith did not become permanent settlers in Canada, it is clear that their experiences in the colony had a lasting effect on their lives, on the lives of their children, and on many members of the Tylee family, who became conversant with all the more important events in the colony. Apart from the two original sojourners, however, images of the colony were formed entirely through correspondence and visits from prominent Canadians.

None of the Tylee family appears ever to have visited the colony. Indeed, Edward Tylee, Pilkington's brother-in-law, was the executor of his estate, but seems to have acted as business manager and colonization agent for Pilkington's township without leaving his London office.

After Pilkington's death, a proposal that a member of the Tylee family visit Upper Canada to attempt to bring some order to Pilkington's affairs came to nothing.

It is difficult, therefore, to know how these middle-class Britons imagined Canada. Smith's daughters may have retained some memories—but even the oldest girl was only nine years old when she saw Canada for the last time. Pilkington's wife had reason to doubt stories of boundless opportunity; after her husband's death, she was reduced to seeking employment as a housekeeper at the Tower of London. Yet even the application for the housekeeping post was accompanied by a reminder that "the late General had landed property in Canada" that, unfortunately, "was left so involved as to be of no *immediate* benefit to the family."[38] Canada remained a possible source of fortune, then, even as Mrs. Pilkington's social status fell, and in general, Smith's and Pilkington's children and grandchildren were clearly brought up in an atmosphere in which references to Canada were not only frequent, but also positive. In addition, the families retained contact with powerful men in the colony who could act as mentors to aspiring immigrants who could thereby hope for an introduction into influential circles.

Robert Pilkington died in 1834 and David William Smith in 1836. Smith's grandson, Robert Tylee, was in Canada by 1838. Only 22 years of age, he was a source of concern to his grandmother, who hoped he would not "dissipate" his money "thoughtlessly," and to whom she "often look[ed] with much anxiety."[39] She need not have worried about him. In Toronto, he was taken under the wing of old friends: William Allan, Chief Justice John Beverley Robinson, and Christopher Hagerman, now the province's attorney-general. By May 1838, he had moved on to other "kind friends in Montreal" who, his grandmother hoped, would not "make him think more highly of himself than he ought to think."[40] Robert soon had reason to think well of himself. By 1845, he had married the youngest daughter of Queen's Counsel David Ross, and he and his wife had settled into a house on fashionable Drummond Street. As a respectable member of the English-speaking business community of Montreal, he soon received a commission in the Montreal Artillery and became a member of the board of directors of the Colonial, as well as the Liverpool and London Insurance Companies.[41] In his study of Montreal commercial life, Gerald Tulchinsky has suggested that service in politics could be a criterion for a seat on the board of such companies, so Robert Tylee's early rise to commercial success may well have been due, in part, to his grandfather's earlier political prominence.[42] In a similar manner, links with the Auldjo family facilitated Tylee's entry into Montreal's business community, for Alexander Auldjo had been an old acquaintance of David William Smith and a frequent visitor to the Smith home in Northumberland. Alexander had died by the time Robert arrived in the province, but the Auldjo and Maitland family trading company continued. By the beginning of the 1860s, Tylee had entered into a new business partnership with Edward Maitland which lasted until his death.

Robert Tylee, successful merchant and a manager of the Montreal Exchange, died when he was just 49 years old. His obituary in the *Montreal Gazette* made specific mention of his relationship to his grandfather, "Speaker of the House of Assembly of Upper Canada during the three first Canadian Parliaments."[43] In the thirty years that Tylee had been in Canada, he had become regarded as a Canadian. When he died while on a visit to England, a Montreal newspaper report of his death lamented that his death had occurred while he was "absent from home."[44] By the time that Robert Tylee died, he and his wife had produced a large family, most of whom settled in the Montreal or Eastern Townships area. Perhaps the most prominent of his grandchildren was Lieutenant-Colonel Arthur Kellam Tylee, holder of the Order of the British Empire and appointed in 1920 as the first Canadian Air Commodore.[45]

We know less about Robert Tylee's second cousin, Robert Pilkington Jr. He was still a schoolboy at the time of his father's death, and it is unclear when he first arrived in Canada. There is a report that he visited Pilkington Township, but no date is given.[46] He may have arrived as early as 1840, but he was certainly in Quebec by 1842. In 1843, he was residing in Montreal.[47] Robert's early career closely paralleled that of his father. Although he could not afford a commission in the Engineers, Robert worked on the civilian branch of the Royal Engineers as a draftsman, producing several maps and sketches preserved, like those of his father, in the British Public Record Office. Whereas his father had become, temporarily, a member of the Upper Canadian political and social elite, Pilkington Jr. became part of the city's circle of merchants and prominent businessmen. There were two reasons for this: first, his cousin, Robert Tylee—four years his senior—opened the door to the English-speaking commercial society of Montreal; second, his marriage to the daughter of Glasgow-born Andrew Shaw broadened his circle of business acquaintances. Shaw was a leading member of Montreal's English-speaking community and also played a major role in organizing social evenings that brought together military officers and civilians. He had a diversity of business interests as a merchant, shipper and president of the Montreal Telegraph Company, and was also a business associate of John Molson's.[48] Perhaps it is not surprising, then, that Pilkington Jr.'s daughter married into the Molson family.[49]

Robert Pilkington Jr. was not destined to be a long-term resident of Canada for he died at the end of the 1850s. But the strong bond between the two original families continued as his son-in-law, John William Molson, took up business premises on the same street where Robert Tylee had carried on his business for twenty years.[50] Indeed, by the latter part of the nineteenth century, all members of the extended Canadian families of the two early sojourners lived in closer proximity to each other than their ancestors had done in Britain.

Thus, both Robert Pilkington and David Smith were finally represented in Canada by established family lines that were truly and permanently Canadian. Members of the first generation may have been only sojourners in Canada, but the migration of their descendants would not have occurred without the continual flow of transatlantic contacts that provided the motivation and opportunity for eventual settlement in Canada. Forced by circumstances or by choice to return to Britain, the early generation had experiences that provided a background of nostalgic reminiscences which must have grown increasingly appealing to their families. Moreover, continuing business and social contacts with leading Canadians eased the migration of their descendants to a new land.

Though mothers and grandmothers may have worried that the new environment would allow two young men to behave without proper restraint, they were not migrants who sought to change the status quo. They came from conservative families, dedicated to the ideals of Empire. They were adopted into Canadian circles whose members were among the early elite of Upper and Lower Canada, and who perpetuated the ideals of Canada as a British colony. In effect, the migration process had continued across the generations. Despite starts, reversals and offshoots, the young men who finally settled in Canada almost forty years after their forebears had left continued to uphold a way of life that had changed very little over the years.

Notes

1. Robert F. Harney, "Boarding and Belonging: Thoughts on Sojourner Institutions," *Urban History Review*, 2, no. 78 (October 1988): 9.

2. Gordon T. Stewart, *The Origins of Canadian Politics: A Comparative Approach* (Vancouver: University of British Columbia Press, 1986), 17.
3. Howard Kushner suggests this motivation for migration in "The Persistence of the Frontier Thesis in America," *Canadian Review of American Studies*, 23, special issue, Part 1 (1992), 66.
4. A. Ross McCormack, "Networks among British Immigrants and Accommodation to Canadian Society: Winnipeg, 1900–1914," *Histoire sociale/ Social History* 17, no. 34 (November 1984): 357.
5. S. K. Johannesen, "Of Dead Grandfathers and Stolen Babies: Social Experience and Moral Reflection in a Norwegian Tale," *Historical Reflection/ Reflexions Historiques* 21, no. 1 (Winter 1995): 14.
6. Carl Christie, "Pilkington, Robert," *Dictionary of Canadian Biography*, vol. 6, *1831–1835* (Toronto: University of Toronto Press, 1987), 583.
7. Louis Gentilcore and C. Grant Head, *Ontario's History in Maps* (Toronto: University of Toronto Press, 1984), 70. The island is now called Fox Island.
8. See, for example, *The Diary of Mrs. John Simcoe*, with notes and biography by J. Ross Robertson (Toronto, 1911), 196, 197, 203.
9. Metropolitan Toronto Library (hereafter MTL), D. W. Smith Papers, B8, 17-19, J. Elmsley to E. W. Smith, 17 February 1798.
10. B. M. Dunham, *Grand River* (Toronto: McClelland & Stewart, 1945), 110. J.R. Connon, *The Early History of Elora,Ontario and Vicinity* (1930) (Waterloo: Wilfrid Laurier Press, 1970), 13, 20. My thanks also to Bruce Elliott, who confirmed that Pilkington sent out a party of artificers from Woolwich in 1815.
11. *Historical Atlas of the County of Wellington, Ontario* (1906) (Belleville: Mika, 1972), 7.
12. Archives of Ontario (hereafter AO), Pilkington Estate Papers, Correspondence, C. Tylee to C. Hagerman, 22 July 1834.
13. *Historical Atlas of the County of Wellington,*7.
14. MTL, Smith Papers, A10, Pilkington to Smith, 12 April 1803.
15. S. R. Mealing, "Smith, Sir David William," *Dictionary of Canadian Biography*, vol. 7 (Toronto: University of Toronto Press, 1988), 811–13.
16. British Library, Northumberland Estate Papers, Reel 313, Folio 109, Smith to Duke of Northumberland, 29 April 1821. See also, Mealing, "Smith, Sir David William," 811–14. For a description of the Small–White affair, see Katherine McKenna, *A Life of Propriety: Anne Murray Powell and Her Family, 1755-1849* (Montreal and Kingston: McGill-Queen's University Press, 1994), 70–71.
17. *A History of Wiltshire*, vol. 10, 260.

18. See, for example, MTL, Smith Papers, A10, Darling to Smith, 30 January 1805, Simcoe to Smith 9 April 180[5?], Pilkington to Smith 15 November 1804, 20 February 1805; A11, Osgoode to Smith 24 July 1803.

19. C. W. Robinson, *Life of Sir John Beverley Robinson* (Toronto, 1904), 94.

20. Ibid., 68, 88, 94, 121.

21. Public Record Office (hereafter PRO), CO 42/336, Smith to Sullivan, 14 April 1804.

22. AO, MS4, Sir John Beverley Robinson Papers, J.B. Robinson to Emma Walker, 30 April 1817.

23. G. Jones, "List of Commanding Officers" in *Weedon Barracks and Depot: Historical Notes* (Northampton, 1982).

24. Squire William Reynolds, *Township of Pilkington*, ed. A.E. Byerly (1866).

25. Connon, *Early History*, 38.

26. Wellington County Museum and Archives, "Declaration, Charlotte Morrison, 'In the Matter of one George Frederick Matthews,'" 30 March 1910. Matthews did not settle in Pilkington Township, but in nearby Arthur.

27. Connon, *Early History*, 24, 38.

28. PRO, CO 42/144, Pilkington to Perceval, 31 July 1811.

29. PRO, CO 700/77 and CO 42/360, Pilkington to Goulburn, 16 May 1817.

30. PRO, Prob11/1840, Last Will and Testament of Robert Pilkington; National Archives of Canada (hereafter NAC), Upper Canada Executive Council, Submissions to Council, RG1, E3, vol. 35, 40–1.

31. Wellington County Museum and Archives, Indenture between Edward Tyler and Donald Cameron, 22 November 1861.

32. NAC, RG 1, E3, vol. 61, 15.

33. PRO, CO 42/376, Smith to Horton, 19 March 1825: CO 42/387, Smith to Huskisson, 11 February 1828; CO 42/392, Smith to Horton, 13 January 1830.

34. General Pilkington to the mother of Squire Reynolds, Dublin, 9 February 1832, quoted in "Old Map gives Elora History," *Guelph Mercury*, 4 November 1924.

35. AO, MS525, Elmsley-Macaulay Papers: 1792-1857, Macaulay to Sir F. Bond Head, 15 February 1836.

36. J. B. Burke, *A Genealogical and Heraldic Dictionary of the Peerage and Baronetage of the British Empire* (1828).

37. MTL, William Allan Papers, Box 2, Smith to Allan, 20 October 1825.

38. PRO, WO 54/898, Sir Frederick McMaster to Colonel Fox, 18 December 1838. (My italics).

39. MTL, Allan Papers, Mary Smith to William Allan, 12 May 1838.

40. Ibid.
41. Montreal *Gazette,* 28 August 1845; 5 January 1846; 8 July 1846.
42. G. Tulchinsky, *The River Barons: Montreal Businessmen and the Growth of Industry and Transportation 1837–53* (Toronto and Buffalo: University of Toronto Press, 1977), 25.
43. Montreal *Gazette,* 12 April 1866.
44. Ibid.
45. MTL, *Biographical Scrapbook,* vol. 3, *World,* 26 May 1920.
46. Connon, *Early History,* 20.
47. For date of appointment and period of service see PRO, WO 54/670, "Returns showing the Pay, Allowances, Length of Service of Royal Engineers in Canada," 1 October 1847. For residence in Montreal, see *The Montreal Pocket Almanac and General Register* (Montreal, 1843).
48. Mackay, *Montreal Directory for 1845-6,* 168; Tulchinsky, *The River Barons,* 20.
49. *Diary of Mrs. Simcoe,* 192.
50. *Lovell's Business and Professional Directory of the Province of Quebec for 1890/91* (Montreal, 1890).

Quest for Independence: The Achomer Crerars' Migration to the Canadas

Duff Crerar

A T THE CONFLUENCE (*ACH' CHOMAIR*) OF TWO SMALL STREAMS FLOWING into Loch Tay lies Achomer, a small farm perched on a steep hillside. Today, it is one of three farmhouses standing along the winding road to Ardtalnaig. Around them, scattered among the flocks of sheep, are nameless piles of rubble, indicating that this small glen was once far more heavily populated. The place bears almost no resemblance to the flat, dry, fertile bottomland in Osgoode Township, Carleton County, Canada West (later Ontario) named Achomer by the Crerars who came there in 1852. The only confluence in view was the junction of two dirt roads. Still, Alexander Crerar, son John, and his son, Peter, insisted on naming the farm after the cottage and pasture they once held from their lairds, the Campbells of Breadalbane. To them, Achomer was a symbol of what they had lost and what they hoped to gain by emigration.

This paper will help to explain why the name of Achomer was so potent to them. It draws partly on a packet of letters passed down since the 1830s within the Crerar family, which were edited and published privately by the late Peter D. Crerar of Waterloo, Ontario; partly upon the work of genealogist David A. Crerar of Vancouver; and partly on my own research in the Breadalbane Muniments held at the Scottish Record Office.[1] It reveals the social and economic circumstances of a Highland cottar family whose response characterized one type of Scottish migration to the Canadas. The story of the Achomer Crerars also reveals how some overseas migrations were probably shaped by prior migrations within Scotland and Great Britain. It shows that the Crerars, like many Scots, had been (in the old phrase) "hopeful travellers" from their emergence around Loch Tay some time before 1600 until their arrival in western Canada at the turn of the twentieth century.

Crerars have been baptized, married, and buried in the Kenmore parish since at least 1608. Over the next two centuries, a growing number of Crerar families worked Breadalbane lands, carted Breadalbane freight, and helped build Breadalbane castles. Eventually, some from Glenquaich and others from Lawers and Crieff made their way to Canada, but the parents of James Crerar and his brother Alexander clung to their ancestral locale along the south shore of Loch Tay.[2] They had always been carters, crofters, and Gaelic-speakers, but in the early years of the nineteenth century, the Crerar brothers chose different paths. Reflecting the great changes taking place in the land, James, the elder, left farming for London and became a clerk for the shipping company of Joseph Adams, living at the Leith and Glasgow wharf on the Thames. Mastering the English language and business culture, making successful loans and small business coups with his growing funds, the lifelong bachelor became both advisor to and patron of Tayside youths seeking employment in the South. Alexander, however, chose to carry on as a cottar in Breadalbane, married Anne Carmichael (their son John was born in 1808), and pieced together a living from several small plots in the Breadalbane officiary of Ardeonaig, just a few miles from his birthplace.

By the late 1820s, the brothers were living very different lives. James took an active interest in his nephews back in Breadalbane, patiently but persistently reminding them that they must eventually abandon Gaelic and master both written and spoken English if they were to advance in life.[3] He often wrote to his brother, offering advice, keeping up with the news and views of his home region, and urging Alexander to send sons John and Gilbert to London, or at least to have them attend the Perth schools, where English as well as other utilitarian subjects were taught. John did study in Perth during the winter of 1831–32, until parental anxieties about his poor health in town brought him back to the farm. In 1843, Gilbert moved to London, becoming uncle James's protégé at the wharf.

Alexander, too, enjoyed initial prosperity. After more than a decade of managing several small fields on various farms (and occasionally requesting rent abatements from the factor, as did almost every small farmer in the Breadalbane lands from time to time), by 1832, Alexander and son John were contemplating an ambitious move to advance the family's fortunes. When a nearby tenant relinquished a sizeable farm in Ardeonaig, Alexander and John made an offer to take it over. At Alexander's urging, James visited the Earl of Breadalbane at his London home and promoted his brother's offer, a service he had performed for his sister and brother-in-law a few years earlier. Although James failed in his suit for Alexander's first choice, Breadalbane offered him the Achomer farm. Despite James's misgivings that Achomer was too expensive to stock and susceptible to early frost, Alexander and John did not hesitate. In mid-June 1832, the Crerars came to Achomer.

They would not have been able to consolidate their efforts and embark on such an ambitious project without James's support. In fact, Alexander and John were counting on him to stock the farm with cattle and sheep, cover the expenses of equipment and building repairs, and pay for the crop already planted by the previous tenants. True to his promise, James cashed in some of his precious government securities (at a slight loss), sending the required £200 north well before Whitsunday (June 10), the traditional day for tenants to acquire their new holdings.[4] Nevertheless, Achomer seemed a worthy undertaking, despite its sizeable rent (at £45 per annum almost nine times the rent Alexander had paid for Balloch, his last cot). It was considered by J. Wylie, Breadalbane's factor, to have pasture for three to six times the number of sheep run on Crerar's last farm, with room for a few goats as well as cattle; it was serviced by a road, and had two shielings in good repair up on the high pasture. Adjacent to Achomer lay the large grazing farm of Claggan, where Crerars had been tenants (and where Alexander himself may have been born). Alexander and John viewed their move to Achomer with pride and expectation: it was twice the size and brought twice the prestige of any farm they had ever rented before.[5]

Whether Alexander and John were ever able to repay James fully has not been recorded: what is certain is that the Achomer project was undertaken on the eve of some of the grimmest years for Scottish cottars in the first half of the nineteenth century. Petitions to Factor Wylie from the 1820s to the 1840s repeatedly pointed to falling wool, cattle, and grain prices as reasons for rent defaults. Cottars and crofters who turned to distilling to raise the cash for rents found themselves increasingly under the hands of excise officials enforcing new licensing laws. Harsh, long winters with deep snowfall throughout the 1830s devastated lamb crops and came down especially hard on tenants with high moorland pastures on the upper slopes of Tayside. Petitions from most officiaries of the Breadalbane estate chanted a litany of dying lambs, seed grain eaten for food, hogs and sheep killed by cold, pastures rendered unfit for cattle and poor prices offered for whatever was brought in from the sodden fields.[6]

Achomer was not immune to any of these disasters, especially those stemming from its higher location and exposure to extremes of winter. In 1835, Wylie raised the Achomer rent to £50. Alexander and John had just succeeded in paying off previous rental arrears. By the end of 1836, however, their petition for rent abatement joined others flowing across Wylie's desk.[7] James Crerar thought that both Wylie and Breadalbane's wife, out of compassion for the tenants in such hard times, were somewhat reluctant to force the pace of improvement on the estates during these hard years. He did not hold the Marquis of Breadalbane in such high regard. The fourth Earl of Breadalbane, under whom Achomer had been acquired, was a relentless improver: abolishing runrig, laying out compact farms, insisting on crop rotation, bringing sheep to the uplands, and doubling rents.[8]

His successor, the fifth Earl and second Marquis of Breadalbane was equally obsessed with increasing revenues, though it soon became apparent that his predecessor had already raised rents as high as the land could bear without more reorganization. Fifteen-year leases were shortened to seven years. Most tenants found themselves farming their holdings "at pleasure." While the Marquis roamed his tracts searching for ores promising mineral wealth, his factor was ordered to remove tenants from lands in Morenish, Kiltyrie, Cloichran, and Glenquaich, a clearance which brought such public outcry (and contributed to the first of many Breadalbane group movements to the Canadas) that the Marquis abandoned mass clearances. Thereafter, a steady stream of his tenants made their way to city or colony.[9]

As Whitsunday 1837 approached, the Achomer Crerars faced relinquishment of their prize. The 1836 crop had been a failure owing to rain and early frost. Breadalbane was deaf to Alexander's petition and the personal entreaties of many other tenants for relief. Anxious letters to James raised the possibility of him sponsoring an offer on a larger and riskier, but conveniently vacant, cattle-grazing farm in Ardeonaig. Alarmed at the prospect of his brother and nephew (who had never been drovers) taking on such an operation with no experience and in such dismal markets, James resorted to his savings. Breadalbane got his rent, and Achomer was preserved.[10] The early 1840s brought some mild prosperity and were lightened by the birth of John's son, Peter, in 1842. As happy as his childhood spent at Achomer may have been, however, Peter's parents and grandparents were bedeviled by harsh weather, poor prices, and, in 1846, a new menace: potato blight.

This time there would be no succour from London. John's brother

Gilbert, now a junior clerk at the wharf, reported that James's health was failing. He died in 1847, and, when Gilbert had finished liquidating his estate, a few pounds sterling and a box of old clothes were all that remained of his legacy.[11] Meanwhile, Breadalbane tenants were facing some of the bleakest years of the decade. Petitions from the local Free Church sessions (Campbell of Breadalbane was the most prominent Free Church laird in Scotland) appealed for funds to help destitute members, as collections failed, schoolmasters and beadles went unpaid and parishes were overwhelmed by care of the poor. In 1847, as leading men of the congregation, Alexander and John Crerar signed the Ardeonaig Free Church petition.[12] Two years later, their names and those of their families had disappeared from the Communion Roll: on Whitsunday, 1848, the Crerars had relinquished Achomer and moved into a cottage near Lochearnhead, living on the little capital they had acquired by the sale of their last crop and farm goods.

Over the next four years, John, his ageing father, and the family refused to accept their reduced circumstances in Scotland. Crerar cousins had been settled in the Huron tract since the 1830s. Other former Breadalbane tenants had been sending back reports of their progress in other parts of Canada West. Repeatedly, they pointed to perhaps the most significant factor in any calculation of the costs and benefits of emigration: land ownership. The prospect of owning real property, an end to terminable leases and interminable Whitsunday quarrels with jealous neighbours, doing away with stipulations from factors and lairds, and of paying no more rent, either by them or their children, must have been decisive for the Crerars.[13] Gilbert Crerar wrote to his brother John, when the decision was made in early 1852, "I have intimated . . . that it is your intention, as well as that of the rest of our Family, excepting James, to emigrate to America . . . many of my Friends coincide with me that you cannot do better."[14] By the summer of 1852, the former Achomer Crerars had bade farewell to Scotland from the quay of Greenock. They took with them their most potent link to the old way of life enjoyed by their family for generations: Alexander's old Gaelic family Bible.

Once in Canada, the family's movements revealed more of their strategy. From Quebec to Montreal, then Cornwall, the family moved on through the Glengarry settlement (staying with Breadalbaners who had come out in previous migrations) toward the settlement of Free Church, Gaelic-speaking former neighbours established in Osgoode Township. On the whole, the next two decades were prosperous ones for the Crerars, thanks to Reciprocity and a ready market for Canadian stock and grain in civil-war New York state. Much of the old-growth forest in Osgoode township had been logged over the preceding generation, so relatively little time had to be diverted to land clearing. Before long, their letters, too, were planting the seed of emigration in the hearts of former neighbours and kin. In 1855, John's wife, Isabella Campbell, wrote such glowing accounts of their life at Achomer that her sister, after listing the kin and neighbours who had emigrated recently, replied, "The greatest Consolation we have now is to hear often from one another, and who knows but we may see you yet in America? We have a break in our Lease in a few years and, if you encourage us we may follow you."[15] By then, Gilbert had decided to emigrate, though not to Canada. He arrived in Australia in 1855, and settled down permanently in New Zealand a few years later.

According to the 1861 census, Alexander and John Crerar had eighty acres under crop and enough livestock to give them a comfortable subsistence on the new farm. Alexander died soon after, passing on Achomer to John. That year, his nineteen-year-old son, Peter, returned from visiting a nearby neighbour, another Breadalbane family, and declared his intention to marry their newborn daughter. Another nineteen years later, after their wedding, he took up full responsibility for the Crerar farm, now known to the community as Achomer, its large barn, elaborate gardens, and brick house becoming a landmark and tribute to the possibilities for advancement enjoyed by Canadian farmers.[16] By then the Gaelic Bible had been laid aside: the Crerars knew only English now.

The Crerars enjoyed a level of security and prosperity unknown to their ancestors. After a brief adventure in the militia fending off the Fenians in 1870, Peter and his large family brought Achomer to its peak of prosperity and prominence. While the dairy farm flourished, his sons sought adventure and fortune in some of Canadian history's most dramatic moments. One son, John, ventured into the Yukon territory after gold. A much younger brother, Gilbert Duff Crerar, chafing under his father's stern rule, eagerly enlisted in the local battalion raised for service in World War I. His first duties with the Ottawa battalion consisted of guarding the ruins of the Canadian Parliament buildings, destroyed by fire during the winter of 1916–17. World War I would cost the Crerars dearly: John, who had enlisted in 1914, was posted missing in action at Passchendaele on November 6, 1917. Duff, by then serving with the 73rd Battalion (Black Watch), C.E.F., was wounded two days before the battle of Vimy Ridge in the same year. Returning to duty with the 13th Battalion, he was gassed in 1918, which permanently impaired his health. Still, he would return to inherit Achomer, though the reconciliation with his father was cut short by the influenza epidemic of 1919. Peter died of the flu within a few weeks of Duff's demobilization.

By then, some of the Achomer Crerars had yet again begun a new Canadian migration. Peter's brother, Alexander, unhappy with his own farm two lots north of Achomer, made brief forays into the Canadian West before the war. Consciously or unconsciously making the same calculations as had his ancestors about carrying on an agricultural way of life with third-class land, he abandoned the Osgoode locale. In 1912, he staked a farm claim in the developing settlement of Grande Prairie, Alberta, and within a year he brought his wife and children to homestead on the northern prairie parkland. His children would establish a number of enterprises in the "last best West," but Alexander perished, with his brother, in the Spanish influenza pandemic.[17]

While these Crerars joined with their former neighbours from Ontario to build Grande Prairie, cousin Duff tried to keep the Canadian Achomer prosperous. By the 1930s, this had become a failing enterprise. Owing to brucellosis and over-extended credit, the Achomer Crerars were notified by the bailiff to vacate the farm in 1933. The 1930s became a time of renewed struggle and adjustment for Duff and his wife, as they pieced together a living from music-teaching, bee-keeping, and local municipal jobs often reserved for veterans. Within a few years, ironically, Duff was able to purchase the old farm rejected by his uncle and resettle in Osgoode Township only two farms away from his boyhood home. But for these Crerars, there would never be another Achomer. The new Crerar world consisted of bee-keeping, running a few sheep (the land was unsuitable for virtually any other type of agriculture), and weathering the challenge of another world war. Real prosperity and independence gradually returned, but only in the next decade, after Duff's death, when his teenage son, Ian, and new bride looked toward the expanding economy of the 1950s.[18]

In the scholarly study of migration, the mechanisms and the strategies of individual families are easily lost from sight because it is their sum that attracts most attention. Perhaps little in the Achomer Crerar story sheds new light on the study of motivations, strategies, and mechanisms of Scottish migration to the Canadas, and yet it is a reminder that behind the trends, charts, patterns, and analyses of scholars lie the decisions, frustrations, and ambitions of individual families. The Achomer Crerars bring to life what recent migration scholars such as Marjory Harper, Marianne McLean, and, before them, J. M. Bumsted have pointed out: Scottish migration was more often brought about by frustration and fear that one day families might drop below the poverty line, not because they were already destitute.

Unfortunately for scholars, what the Crerar documents cannot yet reveal is the role played by women in their migration story. The letters, records, and business documents which preserve their lives were, except for the letter to Isabella Crerar, entirely written or compiled by and for men. Ironically, they were preserved for us by women from the Crerar and Breadalbane clans, who passed them on to successive generations and, in Lady Breadalbane's case, the Scottish Record Office. It will take new methods and new records to rid this chapter of the emigration story of its unrelenting patriarchy.

Some otherwise hidden elements in migration patterns come to light by examining the Crerar story, for example, the crucial role played by James, living and dead. It was his internal migration into the Anglicized and commercialized world of improvement that enabled him to come to the rescue of his rural relatives and probably helped pay their passage to Canada. The Achomer Crerars' struggles, failures, and successive migrations point to similar strategies adopted by others who came to Canada. Like them, most Scottish migrants were not as naive and untutored in Canadian conditions, ways, and means as Canadians once believed. The decision to migrate was always dramatic, but was often based on shrewd calculations and canny appreciations of past experience and future prospects. Intelligence gathered from neighbours with relatives who had gone before, newspapers, printed letters from immigrants to the Canadas, publicity by shipping agents, and, eventually, from the colonial agencies themselves all played their role in the decision.

Nevertheless, the crucial element in the Crerar story, and perhaps in that of many other migrating Scots, was the stubborn refusal to accept the declining prospects of their old way of life. Rather than be hemmed in and forced back down the road to destitution, or obliged to abandon the farm and folkways of Tayside, the Highland cottars of the nineteenth century, like the Crerars, chose to migrate. In many ways, the Crerars reflected the influence of Scottish rural improvement culture, with its ambition and reluctant abandonment of Gaelic folkways and ancient farms. But in many other ways, the Achomer Crerars, in their decisions to migrate, often rejected the agenda which superiors or impersonal market forces sought to set for them. Like many Scots before and after, if the only choice was between emigration and independence, or persistence and declining prospects, then emigration it would be.

Notes

1. Peter D. Crerar, *The Crerar Letters, 1821–1865* (Waterloo, Ontario: privately published, 1996). See also David Anthony Crerar, *Crerar Compendium*, 2nd ed. (Vancouver: privately published, 1996). Copies of the *Compendium* have been placed in the National Library of Scotland, and p. 5 lists libraries in Canada, the United States, Great Britain, Australia, New Zealand, and South Africa which also have copies. The Breadalbane Muniments (GD 112) are housed in the Scottish Record Office (SRO) in Edinburgh.
2. *Crerar Compendium*, 12–15, 175–97.
3. James Crerar to John Crerar, 25 June 1831; also November 1831, and James Crerar to Alexander Crerar, 11 May 1832; James Crerar to Gilbert Crerar, 30 March 1840, in *Crerar Letters*.
4. James to Alexander Crerar, 16 March and 5, 11 May 1832, *Crerar Letters*.
5. On the estimated values, capacities, rents, and boundaries of these farms, see SRO, Breadalbane Muniments, GC 112/14/13/10/12, "Estimated values of Lands, 1829 and Proposed Rents," and Breadalbane Estate Plans and Surveys, in SRO, West Register House, RHP 974/1-2, and RHP 717. Although the estate map and survey were completed in 1769, the boundaries (and often the estimated capacities for cropping, pasture, and livestock) are similar to those of the early decades of the 1800s.
6. SRO, Breadalbane Muniments, Petition of Morenish tenants, November 1837 and Glenquaich tenants, November 1838, GD 112/11/10/5/#s 14 and 30. For a survey of climate and other hardships visited on the Tayside parishes, see *New Statistical Account*, vol. 10 (Perthshire), 454–75, 1078. On the special dangers of farms with high elevations for stock in winter, see GD 112/10/2/4/46, "Note on Breadalbane farms to let, Whitsunday, 1840."
7. Representation and Petition of Alexander Crerar, Tenant in Achomer, Ardtalnaig, 9 December 1836, in *Crerar Letters*. On previous Crerar arrears on Achomer, see SRO, Breadalbane Muniments, GD 112/9/2/2/31, "Breadalbane Estate Arrears and Payments, 1832–1835."
8. "The account I have of the Breadalbane tenantry is truly pitiable, but it

appears the Marquis of Breadalbane does not intend, nor will he permit both sides of the Loch to be disturbed while he lives—notwithstanding the wishes of the Marchioness Earl of Ormilie and the Factor, which I consider a laudable trait in his Character—by making both sides of the Loch into large Farms and throwing many hundreds of poor families on the Wide World without house or home and without the Means to convey them to a more hospitable clime, would certainly be considered an act of Cruelty only equalled among certain Highland Proprietors," James Crerar to Alexander Crerar, 16 March 1832 *Crerar Letters*. For a far less critical description of the regime of the fourth Earl and Second Marquis of Breadalbane, see William Gillies, *In Famed Breadalbane* (Perth: Munro Press, 1938) 196–220.

9. "I notice what you say with regard to the conduct of the Marquess towards the poor Tenantry during his short stay at Taymouth in June last. All of which I fully anticipated, and I agree with you in opinion that it was of little consequence whether you had an interview with him on the same Subject or not. He would naturally enough give you as little consideration as he did to all the rest that waited upon him at that Season of the Year," James Crerar to Alexander Crerar, 25 December 1838, *Crerar Letters*.

10. James Crerar to Alexander Crerar, 25 December 1838 and 19 March 1839, *Crerar Letters*.

11. Gilbert Crerar to Alexander Crerar, 9 October, 11 November and 25 December 1847; also Gilbert Crerar to John Crerar, 18 December 1850, *Crerar Letters*.

12. SRO, CH3/1243, Ardeonaig Free Church Parish Records, Deacon's Minutes, June 1847 to July 1849, also Communion Rolls, 12 July 1847 and 12 May 1849.

13. On the influence of immigrant letters and their wide circulation in Breadalbane as well as Inverness, see Marjory Harper, *Emigration from North-East Scotland,* vol. 1 (Aberdeen: Aberdeen University Press, 1988) 204–6.

14. Gilbert Crerar to John Crerar, 12 May 1852, *Crerar Letters*.

15. Jane McDiarmid to Isabella Crerar, 1 June 1855, *Crerar Letters*.

16. *Crerar Compendium*, 189–90.

17. Ibid., 194–5.

18. Ibid., 190–2.

How to Survive in the West, Young Woman

Joan Bryans

FEMINIST PHILOSOPHY EMPHASIZES THE IMPORTANCE OF FAMILY AND friends in a person's life. Our significant others help to define us as agents in the world; without them we flounder. Their absence not only triggers a sense of emotional loss, it affects our very being. Without them, we lose track of who we are and where we belong in the world. In a very deep sense, without them, we cease to be. Of course, we do not die in the physical sense, but our identity as individuals is threatened. The notion of identity involves not *who* I am, whether a Canadian, or a Scot, a daughter, or a machine operator, but whether *I* am at all. This position can be traced to the work of Herder, the German pre-romantic. In Herder's view, man is born incomplete: "At no single moment can he be said to be the *whole* man, rather he is always in the state of development, of progress, of becoming."[1] Unique self-realization is a continuous, ongoing process; there is no place that one can stop, fully realized. Further, for Herder, we are essentially social beings.[2] Our tie to our true community is essential for self-realization. Without that tie, we wither, becoming stunted or deformed, living an inauthentic life. Herder held that our true community is determined by the culture to which we belong, a culture determined mainly by the language spoken—German, French, and so on.[3] For modern feminists, this true community, now called one's significant others, is taken to be one's family and close friends. Virginia Held defines significant others as "particular flesh and blood others for whom we have actual feelings in our insides and in our skin, not the others of rational constructs and universal principles."[4]

What happens when a young woman leaves her family and friends and sets out across a continent to a new life? What does she do when the physical bond to significant others is broken? Jessie and Annie

Fig. 1. McQueen homestead, Sutherland's River, Pictou County, Nova Scotia.
(Photograph courtesy of the Nicola Valley Archives.)

McQueen, two sisters who travelled west to the Nicola Valley in the
interior of British Columbia in the late 1880s, provide us with relevant
examples. Their home was a farm in Sutherland's River, Pictou County,
Nova Scotia. They came from a large family of eight children presided
over by a kindly if somewhat ineffectual father, Daniel, and a strong
mother, Catherine. Times were tough, and the family always seemed
short of cash; the extra earnings provided by summer visitors never
seemed enough. But it was a close-knit, loving family, with mother
trying to keep a firm hand on her children's affairs even after they had
left home.[5]

Annie, the baby of the family, was the first to head west. She had
attended Normal School in Truro in 1886–87 where, despite illness, she
was granted a teaching diploma. A family friend, the Reverend John
Chisholm, minister of the First Presbyterian Church in Kamloops, wrote
of teaching opportunities in British Columbia,[6] where salaries were six
times those in Nova Scotia. Annie, aged twenty-one, soon decided to
head west. In Victoria, after sitting for further examinations, she was
interviewed and offered the position of schoolteacher at Nicola Lake, a
farming community in the interior of British Columbia near Merritt.
She quickly accepted.

Jessie, her older sister, went west eight months later, at the age of

twenty-seven, after securing a teaching position at the Methodist settlement of Lower Nicola, some twenty kilometers away from Annie's
location. While the distance does not seem like much to us now, given
the rugged terrain and the state of transportation then, it was far enough
to ensure that the sisters could meet only once a week at most, when the
weather was fine.

The initial reactions of the two women to the west and their subsequent behaviour were very different. In her first letter home, Annie
wrote,

> Victoria, July 13th, 1887
> I feel very well here and weigh 106 1/4 lbs. Mr. Davis weighed me this
> afternoon in the Chinese store. Mr. Davis is a widower and both he
> and my minister were here to tea this evening, and if the boys [at the
> boarding house] weren't giving me a fearful time. . . . It makes me
> laugh to see them put on the attitude of brothers. . . . They dose me
> with advice. They tease and fight for me in the same breath. . . . Yes, all
> reports are true: gentlemen are very plentiful over here. Even I, if I
> wished, might have a string tagging at my heels . . . but I don't. (13/7/
> 87, PANS)[7]

When she arrived in Nicola, though, there seemed to be quite a string of
men:

> Nicola, Sept. 1st. Last Wednesday morning, Mr. George Armstrong
> came in to ask me to go to Quilchena with old Mr. & Mrs. Howse and
> himself. He had a double-seated buggy with two horses, so we had a
> gay drive. I drove nearly all the way. . . .
>
> Next morning, Mr. Carpenter came tearing in to say that there
> was to be a cultis pot-latch at the rancheree above Quilchena. . . . Well,
> of course, I said "Yes'r, I'll go!" . . . He is a good man, and an awfully
> jolly one. . . . We got to the Quilchena hotel about 5 o'clock, had tea
> there, lovely whips and such cake!!! then went on to the pot latch. . . .
> We had a lovely drive by moonlight to our home. . . .
>
> Mr. Carpenter has been suffering fearfully from headache today
> but I am as fresh as a daisy. I am aggravatingly well they think. (1/9/
> 88, PABC)

There was little talk of her work or domestic arrangements, but many
descriptions of her various escapades.

Fig. 2. Annie McQueen. (Photograph courtesy of the Nicola Valley Archives.)

Fig. 3. Jessie McQueen. (Photograph courtesy of the Nicola Valley Archives.)

> I forgot to tell you of all that went on up at Moore's. . . . We played and sang for dear life, and Reid teased me and worried me until I was nearly possessed. In the morning after breakfast Mr. Moore took the notion that he would teach me to shoot. The guns were dragged forth and loaded and although I was scared to death I meekly walked out with the rest of them. They put up a target one hundred yards off. I believe I would have backed out most ignominiously, only Reid came dashing up behind me and grabbed my shoulders saying "Let me support you, you are fainting!" It made me so mad that I boldly walked up and grabbed the gun, squinted along it after the most approved fashion, to make sure I was aiming at the bull's eye and fired!!! To my great surprise I didn't mind it a single bit. Of course I didn't hit anything but the straw stack. Anything as small as the bulls-eye was beneath my notice. (to Jessie, 1/9/88, NVA/ PABC)

Other escapades were described, almost always involving men.

Annie's enthusiasm was infectious and her embrace of the freedom to be found in the west appeals to us today. But the social norms and morality of the day made her behaviour risky, if not downright danger-ous. At a time when a reputation was all that a poor working woman had to protect her, Annie's actions were foolhardy in the extreme.

There resulted a flurry of letters among the family. One sister wrote to her mother,

> Mother dear, about Annie, I could shake her for giving you a moments worry about her nonsense. She wrote me too. She described three of her would-be adorers and says, "If worldly wealth were all one wanted in a husband one would be easily suited here . . ." (from Liz, 1887, PANS)

Other sisters tried to assuage their mother, but she remained outraged and wrote sharply to Annie. It seems to have had the desired effect: Annie's next letter home takes a very different tone.

> Dear Mother, Your letter safely to hand last Wednesday. . . . My plan is to work up to the top of the ladder in the interior. Already my name as a teacher has gone a good distance further than the length of Nova Scotia and I am determined to work up. Then my health is good, and the people are very kind. Kamloops school will be open to me shortly. . . . Salary the same as here, board at Rev. Chishom's $15.00 per month. (16/11/87, NVA)

Fig. 4. A general view of Nicola Lake in 1899. (Photograph courtesy of the Nicola Valley Archives.)

Annie never went to Kamloops to teach. As we shall see, the west would gain a hold over her unrelated to her career.

Jessie's initial reaction to the British Columbia interior was very different. While she thoroughly enjoyed the train trip out, her good mood vanished when she arrived in Kamloops.

> Kamloops itself I don't like much, it is so dry and dusty and cooked-up looking. It is a straggling bit of a town—two or three houses and hotels near the Station, and a few more about a quarter of a mile further along the road. There seems to be a scarcity of paint, and the unpainted buildings don't turn a soft grey as they do at home but are more the colour of toast . . . A dismal tint, I think.

Then, on the road to Nicola:

> Gilmore's Hill near Nicola is . . . a terror. The road winds along by the side of that 15-mile lake and was built without a thought of anything but cheapness, so its just wide enough to take one carriage—the mountain on one side and the lake on the other—ten, twenty, and in some places, even a hundred feet below. And I lived through it all, and wasn't very nervous, but I don't want to go over it very often.

Of her new home in the house of the Harvey Woodwards in Lower Nicola ($18 a month, washing included) she remarked, "I think I'll be comfortable and will like it well enough but as to liking any place better than home I never did and never will" (27/3/88, PANS).

Everything was wrong. While she could get a glass of milk anytime she liked (something not always possible at home), she grumbled, "The milk is blue, blue to what we have at home. The cattle are so poor, and the calves get the best of it anyhow" (14/4/88, NVA). Choke berries and apples also failed to make the grade. "B.C. [choke berries] haven't half so much meat on them as ours, and I never want to taste them. How does the apple crop look? We have had some here, from Spencer's Bridge. They look like those from George's tree but are as soft as butter—wouldn't keep a week" (22/8/88, NVA). This was the produce of an orchard that was to win gold medals around the world and whose apples drew the attention of Edward VII. Then, there was the dust (17/5/88, NVA), the dreadful mosquitoes (28/5/88, NVA) and the excruciating heat (22/8/88, NVA). Above all, the landscape was wrong:

I can't get used to the dark hills and rocks—I don't know what it is I miss, but there seems to be such a lack of brightness somehow—perhaps it's the want of water that makes the difference—a sheet of water I mean, like the river and harbour at home. The river here is a rushing dirty thing only showing itself here and there among the hills and bushes. (14/4/88, NVA)

No, she concludes, "B.C. may be good enough but it doesn't come up to N.S. in any way" (1/10/88, NVA). Her feelings are strong: "If hatred to a place would make me leave it I don't think I'd have stayed more than three weeks in the Valleys, not to mention such a length of time as three months" (11/6/88, NVA).

It was wrong because it was not home. Over and over she expected to see a "home scene," as she called it, either in the physical geography or in the behaviour of the people, but she was disappointed. Where others were lacking, she herself tried to establish Sutherland River in Lower Nicola whenever possible, in her habits, her dress, or the behaviour of those she could influence (the servants, the schoolchildren), and she lamented when her efforts failed.

While she tried establish Sutherland River in Lower Nicola, she also endeavoured to retain her presence, connection, and influence in Sutherland River. The following passage is typical: "I'll be so glad if you'll get some help with the barn this winter, I've been thinking of you all, getting fires kindled and the beasties looked to, in the cold mornings. Tell me how many cows are giving milk, do the hens lay . . .?" (3/12/88, PABC). She asked innumerable questions about the doings of family, friends, and neighbours. She advised on various household problems, commissioned small tasks to be done—the knitting of socks, the purchase of a pair of shoes—and sent money to help with the household finances.

She was dreadfully homesick: "I don't want to think back any more than I can help for fear I get homesick. That last sentence isn't very idiomatic—not to say idiotic—but you know what I mean, so that's all right. I've had no settled homesickness yet, though I've had to swallow at various times, lumps about as big as a barn" (29/3/88, PANS). The passage is typical. She recognized homesickness as something to be kept at bay—tried to be brave and shrug it off, yet never quite managed. Her letters are infused with yearnings of home. She read her Bible every night and comforted herself that she was reading the same pas-

Fig. 5. The school at Nicola Lake where Annie taught. (Photograph courtesy of the Nicola Valley Archives.)

sage that was being read at home. As school holidays approached, she remarked, "Looking back over what I have written about looking forward to holidays it's struck me all at once—what's the good of holidays to a body when you can't get home? I take blue streaks and bright streaks turn about without any apparent cause—I must scuttle to bed before this blue streak develops further" (14/4/88, NVA). That bed stood in the corner of her room, beside the window which faces East, "my Jerusalem in very fact" (14/4/88, NVA).

She seemed to get some comfort in memories of her Jerusalem:

> I think I can see our garden now—that long grassy strip behind the house with the branches of the trees sweeping it. (25/6/88, NVA)

> I was reading aloud a description . . . that brought the little old dog to my mind, and I thought I saw him trotting to the gate to meet me, with his little tail a'wagging and his brown eyes a'winking. (8/8/88, NVA)

Letters sustained her. While Annie was fairly haphazard in her letter writing, though usually managing one every two weeks or so, Jessie wrote two or three long letters a week, sometimes ten to fifteen pages in length. She was aware of her need to keep in constant contact with home: "I must write to you every week though. I couldn't pull through otherwise" (14/4/88, NVA). She was also demanding about getting letters in return, placing quite a burden on a mother who had other children in need of letters, not to mention a farm to run. Mother never complained outright but tried to wean Jessie off her constant letter writing when as many as forty or fifty pages a week came her way.

In their differing ways, both young women were floundering. In this period, they were desperately trying to keep in contact with significant others. Annie did it by filling her life with people—mostly men— finding a substitute for the intimacy of home wherever she could through a sort of instant friendliness to any and all who came her way. Jessie, emotionally blind to those around her, reached out across the continent to those at home in a desperate attempt to keep those ties as strong as ever.

Some months after their arrival in British Columbia, a second phase began. For Annie, it occurred after her mother reprimanded her about the wild life she had been living. Just six weeks later she wrote, "Mother what would you say if I told you that by-and-by I was going to marry a

Fig. 6. Mr. James Gordon and his new wife Annie (Nee McQueen). (Photograph courtesy of the Nicola Valley Archives.)

B.C. business man, one who is nice, steady, clever, and wealthy into the bargain! Mind, I don't say that this is the case, but what would you say if it were?" (7/1/88, PABC).

Mother was not at all pleased with the idea, and accused Annie of thinking only of herself. Annie replied, "I don't think I am as selfish as you think me, I try not to be, and your letters make me feel very badly. I hadn't any idea of 'caring particularly for Mr. Gordon' until it was too late, but if you say you don't want me to marry him, I'll obey you, without a word" (16/3/88, NVA).

Mother was persuaded by the Kamloops minister and by Jessie that James Gordon was a respectable gentleman with many good qualities. But she seems to have kept aloof from him for a long time—perhaps because it was all happening away from her intimate control. However, a cautious truce between Annie and her mother was eventually established. Interestingly, the permission of Annie's father was sought only ten months later, when the wedding was but weeks away.

Able to see her fiancé only occasionally on weekends, Annie settled down during her engagement. Her letters brimmed with news of her work at the school, in which she took great pride, of singing at local Methodist socials, and of the general round of village life. It was a happy period. But as the wedding approached and she faced the prospect of giving up her work, Annie's thoughts turned to home. Her letters began to resemble Jessie's:

> How are you all at home anyhow? It seems an age since I had a word from you, and it just makes me real lonesome. . . . Dearest mother, I miss you more now than I ever did since I left home. If I could only be with you for even ten minutes, I wouldn't mind so much. (10/11/88, PANS)

She wrote one last letter as a single woman:

> I feel a bit lonely over leaving the school, and the children, the people too have been very kind to me and I feel sorrier to leave than I ever thought I could be. I have laboured hard among them and feel reluctant to lay down my work, and begin in a new place. . . . I feel nervous over the coming event, but I will not feel it so trying as I imagine. (26/12,88, NVA)

Annie's disconnection was short-lived. After her marriage to Jim Gordon, she moved to Kamloops and set up a home. Jessie wrote on her first visit there some six weeks later:

> Nan does very well in the housekeeping line and had her weeks' work all done up in expectation of my arrival. . . . She is quite settled down and doesn't care for "running around:" at all—wants to keep her

house nice, and have things comfortable for Jim when he comes in. He
isn't half so care-worn looking as he used to be, and I guess they both
think they are as happy as clams. (13/2/89, NVA)

Annie had been in the British Columbia interior some sixteen
months. The first baby was born nine months later, and two others
were to follow. Her letters became very infrequent. They were full of
descriptions of long nights of babies' colic and teething, of days when
she would see no one except her immediate family, of trying to clothe
them all with scant resources. Eventually things improved, a servant
girl was hired, the children grew. Through it all, despite the hardships
of raising three young children under such conditions, Annie was
essentially happy, at home in the west.[8]

Jessie, however, was worse than ever after Annie's marriage. She
remarked, "Even if I didn't see [Annie] every week, I always knew she
was there and could be seen in a pinch" (24/1/89, NVA). The first
indication of Jessie's solution appeared in a letter written two months
after Annie's wedding. Jessie had been staying in Lower Nicola, a
Methodist settlement mostly made up of members of the extended
Woodward family. She had been boarding with Mr. and Mrs. Harvey
Woodward. They had previously been described as having "six or
seven children, I forget which," including a small child called Fred,
about a year old. Until this time, descriptions of the family had been
brief and rare, and the child hardly mentioned. But now, we find Jessie
remarking, "Small Fred has just climbed up on my lap. He. . . . sometimes refuses to go to his mama from me" (4/3/89, NVA).

Jessie began to dote on Fred, a loving child, to the point that one of
her sisters remarked that he had a bigger share in her affections than
any of the ranchers could ever have. Jessie agreed (18/3/89, NVA). Her
letters began to fill with descriptions of life in the Harvey Woodward
household (always so-called to distinguish them from the Marcus
Woodwards, living nearby), and of all their comings and goings. She
said of Mrs. Harvey "If I were her eldest daughter she couldn't be
kinder" (22/7/89, PABC). A new baby was born, referred to as "the
baby" (9/9/89, NVA), Fred became "my boy" (9/9/89, NVA), Mr. and
Mrs. Woodward senior, who lived nearby, became "Grandpa" and
"Grandma" (29/8/89, NVA).

A few weeks later she wrote, "We had our christening here, Saturday evening and supper afterwards. Counting babies and all of our
own family, there were thirty in the house" (29/10/89, NVA). The

phrases "*our* christening," and "all of *our own* family" reveal that Jessie had embraced the Woodwards as her own family.

Her opinion of British Columbia changed radically following this identification. In the spring she remarked, "The ground is taking a greenish tinge and by the end of the week it will be as green as we can expect to see it. It is emphatically "a country without grass" but I am getting used to it" (18/3/89, NVA).

In the fall she wrote,

> There is not much sign of the threatened famine on this ranch. There are good big stacks of hay, bins of wheat, sacks of flour, a root-house full of potatoes, and between them Mr Harvey and Grandpa killed fourteen hogs. Grandpa took two of them but the remaining dozen were all cut up here into hams, bacon, sausages, lard, potted head, and everything else that pig could be made into. We've had spare rib enough to spare and I don't like to say how many pounds of soap are being made.
>
> They are still milking one cow, so we haven't come down to condensed milk yet. I am patriotic to the back-bone, but I prefer B.C. milk straight from the cow to the best Truro condensed milk. This is a very different country from Nova Scotia. Looking out of my window, I can see a field that Mr Harvey ploughed in the early part of the summer, after the hoppers swept it. There is not a vestige of anything growing on it, and yet it is good ground and gave a fine crop of potatoes last year. (13/11/89, PABC)

By adopting the Woodwards as her own family, Jessie, albeit tenuously, was beginning to forge a bond with a new set of significant others and to find a way of surviving in the west.[9]

Notes

1. J. G. Herder, "Essay on the Origin of Language, Part 1," in *On the Origin of Language*, trans. J. H. Moran and A. Gode (New York: F. Ungar, 1966), 156.
2. See J. G. Herder, "The Origin of Language, Part 2," in *J. G. Herder on Social and Political Culture*, translated and edited by F. M. Barnard (London: Cambridge University Press, 1969), 161–3.
3. There are, of course, many problems with this view, given that persons

who speak the same language may not necessarily share the same culture, and vice versa.

4. Virginia Held, "Feminism and Moral Theory," in John Arthur, ed., *Morality and Moral Controversies* (Englewood Cliffs, N.J.: Prentice-Hall, 1993), 73–84, 77.

5. That closeness has benefited us greatly, for not only did they all write to each other regularly, they kept each other's letters, as did their successors. Today, there are, I believe, over two thousand family letters, cards, diaries, and the like in the archives from the period, including over two hundred letters written to and from British Columbia. More are being discovered— one was found in Saltspring just last year. This paper is based almost entirely on the letters to and from B.C., and I would like to thank Dr. Jean Barman of the University of British Columbia not only for introducing me to the charming McQueens in the first place but also for her great kindness in making typed transcripts of all the British Columbia letters available to me.

6. The letter is described in Relief Williams MacKay, *Simple Annals* (Pictou, N.S.: Advocate, 1986). The book, by a great-niece of Annie's, is a wonderful source of McQueen history.

7. The following abbreviations are used to indicate the location of the original letters:

   NVA : Nicola Valley Archives
   PABC: Provincial Archives of British Columbia
   PANS: Provincial Archives of Nova Scotia
   Unless otherwise mentioned, the letters are written home to Mother.

8. Annie went on to live a long, interesting, and productive life in British Columbia. She died in Victoria in 1941.

9. Jessie's struggle to maintain her identity in the west by no means ends here, but the rest is a story for another day.

"It's an Odd Country": One British Family's Response to Social Attitudes in British Columbia, c. 1890–1914

Donald F. Harris

SEVERAL MEMBERS OF AN EXTENDED FAMILY FROM THE SHROPSHIRE-Flintshire borderland emigrated to British Columbia toward the end of the nineteenth century. In the old country, the Lees were people of substance and local standing: farmers with broad, fertile acres, justices of the peace, prosperous land agents, lawyers, clergymen.[1] To define class in Britain is a frustrating, and sometimes futile, task. This article describes the Lees with an old-fashioned word that they might have used themselves: gentlefolk.

By the late nineteenth century, the Lees were troubled by the question facing many of their class: what to do for their sons—and daughters. Matthew Henry Lee, vicar of Hanmer, had six children; four went to Canada.

The seven children of the vicar's cousin, William Henry Lee,[2] also had cause to think of emigration. Their father had been a land agent, in prosperous partnership with another cousin. His house, Oak Bank, was set in a small estate of forty-four acres, and the 1881 census listed three servants there.[3] However, William Lee wanted to have an agency of his own, and in 1881, the family moved about seven miles to a smaller house in Shropshire, not far from the market town of Whitchurch. Alas, William died within seven years, aged only forty-five, leaving little to his widow, Agnes.[4] With those of her children who had not already left home, she moved into Whitchurch to live at the end of a newly built terrace of narrow, four-storey houses, with tiny yards at the rear. While there would have been enough rooms, albeit all small, and though the census recorded a live-in servant girl, compared to Oak Bank the new house reflected the family's reduced circumstances. Mrs. Lee remarried, but was soon widowed again, with little improvement to her financial resources. One son, Hugh, became a solicitor in Whitchurch; he remained a bachelor, and she lived with him. Of her seven children, three sons and one daughter emigrated to western Canada: one to Manitoba and the others to British Columbia.

Agnes Nash (as she became by her second marriage) stayed in Canada from January 1913 to November 1914, visiting her children and two stepsons who had emigrated to Alberta. The visit was paid for by her son-in-law, Norman Lee, eldest son of the vicar of Hanmer, who had married her daughter, Nessie. At the time of their marriage in 1902, Norman already had a prosperous ranch and trading post in the Chilcotin Valley of British Columbia and was something of a legendary figure. During the Klondike gold rush, he had driven a large herd of cattle a thousand miles north to the Teslin River, where he slaughtered the survivors, built two large scows, and began to sail the carcasses down the five hundred miles to Dawson City, only to lose them all in a storm. Norman got back to Vancouver, by his own account with nothing but a blanket roll, a dog, and one dollar. But he arranged credit, got back to his ranch and trading post, repaid his debts, and soon had a herd of a thousand fine cattle. By the time his mother-in-law arrived, he and Nessie were in the process of selling up and retiring to Victoria— something they were to regret, and eventually to rectify.

During her stay in Canada, Mrs. Nash wrote almost once a week to her son in Whitchurch.[5] She was a perceptive observer. Reduced circumstances had not made her forsake the values of her class, but any critical comments were made without malice. Moreover, her determined stamina was matched by a willingness to work hard in circumstances as she found them, rather than complain: at sixty-five, she was always ready to take on more than her share of domestic tasks.

She was not one to tell the colonials how much better matters were ordered in England. Only one custom appalled her. While she was in Victoria, she heard of the death there of someone she had known in England.

> Poor George Gellings, he had wanted to marry Lillian [one of her daughters], but she wouldn't have him. I got a great shock, the coffin had a glass lid and there lay the poor lad in his dress suit with white shirt, collar and black tie, it was too horrible. I can't think how English people can conform to such a horrid custom.

Only thoughts of an English garden made her homesick. At Nicola, after a drive into the mountains, she wrote,

I never saw such beautiful flowers as we gathered, of course all wild, orchids, sunflowers, michaelmas daisies, columbines, pea vines, coreopsis, gladias [sic] and such glorious wild roses, and yet no one seems to have a decent garden . . . just a few pansies. I think it must be that the men have no time to attend to it. I just long to see our sweet garden at home.

A few days later, she was given some sweet peas, "and I just could have cried, they seemed like a whiff from home."[6]

She occasionally chided colonial manners, but only gently. She stayed a while with a stepson at Carbon, fifty miles northeast of Calgary. He had married a Canadian farmer's daughter, and Mrs. Nash praised her virtues:

Very pretty . . . she keeps house and babies spick and span, [but] the meals are served Canadian fashion, which isn't what one likes. However, she is a good cook, and if the man who works for them eats with you and uses the same fork for his meat and pudding, why you get accustomed to it.

Mrs. Nash recognized that she was in a country very different from England, but never suggested that the differences made Canada any the worse. In one of her first letters, written from the Chilcotin, she wrote, "This is an odd life, but has its attractions, and I can quite see that Norman could never be happy in any other country."

She did, however, understand that a different sense of freedom in pioneer Canada could make heavy demands on the womenfolk. At Hanceville: "Nessie has gone to nothing, worried and worn out." And at Nicola: "Amy [her daughter-in-law] is going away for a week. She is just worn out, and I can see to things whilst she has a holiday away from the children." And she did indeed "see to things." Visiting Norman's bachelor brother at his Chilcotin ranch: "Penrose is away all day branding horses. I have had a huge wash, then I cooked a brace of willow grouse and made a pudding for dinner." She noted the calls upon up-country hospitality: "This is a place where people are continually coming and going and beds have to be ready." And a month later: "The house is full tonight to overflowing and Agnes [a visiting granddaughter] has to go up to the Hances to sleep."

If Mrs. Nash sometimes found British Columbia "an odd country," it was because the social environment disturbed her notions of class. She was observing new patterns of behaviour. She did not condemn, but sometimes seemed bemused at the absence of her old-country certainties.[7] Visiting a son in Nicola, she wrote, "When he can afford it, Alf will buy paper and the Vicar will come and paper inside the house. It is an odd country." She visited a newly married couple: "The man, who is the son of a doctor at Burton-on-Trent, helped last winter here to build out-houses, and the girl, who came out from England two months ago to marry him, is a clergyman's daughter."

"Fancy," she wrote from Victoria, "the one servant has £60 a year and I do the cooking." And in another letter,

> Out here one hardly ever has more than one servant or one China Man [sic] in the house. It is quite wonderful to me the amount of work just one does, but the wages are huge, our young Scotch maid, Elsie gets £5 a month. Isn't it awful? . . . Elsie always has Sunday out after she has washed up the dinner things.[8]

She found several gentlefolk emigrants who, lacking the skills or capital necessary for quick success in British Columbia, were working at jobs which they would have considered far beneath them in England, hoping soon to find something more rewarding or congenial. She did not tell of any who complained. An Old Etonian in his sixties, who "knew all the best people around Whitchurch and Malpas," was tending a vegetable garden for his keep, while trying to arrange a land grant for his son. Another Old Etonian was a hired man on a ranch, living on a diet of salt beef, beans, and potatoes, and grateful for a supper Mrs. Nash prepared for him. Yet another Old Etonian ("We seem to meet so many out here," she wrote) had become a motor mechanic and bred fox-terriers for sale.

Mrs. Nash could recognize a gentleman, and those Old Etonians had not forfeited their status in her eyes. She thought that a Mr. Temple, who had money to buy Norman's ranch, was "a bounder," whereas Temple's assistant, a Mr. Marryat, "knows the rector of Malpas [the parish in which Oak Bank was then situated], and is a gentleman." (As it turned out, she was right about Temple.) Not that being a gentleman was everything. Her granddaughter Kittie, whom Mrs. Nash had taken to Canada with her, soon received an offer of marriage from a man at Alexis Creek. "He is a gentleman but a fool, and I hope she refuses him." She did.

By 1913, even in the more isolated parts of British Columbia, gentlefolk emigrants need not have had such a painful feeling of "leaving the world" as Jane Floyd has described in her study of women in earlier frontier life.[9] However, Mrs. Nash was aware of the need to avoid the depressing effect of social isolation in a pioneer environment. When her son at Nicola, in the provincial civil service, was transferred to Alberni, she was pleased to report, "He likes his new home. The vicar and his wife are very nice and Alf had a lot of good introductions so they have soon got into a good set."

Getting into "a good set"—that was important. When she went to Victoria with Nessie and Norman, Mrs. Nash may have worried about Norman's foolish business ventures, but her letters leave no doubt that he and Nessie were in the right set. On December 16, 1913, she wrote,

> Norman and Nessie went to have tea with Sir Richard McBride, the Premier. . . . Then Norman had to go to see the [Lieutenant] Governor. Most of the rich swells of the neighbourhood have called on us, Norman having known their parents.

On May 10, 1914:

> The Miss Duponts leave shortly for England. . . . They are old-timers here and have asked so many of the best people to call upon us. People come here by dozens to tea on Sunday and we make it a kind of picnic as Elsie always has Sunday out after she has washed up the dinner things.

Mrs. Nash wrote of going with Nessie to have tea with the Honourable Mrs. Martin, and of being at the premier's reception at the Empress Hotel. She found him "a charming man," but added that he was "entirely self-made."

In the interior of British Columbia, Mrs. Nash noted the absence of old-country attitudes toward class; but in Victoria, at least, she found what Patrick Dunae has described as "a style of society that made visiting Englishmen and gentlemen emigrants feel at home."[10] Canada was not to be without a class structure of its own. Not that all of whom Mrs. Nash called "the best people" were wealthy in Victoria, an expensive city: in December 1913, she wrote of going with Nessie to a bazaar "in aid of the Victoria Club for gentlewomen who are badly off." The experiences of her granddaughter, Kittie, demonstrate some of the problems which faced gentlewomen emigrants of little wealth, who lacked any training for colonial life. Kittie was willing to work hard, and in the Chilcotin she took the only available employment, looking after two "sweet little girls" with "kind people, though not gentlefolk," at $25 (about £5) a month. The job did not last. In January 1914, Mrs. Nash wrote, "Kittie has a post at Port Alberni to look after a little girl. It is only £3 a month, so if we hear of anything better she will leave at once. Work is very difficult for girls out here." What Mrs. Nash meant was "difficult for girls of Kittie's class." Her grandmother might think of Kittie as a governess, or as what is today called a nanny, despite her lack of any training in child care; in reality, she would be expected also to do the work of a domestic servant.

The job at Port Alberni lasted less than three months: the family could not afford to keep her. Kittie might have had hopes of better prospects in Victoria, where well-bred "lady helps" were employed by some wealthy families, and it has been shown that her aunt and uncle had well-connected friends there. However, any such hopes were quickly dispelled, and Mrs. Nash considered her fortunate to be offered what was essentially a general servant's job with the wife of the proprietor of a private school, at £6 a month.

> Mrs. Ward and Kittie will have everything to do. Fortunately there are only two boarders, but there is the big schoolroom to clean daily. She says Kittie can come up here (it is only three minutes walk) every evening, and every Sunday for the afternoon and evening, so it will not be a hard post.

Kittie, for want of any better opportunity, became a domestic servant, something that would have been unthinkable in England.

Kittie's aunt, Nessie, found a much more fulfilled liberation from English conventions. Newly married, her first months in Canada were hard to bear, facing the fact that she had committed herself to a strange and seemingly threatening environment. Nessie later described her shock at arriving at the Hanceville ranch to join her husband, after a seven-day sleigh journey from the railway at Ashcroft:

> A house built of logs in the midst of a wilderness, with a trading post just across the road. This was my home in the New World. Having come straight from an English drawing room I was soon very home-sick, especially when Norman talked pidgin-English to the Chinese cook and various dialects with the Indians. But I never let him know I was unhappy in the home he had provided. Riding was one of my

greatest joys, and I often rode out to the old Indian cemetery nearby. There I'd sit on the rail fence and cry my heart out. But gradually I settled into my new life and learned how to deal with its many problems, and now I wouldn't change for anything in the world.[11]

She coped well with many problems. She actively helped her husband through an unfortunate period in Victoria when Norman, who should never have left his ranch, made foolish speculations in automobiles and real estate. On one occasion, while Norman was away in Vancouver, she heard that the company holding his cars was going into liquidation. In a letter to her brother in Whitchurch, she told how she "flew to a lawyer," and went with a Major Pottinger and three drivers to the garage. "We found parts of each motor had been taken off so that they couldn't work, and none of the heads of the firm could be found, but at last we got each car removed to another garage. The lawyer complimented me on securing the cars; he never thought I would."

In 1919, Norman and Nessie regained possession of the Hanceville property, the purchaser (of whom Mrs. Nash had had so low an opinion—"a bounder," "no gentleman") having been unable to keep up the payments. Nessie shared with her husband and their adopted son in the hard work which restored the ranch and store. In 1927, when she was fifty-five, she opened a women's-wear store in Williams Lake, some fifty miles from Hanceville. She continued to live at the ranch, but had an apartment at Williams Lake so that she could keep a firm eye on her businesses. She lived until 1958, a widow for some twenty years, much respected in the district.

Despite many hardships, emigration for Nessie was a liberating experience, giving opportunities to make full use of her talents and strength of character. She was one of the fortunate gentlewomen emigrants, and Norman was well established in British Columbia when they married.[12]

Nessie's brothers and cousins in Canada all found, through hard work and struggle, what must be called fulfilment. Tom ran his store at Alexis Creek until his death in 1946, through good times and bad. Alfred, after an up-country career in the provincial civil service, retired as County Court Registrar at Alberni and then engaged in real estate development, he and his musical wife both well respected in the district.[13]

Nessie's brother-in-law, Penrose Lee, remained in his sod-roofed house on his Chilcotin ranch until his death in 1960: "the land of my heart," as he called it. He never married, and his sister Helen came to keep house for him after spending twenty years in San Francisco, some of that time as a Pinkerton detective. She stayed with her brother until her death in 1954, aged ninety-two.[14]

Not all of those Old Etonians pursuing unaccustomed careers were as successful as the Lees, and Kittie, who did not return to England with her grandmother, had to wait until she was rescued by marriage. However, when note has been taken of the failures, I would argue that Canada offered the sons and daughters of gentlefolk the opportunity for liberation from class conventions and class pretensions. Tom Lee served briefly in the Mounted Police. Had he remained in Shropshire, it is unlikely he would have enrolled in the County Constabulary, still less likely that he would have become a Whitchurch shopkeeper. Yet when he was about to open his general store at Alexis Creek, his mother described the venture as "a splendid chance"—and so it proved. Nessie would almost certainly not have had a milliner's shop in Whitchurch. Neither Norman nor Penrose could have afforded an English farm of the size or scope (or beauty) of their Chilcotin ranches.

The emigrant farm labourer or domestic servant had the opportunity to achieve liberation from the social restrictions of his or her humble class. Emigrant artisans might find better material reward for their skills. For the Lees and their like, men and women both, Canada offered the chance of new ways to make one's way in the world: new forms of freedom, including the freedom from constraints imposed by old perceptions of status.

Notes

1. For details on the Lees in Britain and Canada, see D. F. Harris, "The Lees of Oak Bank in Western Canada" (unpublished manuscript, 1993). Copies deposited in Shropshire Records & Research Centre, Shrewsbury (hereafter SRR), and the B.C. Provincial Archives.
2. The name Henry is from two ancestors, Philip (1631–96) and Matthew (1662–1714) Henry, father and son, theological scholars. See Leslie Stephen and Sidney Lee, eds., *Dictionary of National Biography* (London: Oxford University Press, 1973), vol. 9, 574–7.
3. The house, now called Whitewell Lodge, has been enlarged in this century, but when I was shown over the property by the owner, who remem-

bered with affection Lee's widow, it was evident that the family had lived in some style.

4. Agnes Tulloch was the daughter of a Scots army officer. Her uncle, The Reverend John Tulloch, was principal of St. Andrew's University, and a first cousin was principal of Aberdeen University and a chaplain to the Queen in Scotland. Matthew Henry Lee, Vicar of Hanmer, and his elder brother, William Henry Lee's partner in the land agency, both married Scottish wives.

5. All these letters, and some to Hugh from her children in Canada, are in SRR, "Letters from B.C.," 2794/42.

6. Cf. Catharine Parr Traill, writing of the lonely wife in her cabin: "She thinks of the flowers that she loved in childhood . . . and what she would not give for one of those old familiar flowers! No wonder that the heart of the emigrant's wife is sometimes sad, and needs to be dealt gently with by her less sensitive partner." *The Canadian Settler's Guide* (Toronto: New Canadian Library Edition, 1969) 11–12.

7. She must have felt much the same as an "old colonial hand" who complained to me in Malaya in 1950 that "one no longer knows who's who and what's what."

8. Visiting English gentlefolk often expressed indignant surprise at the high wages paid to servants in Canada. Arthur Greg in 1922 found Montreal "frightfully expensive. . . . A chauffeur with just one car gets about £15 a month—£180 a year." (Chester RO, DDX 511/8)

9. Janet Floyd, "Leaving the World: Narratives of Emigration and Frontier Life Written by Women in Upper Canada and the Old Northwest" (unpublished Ph.D. dissertation, University of Sussex, 1995). In 1906, Grace Lee visited her brothers, Norman and Penrose, in B.C., and on her return told meetings on behalf of the New Westminster and Kootenay Missionary Association that at one time her brothers had gone almost nine years without seeing a clergyman or attending a place of worship. "We in this country cannot imagine into what state people drift into [sic], living in these conditions." (Parish Notes for Hanmer and Tallarn, *Ellesmere Deanery Magazine, March & April 1907*. SRR).

10. Patrick Dunae, *Gentlemen Emigrants: From the British Public Schools to the Canadian Frontier* (Vancouver: Douglas & McIntyre, 1981).

11. From the foreword by Eileen Laurie in G. R. Elliott, ed., *Klondike Cattle Drive, The Journal of Norman Lee* (Vancouver: Mitchell Press, 1960). Copy in B.C. Provincial Archives, NW 971.chi.

12. Susan Jackel doubted if the majority of English gentlewomen who emi-

grated to western Canada "found either success or freedom." *A Flannel Shirt and Liberty. British Emigrant Gentlewomen in the Canadian West, 1880– 1914* (Vancouver: University of British Columbia Press, 1982), xxvi.

13. William, the first of Nessie's brothers to emigrate, went to Boissevain, Manitoba. Helped by a Whitchurch friend already settled there, he worked at various jobs before starting up a farm of his own, but after five years of poor returns (his crop was hailed three years running), he sold up, moved with his family to Toronto, and despite financial hardship qualified as a vet. He returned to Manitoba, and as "Doc Lee" earned respect and affection not only for his work, but for his generosity and participation in local affairs. "A veritable prince of a man," was the local newspaper's verdict when he died. (Sources in Harris, "The Lees of Oak Bank").

14. Her other brother, Robert Warden Lee, after a First at Balliol, a brief period in the Ceylon Civil Service, and a fellowship at All Souls, became dean of the Faculty of Law at McGill University in 1914.

From Eastern England to Western Canada: Illustrations

John F. Davis

On April 9, 1906, after a farewell service at Beverley Minster, where each had been given a pocketbook containing a New Testament and Psalms bearing the Beverley coat of arms embossed in gold, as well as gifts of clothes, fifty would-be emigrants were led by the town band as they marched from the Guildhall to the railway station. Arriving in Liverpool by train the following morning, they sat down to a restaurant breakfast, paid for by a former Beverley resident, before setting sail for Canada. The group of fifty-five had been selected and approved by a doctor from sixty-five original applicants. The original plan had been to go to Winnipeg, but they initially went only as far as western Ontario. They were met by Church Army representatives upon their arrival in Canada. It was reported that all the men had undertaken to repay their passage fare within eighteen months, "their employers in Canada being authorised to deduct the amount from their wages and forward it to the Church Army." Thus, the *Beverley Guardian* in 1906 reported upon one of the larger group movements from east to west. The heading on 7 April had been:

> Beverley Emigrants to Canada
> Fifty to Depart Next Monday
> Farewell Service at the Minster[1]

The story did not end there, for in late May and June, the paper published excerpts from letters written home by some of the men, most of them working on farms in southern Ontario.[2]

The purpose of this paper is to discuss the evidence for emigration from eastern England to western Canada over the thirty-five years preceding the First World War using material gleaned from a not very scientific sampling of journals and newspapers over a period of years. The regions considered are very crudely defined. By "Eastern England" I mean an essentially rural and agricultural area east of the Pennines, north of the Thames and south of the Tees, while the term "western Canada" is used to describe what would become the three prairie provinces, British Columbia, and also western Ontario. My defence for including western Ontario is that would-be immigrants were frequently advised to go to there first so that they could experience the Canadian way of life and farming methods before heading west.[3] The period 1880 to 1914 coincides with the opening up by the railways of the prairie provinces. The need for farm settlers was great, while surplus labour was available on English farms as methods and conditions changed and as farmers' younger sons, tenants, and farm labourers looked for possible ways of becoming their own bosses.

Conscious of the need to promote settlement, Canadian national and provincial governments and business organisations sought various mechanisms to advertise the attractions and advantages of Canada as a destination, offer advice, and dispel fears. The widest coverage was from advertising through the press. Newspapers provide researchers into migration with a wealth of material.[4] This paper represents the fruits of working through editions covering a range of years of some thirty regional newspapers and journals.

Newspapers frequently carried advertisements from the main shipping lines, such as the Allan Line and the Royal Mail Line. Examples exist in the *Retford and Gainsborough Times* and the *Worksop and Newark Weekly News* of January 3, 1890, which listed agents in Brigg, Gainsborough, Grimsby, Retford, Scunthorpe, West Retford, and Worksop. Not all advertising targeted people going to Canada to stay and work; the summer issues of this and other papers for 1890 and 1891 refer to tourists and sportsmen. Round-trip tickets were offered, combining excursions to Niagara Falls and "the wonderful scenery and sporting delights of the Rocky Mountains and B.C."

Readers of the *Sheffield Telegraph* in 1904 and 1905 had ample opportunity to gain some picture of work, life, and prospects in the area of Lloydminster, now on the boundary between Alberta and Saskatchewan. Over sixty articles appeared, some filling a whole page, often accompanied by pen sketches. These dealt with life in winter on the prairies, railway construction, an Englishwoman's experience, tips for would-be settlers, and much else.

Some years earlier, the *Boston Gazette* carried an item under the title FREE GRANTS OF LAND IN MANITOBA AND OTHER PROVINCES OF CANADA. This article commented on the reports of twelve British farmer delegates who had visited Canada that year and also on pamphlets issued under the authority of the Imperial and Dominion governments. These pamphlets offered "full information as to land regulations and bonuses granted to settlers who take up land in Manitoba, the North West Territories and British Columbia, openings for capitalists, demand for labour, rate of wages, [and] cost of living. . . . [A]ll the particulars may be had post free from the H.C. of Canada."[5] The bonuses were given to settlers and their families to help to defray some of the costs of the move. Thus, a range of material was available to the prospective settler in 1890.

A column in the *Eastern Daily News* of February 1, 1898 was titled, "FROM MANITOBA TO NORFOLK: The Brandon of the Far West; Where agricultural depression is unknown." The column reported a conversation of the previous day with a J. S. Frier of Norbury Farm, Brandon Hills, Manitoba, who was visiting England after a ten-year absence. At thirty-three, he had sold up in England and moved to Canada with his wife, family and mother. There, he had bought a homestead near both market and railway, paying $10 an acre. He had prospered, and he now had two farms with elevators near each. He reported that soils were fertile and schools and churches good. Frier recommended that a person with approximately £400 could make a good start, and further advised newcomers to work on a Canadian farm to get experience of Canadian conditions and save wages to buy land and equipment.[6]

A footnote to the column mentioned that J. S. Frier had lectured at the Norwich YMCA on January 29, 1898, and at Old Catton on January 31. National Archives searches reveal that he also lectured in Lincoln and Yarmouth, as well as on similar tours in 1899 and 1903. He was one of the farmer delegates who came to England, visited various parts of the country, and spoke in favour of emigration to the farmlands of Canada. The Canadian and provincial governments, as well as the railways, encouraged and largely financed such visits for a number of years, though at times they had to be rather explicit as to the amount of work they expected to be done. It was not to be seen as an easy ticket for a trip back to the old country.

Lecture tours by both Canadian government officials and farmer delegates were a major source of information and allowed the advantage of face-to-face contact and the opportunity to ask questions to elucidate particular points. Concern had been expressed by Canadian officials in London and Ottawa about the danger of biased reports from railway or government officers promoting the merits of western emigration. So why not get farmers to do the work? They would know the problems of farming the prairies and the issues that concerned farm labourers, tenant farmers, or others in Britain contemplating a move. Obviously, the farmer-delegate system had shortcomings, but it meant that a practising farmer could give valuable information to audiences gathered to hear him, sometimes in the market town or village from which he had originally hailed. Therefore, the government and railways sought suitable, successful men as delegates who were prepared to make the journey to England, sometimes leaving their farms in the care of family or farm workers. The other side of the plan involved getting groups of farmers from Britain to visit Canada on organised tours on the understanding that when they returned they would publish a report (often widely quoted in the local newspapers) and perhaps give lectures, which might be accompanied by illustrations.[7] In 1893, a group of twelve British delegates visited the prairies for a month; of these, six were from eastern England.[8]

For some, the idea of travelling to Canada and seeking work was very daunting. Therefore, in a number of cases, organised parties were arranged and escorted. Returning farmer delegates often took on the job of escorting parties. The *Thirsk and District News* carried the following advertisement on January 5, 1906:

> Mr. Howells, Manitoba farmer, returning 23 February, Mr Wood, 8th March will take parties, Single and married men. Situations provided. Pay own fare. Enclose envelope. W. Rumsey Esq. Shrewsbury.[9]

Emigration was also promoted with stalls and advertising wagons (and later vans) at major agricultural and country shows. The *Cambridge Daily News*, June 25 and 26, 1894, carried a column headed:

THE ROYAL SHOW
THE GOVERNMENT OF CANADA

The Govt. of Canada, with characteristic enterprise, are well represented. Mr John Dyke, the Canadian government agent in Liverpool is in charge.

It goes on to say that the exhibition on Stand 4 was by the High Commission in London on behalf of Ottawa, Manitoba, and the North-west Territories, represented by "magnificent displays of grain and grasses." Such stalls were staffed by emigration officials, or national and sometimes provincial government officers on hand to answer questions. These "Exhibition vehicles" carried exhibits of equipment, farm produce, and pictures, and dispensed literature. The *Norfolk Weekly Standard and Argus* for July 29, 1905, advertised that there was a motor vehicle touring the United Kingdom providing pamphlets and other materials, and that an officer would be on hand to give information and advice to those intending to reside in "BRITAIN'S GREATEST COLONY." The tour was organised by the Commissioner for Emigration to Canada, 11–12 Charing Cross. The vehicle visited Aylesham, Fakenham, Kings Lynn, and Norwich. Unfortunately, I have been unable to unearth the itinerary of any travelling exhibits in the eastern counties, although I did find some for southeast England.

Although the climates were different, eastern England and the Canadian prairies had one thing in common: both were grain-growing areas. The numerous references in the press to the grain crops and possibilities of farming in Canada would have struck a particular chord. The size and quality of the wheat harvest, referred to frequently, was, of course, a sort of barometer of Canadian prosperity. The *Norfolk Weekly Standard and Argus* of August 26, 1905 advertised "CANADA'S WHEAT HARVEST, 100M. BUSHELS OF WHEAT." The *Malton Gazette*, on July 8, 1905 reported a speech by Lord Strathcona at a banquet in London:

> People came somewhat slowly at first but since the CPR joined the two oceans prosperity has gone on by leaps and bounds. In the North-west province 35 years ago there was not a bushel of wheat sent out, but, on the contrary, all that was needed had to be brought from neighbouring states. Last year reports of 50,000,000 bushels of wheat are expected, and this year's harvest should be nearer 75m or perhaps 100m.

Newspapers also frequently contained advertisements asking for harvesters.[10] There was, however, an obvious danger in responding to "harvest call" advertisements. While some offered permanent situations, many were just for the season. Unless one went out in an organised party, there was also a danger that more men would turn up at the farms than could be used. The *Lincoln, Rutland and Stamford Mercury* carried an advertisement on August 10, 1906, from the Canadian Labour Bureau of Liverpool, which promised that men were "wanted in large numbers for harvesting. High wages, cheap fares." Yet no one would know when all of the two hundred or five hundred men needed had been already hired, a situation that hints of conditions similar to those in *The Grapes of Wrath*.

The *Herts and Essex Observer and General Advertiser* carried a "special notice" on October 28, 1905:

CANADA
LAND FOR ALL
WORK FOR ALL
HOMES FOR ALL

A lecture on the above subject, illustrated by a splendid selection of slides will be delivered by Dr John Robbins of London (Resident in Canada for 25 years) at the British Schools, Sawbridgeworth on Tuesday 31 October at 8 p.m.

The slides were of the Winnipeg area between 1874 and 1905. The following week, in reporting the lecture, the paper wrote that Dr. Robbins had said there were some who should go and some who should not. "Born grumblers and people with an indisposition to work should stay here." He said that cheerful, hard workers were wanted, that Manitoba and the Northwest Territories had a hundred million acres of land for wheat, and that every male over 18 was entitled to 160 acres to farm. He suggested that immigrants go to Ontario first to get experience of life in Canada and then "proceed to the Great West beyond." Dr. Robbins was described in the *Boston Independent* and in the *Lincolnshire Advertiser* of January 23, 1904, as a Canadian expert and an agent for the CPR Steamship Company.

Earlier, on February 3, 1900, the *Louth and Lincolnshire News*, the *Louth Times,* and the *Mablethorpe and Sutton on Sea Advertiser* carried the following advertisement:

WANTED IN CANADA
Capitalists and persons with moderate incomes. Farmers, farm labourers, young men desiring to learn farming, domestics.

FREE GRANTS OF LAND
IN MANITOBA AND THE NORTHWEST
Crown lands in other places. Pamphlets etc from Allan, Dominion or Beaver (Elder Dempster) Lines, CPR or Can Govt— 15 Water St. Liverpool.

Not all references to places where one could obtain information were quite so distant from the eastern counties. A whole series of more accessible agents operated in eastern England.[11]

Other advertisements were specifically directed to those with capital. The Alberta Land Company, which had a northern branch in New Street, York, advertised in the *York, Thirsk and District News* on February 15, 1908, and then regularly until April 4, 1908, as follows:

ALBERTA, CANADA ; ATTRACTIVE FARM FOR SALE.
640 acres of which 155 under cult.—excellent wheat land, wooden house with stone foundation, farm buildings, stabling for 13 horses. Good water from 3 wells and 7 miles of fence erected. 40 strong herd of shorthorns, 28 horses etc and all necessary farm implements. Value of equipment and stock c £1,600. A crop may be taken this year and could make a profit of £500–600 and after this year £750–1000 if a good year and sales good. Details from Alberta Land Co.

Obviously, such a farm would appeal only to the more affluent, although it indicates that some farmers were already prospering, and that those with capital could acquire a well-established farm. The same company advertised Canadian fruit farms in Nova Scotia and British Columbia in the same paper on April 18, 1908. British Columbia was also promoted as a destination in the *Lincoln Gazette*. The province was described in glowing terms in an advertisement which ran for six weeks from May 2, 1908. It was a

most desirable country for British people to settle in. Climate healthy and delightful, splendid scenery, great fisheries, free education. Good Laws. Fine land well adapted for fruit farming, dairying and mixed farming. Details T. H. Turner, Agent General, Salisbury House Finsbury Circus.

Whether directed to labourers or more substantial farmers, such adver-

tising tended to focus on the agricultural community, and there was frequently a direct or implied request for experience.

However, a large number of emigrants set out under different auspices. Children's homes and their role in emigration to the Dominions is a large and sometimes emotive subject, but it is appropriate to record here that a number of references in letters to editors concern farm workers settling into Canada and meeting with Dr. Barnardo's and other children who had been placed on Canadian farms.

A whole range of other organisations existed to try and help people in need to find situations and work in Canada. The *Lincoln Rutland and Stamford Mercury*, on December 21 and 28, 1906, carried a front-page advertisement:

> TO THE WEST   TO THE WEST
> TO THE LAND OF THE FREE
> CANADA IS THE COUNTRY OF OPPORTUNITY.

It asserted that over ten thousand emigrants had been recently and happily settled by the Salvation Army and that the Dominion still wanted more. It stated that work was still plentiful and prospects abundant.

> The Army has chartered two SPLENDID VESSELS usually engaged in the Atlantic passenger service for EIGHT SAILINGS in Spring 1907 leaving Liverpool February, March, April and May. Carrying passengers to Canada and the USA. Temperance. No gambling. WORK ON LAND guaranteed. Exceptional opportunities for women. . . . Passengers other than salvationists welcome. 3rd class £5.10.0; 2nd class £8.0.0, Details Col. Lamb, 27 Queen Victoria St.

While the advertisement did not make it clear how many would be going to the prairies, it shows a relatively organised method of travel and support for those seeking work. Admittedly, the Salvation Army had a mixed record of success with placements, for although work was found for all or virtually all, not all who went out—especially those on fares initially paid by Army well-wishers—knew farm work. Once on the farms, some disliked both the relative isolation of rural life and the nature of the work, and they soon moved to the towns. Some organisations, such as the Church Army, made a point of providing farm work training for those planning to go to Canada. This helped to undercut criticism that masses of unemployed and urban workers were being sent out to work in unsuitable rural occupations.[12]

Awareness of Canada was also promoted through advertisements placed by the Canadian Pacific Railway. The *Lincoln Gazette* carried a series of such advertisements between January 8 and April 2, 1910. These indicated where the head office of the CPR could be found and added "local agents everywhere." These advertisements illustrated Canadian life with pen-and-ink drawings, including pictures of the S.S. *Empress of Britain*, the Canadian Pacific Railway, team ploughing, threshing, Winnipeg with tram lines, team cutting hay, man digging near a cottage, and a CPR express train. In addition to emphasising the importance of the CPR to Canada, these advertisements reassured would-be emigrants with images of urban life and farmers successfully established on the land.[13]

From time to time, the papers throughout the period carried letters, or excerpts of letters, reporting on the progress of local residents who had gone to the west and started farming. One example among many was that of a Mr. C. Olle who, having left Boston in June 1904 and settled west of Winnipeg, wrote a letter to the editor of the *Boston Guardian* published on August 5, 1905. It is a detailed letter giving impressions of the scenery, rural landscape and Olle's own farming activities. Such letters were highly prized by officials, and some were published in government booklets. The Olle letter, preserved in the National Archives of Canada, is among a collection of cuttings from around Great Britain. These often contained details of a press release from the Commissioner for Emigration for Canada underscoring an enormous demand for labour in western Canada for the harvest and offering reduced price fares. Others detail prospects in Canada for immigrants during the 1905 season, and provide directions for obtaining further details.[14]

Thus, in the late nineteenth and early twentieth centuries, the prospective migrant from eastern England to western Canada could gain some idea of what to expect. By visiting displays at agricultural fairs and exhibitions, by attending lectures given by farmer delegates or Canadian officials, and especially by reading the newspapers, the careful emigrant could come to a more informed view. In the end, of course, the final decision to go or to stay was often influenced by factors beyond the control of the prospective migrant. How many left eastern England to go "To the West, To the West, To the Land of the Free" we do not know precisely, but certainly many did go and did succeed.

Notes

1. *Beverley Guardian,* March 31 and April 7, 1906.
2. Issues of the *Beverley Guardian* in May, June, and September, 1906, carried letters from some of these men who had found farm placements in various parts of southern Ontario. Not all went to farms. Some apparently found work in sawmills. These letters, all favourable in tone, describe the type of work available, and wages, although a close reading suggests that the work was not always year-round. One man working on a farm near Oakville was getting £4.00 monthly for an eight-month engagement (see June 30, 1906). A Mr. Cobb from Heckston, Ontario, was getting £4.00 monthly plus board, while Mr. Ward of Oxford, Lakeside County, was getting £50.00 per annum, all found (see June 2, 1906). Another letter spoke of having a good job in a tanning yard, another of work on a fruit and dairy farm. Some were almost certainly gaining experience for a possible move west.
3. *Herts and Essex Observer,* November 4, 1905.
4. See, for example, Marjory Harper, *Emigration from North-East Scotland* (Aberdeen: Aberdeen University Press, 1988), and John Davis, "The Printed Word as a Vehicle for the Encouragement of Emigration," *Journal of Canadian Studies* 8 (1992): 70–82.
5. *Boston Gazette,* June 3, 1890.
6. *Eastern Daily News,* February, 1, 1898.
7. *Lincoln Gazette,* January 3, 1891.
8. The eastern England delegates were from Ruddington, Notts. (175 acres); Wingerworth, Yorks (58 acres); Towcester (1000 acres); Oakham, Rutland (61 acres); Baldock (400 acres), and Thirsk (388 acres).
9. On April 6, 1906, a similar advertisement appeared, but with Mr. Fulton of Manitoba leading the party, and a Mr. Rogers in May. The *York, Thirsk and District News* carried an advertisement on February 16, 1906 from the Canadian Labour Bureau of 45 Great George Street, Liverpool, asking for "200 experienced and inexperienced farm hands, 100 domestics and others. Work guaranteed. Pay own fare. Personally conducted party by Mr. Tweed leaving 27 March." Rumsey of Shrewsbury was very active in the farming emigration business and frequent references to him are found in the 1905 and 1906 issues of the *Lincoln, Rutland and Stamford Mercury* and in the *Herts and Essex Observer and General Advertiser.*
10. On August 10, 1908, the *Lincoln, Rutland and Stamford Mercury* carried an advertisement from the Canadian Labour Bureau in Liverpool for "men wanted in large numbers for harvesting. High wages, cheap fares." Two

months earlier, on July 6, 1906, the same paper advertised for "CANA-DIAN HARVESTERS, SETTLERS. . . . Mr. Brewster Compton of Canada has guaranteed situations for 180 men. Harvest £5–8 a month; yearly £40–60, July and August parties. Pay own fare." This advertisement appeared for the next five weeks.

11. These included Dolby Bros, Shipping agents of Stamford (*Lincoln, Rutland and Stamford Mercury,* March 3, 1905); Sanderson's Booking Office, Kings Walk, Nottingham (*Norfolk Weekly Standard and Argus,* January 31, 1908); King, Haymarket, Norwich (same paper February 14, 1908); Waddington and Son, Estate Agent, Cark St., Leicester (*Lincoln,Rutland and Stamford Mercury* May 4,1906); and Robert Jacques Shipping and Insurance Agent, Alexandre St., Scarborough (*York, Thirsk and District News* 28 January 1907). The same paper on February 4, 1907, lists the Allan Line and other shipping-line agents as being at Thirsk, two in York, as well as Scarborough. In 1908, Otley was added to the list.

12. National Archives of Canada, RG76, vol. 371 File 504791 C 10271. The Salvation Army's 24th Annual Report for 1905 stated that the Army had a farm colony at Hempstead in Essex covering 740 acres where men were receiving training in farm work before emigrating.

13. A Canadian government list of steamship agents in 1907 included 31 in Yorkshire, six in Lincolnshire, and one each in Derbyshire, Huntingdonshire, Northamptonshire and Nottinghamshire. NAC, RG76, vol. 49, File 595171 C 10298.

14. NAC, RG76, vol. 49, File 412815, C 4789.

"Foreigners Who Live in Toronto": Attitudes toward Immigrants in a Canadian City, 1890–1918

Richard Dennis

IN SEPTEMBER AND OCTOBER 1897, THE TORONTO *MAIL AND EMPIRE* PUB-lished four substantial articles on successive Saturdays, investigating the major social and economic issues of the day as they affected the city. The first, on September 18, was titled "Crowded Housing, Its Evil Effects. The Conditions in Toronto a Menace to the Public and a Grave Source of Danger. The Problems of Great Cities Here in Embryo." The last, on October 9, was "Toronto and the Sweating System. Dangers Which May Arise and Evils Which Already Exist Clearly Described— The Warnings of Other Large Cities." Sandwiched between them were two articles, on September 25 and October 2, 1897, which together went under the title of "Foreigners Who Live in Toronto." Although the articles were unsigned, they were all penned by the then twenty-two-year-old William Lyon Mackenzie King. King had recently returned to Toronto from Chicago, where he had been taking courses in sociology and economics while working on his master's thesis on the International Typographical Union and participating, briefly, in the social work of Hull House, Jane Addams's settlement house situated in the heart of the city's immigrant slums. King's experience at Hull House had con-firmed that practical work in the slums was not his forte, and on his return to Toronto he was more interested in researching labour rela-tions at first hand in the city's sweatshops than in visiting the immi-grant districts. His articles on "foreigners" therefore depended rather more on secondary sources and meetings with clergy and social work-ers than on talking to newly arrived immigrants. Subsequently, he was commissioned to undertake further research on sweating, producing a government report on "The Methods Adopted in Canada in the Carry-ing Out of Government Clothing Contracts," published in 1900, the year that he became editor of the *Labour Gazette* and deputy minister of labour in the Laurier government. But his work as a civil servant subsequently brought him back into contact with the "immigrant problem," especially in the context of government control over Asian immigration into British Columbia.[1]

However, this paper exclusively concerns the articles on "Foreigners Who Live in Toronto." It reflects on some of the themes raised by King in his two articles, especially regarding the social geography of Toronto immigrants at the end of the nineteenth century, their situation in the housing market, and their ownership of property.[2]

How were "foreigners" to be defined? The 1891 census had recorded around 35 per cent of Toronto residents as "foreign-born," but the vast majority came from England, Wales, Scotland, Ireland, or the United States. To most commentators, they did not count as "foreign." In King's words,

> These people are, however, so nearly akin in thought, customs, and manners to the Canadians themselves, in fact so indistinguishable from them in most respects, that in speaking of a foreign population, they have generally been disregarded altogether. . . . [W]ith the exception of maintaining a few national societies, their foreign connection is in no way distinctively marked in the civic life.[3]

This was the key to King's interest, and the reason for treating "foreigners" as a "problem," just like slums and sweating. Were foreigners likely to prove "an evil for this city" or would they turn out to be good citizens, "a strength to the community"? It also meant that some second-generation migrants could still be regarded as "foreign," and that *some* English- and American-born migrants *were* "foreign" if they were Jewish or "coloured" or southern or eastern Europeans who had been born in Britain or America en route to Canada.

King's model, for good and ill, was the United States, where "a large percentage of the foreigners have been anything but a desirable class," "aiding in the development, if not in the creation, of dangerous slum districts." Dangerous to whom, we might ask—to themselves, through their occupancy of property that was already unhealthy, unsanitary, dilapidated, and exorbitantly expensive, thereby denying them the chance to save for the future, or to the "host" population and to civic society as a whole? King's perspective, apparently laying some blame on the immigrants themselves for the slum conditions in which

Table 1. Statistics Quoted in *Mail and Empire*, 25 September 1897

City	% city-dwellers foreign-born	% slum-dwellers foreign-born
Chicago	41	58
New York	42	63
Philadelphia	26	60
Baltimore	16	40

they found themselves, was typical of North American writing, but was based primarily on the crudest of ecological correlations—the fact that foreigners tended to be concentrated in slums (see table 1). If nothing else, we might question how slums were defined.[4] There was probably some circularity of argument in using "foreign-born population" as one indicator of the existence of slum districts!

At least two inferences followed from these figures. First, it was assumed that moral degeneracy paralleled physical degeneracy (and hence the eugenicist fear that the population as a whole would be progressively "enfeebled," compounded by the "race suicide"—the declining birth rate—of the better-off, physically and morally superior population in the suburbs). Second, concentration in slums was a very obvious form of residential segregation, but the residential segregation of "foreigners" was undesirable because it inhibited assimilation: it allowed newcomers to avoid having to learn English and, more generally, it meant that they took no part in civic life.

As yet, of course, immigration to Canada and the inner-city problems of still quite small Canadian cities were modest compared to those of major American cities. But, King noted, "Winnipeg is fast becoming a second Chicago . . . marked out by its numbers of foreigners,"[5] and "it is indeed questionable whether Toronto and Montreal will not admit of like comparison with Baltimore and New York."

In fact, while immigration was associated with housing and economic problems in American cities, "the better class of foreigners have been a source of wealth to the United States, have aided materially in its industrial and commercial prosperity, and have, in fact, led the Government of the country to adopt a strong immigration policy for the augmentation of their numbers." So how was the balance sheet working out in Toronto?

King enumerated a succession of "foreign" groups—Germans, Jews, Italians, French, Coloured, Syrians,[6] and Chinese—in each case discussing the same range of issues: their immigration history, their economic circumstances, their employment by city or other level of government, for example as policemen or postmen, their geographical distribution across the city, their housing conditions, including their ownership of property, their propensity to save or invest, their affiliation to "ethnic" societies and the availability of "ethnic" benevolent societies which limited their dependence on city or public charities, their religious separatism, their reputation for criminal behaviour, their political and trade-union involvement, and their attitude toward education. On the basis of these indicators, he could conclude whether their presence was to be encouraged, whether their immigration was in the city's best interest.

Rather than follow his discussion group by group, we shall focus on just a few critical indicators. The total population of Toronto in 1897 was about 190,000, rising to 208,040 in 1901. The 1901 census recorded 6,028 persons of German origin (3% of the total population), 3,090 Jews (1.5%) and 1,054 Italians (0.5%). Given that Italian and Jewish immigrants were mostly recently arrived, while non-Jewish German settlement had slowed, King's estimates in 1897 seem sound (see table 2). But he appears to have underestimated the "French" (actually French-Canadian) population at no more than 800; the census recorded 3,015 in 1901.[7] Either the number of Chinese was increasing very rapidly or King also underestimated their number, for in 1905, Toronto's *Saturday Night* estimated the Chinese population at 600–700, ten times King's estimate. As well as 220 Chinese laundries, *Saturday Night* also identified seven Chinese restaurants and a dozen other stores; but the population was still almost 100% male.[8]

Tables 3 to 6 paraphrase King's comments on the economic contribution, residential distribution, housing conditions, and tenure of different groups of "foreigners." Where it seems important to indicate not only his evidence but his *attitude* toward the evidence, King's precise wording is retained.

As well as describing the occupations of young black males, King also noted the "colour prejudice" that they suffered, the misfortune "caused by almost total cessation of employment by city hotels of coloured help," and the necessity of "leaving for the other side" (i.e., moving to the United States). "In the United States their labour and ability seems to be more appreciated. They hesitate before seeking positions here, as they claim to find the white man is almost universally favoured. ... [O]ne of their number, after having practised for six months in the band of a city regiment, and after having been granted

Table 2. How many, how long, where from?

Group	Mackenzie King's Comments		
	How many?	How long in Toronto?	Who and where from?
Germans	6,000	Most pre-1885	many had arrived via the U.S.
Jews	2,500	Nearly all since 1850	three-fifths Polish, Russian, 400–500 German, 200–300 English
Italians	700–800	30 years ago only 12	Recruited for CPR construction many now leaving for the US
French	< 800		Many French-Canadian [n.b. King includes them as "foreign"], + many from US; only about 6 families directly from France
"Coloured"	800		still a few (c. 15) who were escaped American slaves, but most of the young "coloured" had been born in Canada
Syrians	50–60	Arrived during last 7 years	
Chinese	> 60	Doubled since 1891 but some resident as long ago as 1871	all men, though there had once been 3 women

his uniform, was refused admission when about to be sworn in, and given, as a reason, that he might look 'like a black horse among a lot of white ones.'"

King's descriptions may seem to us too stereotypical to be true— the Jews ran the second-hand stores, the Italians peddled fruit and music, the Chinese ran laundries, and black Canadians manned the trains. But, as Harney has noted of Italian immigrants in Toronto, they "did the jobs that Canadian society expected of them."[9] This was the best, or at least the easiest, way to get on.

Overcrowding (table 5) was not simply a matter of persons per room. King's comments on the Italian community reflected a pattern of seasonal migration, whereby dwellings might be temporarily over-crowded, and the proliferation of Italian boarding houses, where new arrivals were accommodated.[10] An outdoor way of life, practised by

Table 3. Economic contribution

Group	Mackenzie King's Comments
Germans	Most were mechanics in a wide variety of manufacturing, but some owned major commercial and wholesale establishments. They were prominent, as both proprietors and employees, in piano-making, brewing, cigar-making, showcase manufacturing, and fur and jewelry trades.
Jews	At least 20–25 English and German Jews were commercially prominent, but the great majority were in lesser "mercantile pursuits," especially in the clothing trade, making and selling jewelry and watches, diamond-cutting, hardware, and the manufacture and sale of boots and shoes. Jews owned almost all the city's second-hand clothing stores and junk shops. Polish and Russian Jews dominated the rag and scrap iron trade, and owned four of the city's eight pawnbrokers. They also included ready-made clothing contractors and some proprietors of tailoring establishments.
Italians	About 60 ran fruit and vegetable stores, and nearly 150 were employed as peddlers, whether with horse and cart, pushcart, or basket. They managed nearly all the banana trade. About 30 were professional musicians, 11 owned street-pianos, and three or four played hand organs; others worked in the shoe trade or in tailoring.
French	Most worked in factories. One firm employed nearly 100, another 50. A few ran "profitable business concerns of their own." Some worked as hairdressers, printers, tailors, or shoe-makers, a few as barbers or bookkeepers, and there were "one or two doctors, and a blacksmith."
"Coloured"	"Of such as are employed," some were in the Pullman car service, possibly more were barbers, four were letter carriers, others were waiters, restaurant keepers, or day labourers. There were also a photographer, an ice-merchant, and a coal merchant. Many did odd jobs, and "possibly one-third are without steady employment." "Coloured" women did "a good deal of work" and seemed to have "better opportunities for employment than the men," as house-servants, laundrywomen, or dressmaking and sewing at home.
Syrians	"The men are lazy and inclined to be dirty and quarrelsome. They allow their wives to do most of the work." The latter sold small trinkets, or went "into the country often with a baby in their arms, and [bought] clothing of the farmers," to be sold on their return to the city.
Chinese	Apart from one Chinese grocery store on Yonge street, all were engaged in the laundry business.

Table 4. Residential distribution

Group	Mackenzie King's Comments
Germans	"of great importance is the fact that they are scattered pretty fairly over all parts of the city, and have not congregated in any one particular locality. In this regard they prove a happy exception to some other foreigners, who are . . . grouped into small colonies. By being spread out their interests have become those of the city at large rather than of any particular group."
Jews	Were scattered over all parts of the city, but with "a decided tendency towards grouping amongst the poorer members." York Street and part of the south side of Queen constituted Toronto's "Petticoat lane"; Polish and Russian Jews were concentrated in the lower part of St John's Ward.
Italians	Also concentrated in St John's Ward, especially on Chestnut, Elm, Edward, and Agnes Streets and Centre Avenue. A few were to be found on Queen Street West, the north end of Dufferin Street, and on Mansfield Avenue.
French	Most were in Ward Two, around Seaton and Sackville Streets, between King and Queen, but others lived in Parkdale, and "odd ones [were] scattered about in other parts of the city."
"Coloured"	The largest numbers were "grouped together" in St. John's Ward, especially on Chestnut and Elizabeth Streets and Centre Avenue; but some lived in suburbs where rents were cheaper and sanitation better, and in Parkdale, especially if they were in railway employment.
Syrians	Lived "near the north-end of Chestnut street."
Chinese	Lived "in all parts of the city."

many southern and eastern European migrants, also gave the impression of high population densities, since it contrasted so markedly with British reserve and privacy. And the noise of migrants on the streets, whether in animated conversation, making music, playing games, or peddling their wares, reinforced fears that less conspicuous Britons were being "crowded out." In an article in *Saturday Night*, describing an early-evening stroll down Centre Avenue, almost every word was value-laden. First, the walkers passed hundreds of children, "screeching at play; fighting at ball; rolling in the dry garbage of the street; promiscuous, happy and unwashed." Farther along the street "sat a score of women, some busy, others gossiping in Yiddish or Russian . . . while the bearded men folk stood about in groups jabbering near the alley-

Table 5. Housing conditions

Group	Mackenzie King's Comments
Germans	Large families, but little overcrowding; few, if any, live in rear cottages.
Jews	Large families in small houses, many in rear cottages; rare for two families to share the same house; "after school hours the streets are filled with their children."
Italians	Large families and crowding: "During the winter season there have been as many as forty or fifty Italians living in a single house on Chestnut street. Two or three families in one house is not uncommon."
French	"do not crowd in their houses." "[O]nly a few live in rear cottages."
"Coloured"	"seldom that much crowding is found among them'; a minority lived in rear cottages.
Syrians	"They crowd together, often in a disgraceful condition."
Chinese	Most lived in groups of 3 or 4 in the small shops they used as laundries.

Table 6. Property ownership

Group	Mackenzie King's Comments
Germans	"hold a good deal of property in the city, many of the mechanics owning the houses in which they live."
Jews	Many saved a fixed proportion of their income, some hoarding what they saved, others using city banks. As yet they had been unable to accumulate much property, though some wealthy English and German Jews had considerable property holdings.
Italians	About 50 owned their own houses. Almost the entire block of well-built brick houses on the north side of Elm Street, between Teraulay and Elizabeth streets, was owned by Italians; in other districts, their houses were "usually the most substantial in the immediate surroundings." The total value of Italian-owned property in Toronto was estimated at nearly half a million dollars. Of all the foreigners in the city, the Italians had been the best depositors in the Government Savings Bank.
French	"own but little property, but a good many have effected small savings."
"Coloured"	They had not saved much money, but a few owned a little property.
Syrians	"They save practically every cent they make."
Chinese	"own no property, but some have small earnings stored away, and a few keep their money in the bank."

ways." Then into "the Italian precinct": "The street was even more noisy here. The men smoking in groups talked faster; the women laughed more; the children were even more animated, and from sundry windows came the noise of disgruntled accordions."[11]

King noted that, by 1897, few Jews had accumulated much property (table 6). Yet by 1909, many more, including some who had arrived in the 1890s, had substantial property holdings, not only in St. John's Ward, but throughout the city. He also referred to the Italian ownership of part of Elm Street. In 1899, Italians owned 7 and in 1909, 12 houses on Elm between Elizabeth and Teraulay (now Bay) Streets. More Italian-owned property, including hotels and boarding houses, was located a block west, at the intersection of Centre Avenue and Elm Street.[12]

The picture painted by King was—apart from the Syrians—broadly positive. Immigrants were to be welcomed, even encouraged. They were all seen as favouring education, as a result of which, the children—if not their parents—became fluent in English. They were applauded for their thrift—except the Syrians, for whom it was a sign of greed, as they were not prepared to pay even for the basic necessities of life—and honesty. They were almost all law-abiding, except where the pressures of overcrowded slum life provoked disputes between neighbours. They had a modest, usually insignificant impact on the political life of the city. They belonged to ethnic societies which reinforced a sense of community, albeit sometimes at the expense of assimilation. Even the Chinese were welcome: "They are but little trouble to the city, and while their numbers are small are more of a convenience than a nuisance." Other groups were accorded a much more enthusiastic reception: of the Germans, "there can be no doubt that the city at large, as well as individuals, has shared in their prosperity. A steady German invariably makes a good citizen, and the Germans in this city belong to the thrifty and desirable class." King had been born in Berlin (now Kitchener), the heart of Ontario's German community, so he could claim first-hand experience in making this evaluation.

The principal barrier to immigration seemed to be a lack of enthusiasm on the part of government, compared to the aggressive recruitment of German families by American agents, although King also noted that more stringent United States regulations were likely to lead in the future to more Italian families settling in Canada. His main concern was the effect of residential segregation. With respect to Jewish immigrants from both Europe and the United States, "the only immediate policy which it seems practicable to adopt is to check as far as possible the tendency to group, or the formation of a foreign section, in any part of the city. Only by spreading these foreign elements are they likely to become adapted to the new surroundings and properly assimilated with the general community." He reiterated these points in his conclusion to the following week's article:

> With the children the hope of the future lies, and if, as present indications are, they get the advantage of a fair education, and are kept in proper moral surroundings, there is no reason why they should not be, as many of their parents already are, the best of citizens. The city will have to watch closely its crowded centres, for, as already pointed out, it is in the crowded parts that most of the foreigners have congregated. Whatever is done for them in the respect of better housing or otherwise will be for the profit of the city at large.
>
> It needs hardly be again repeated that the foreign element should be spread out wherever possible over the whole city, and prevented from becoming communities by themselves. This is the surest guarantee that their interests will not become self-centred, but be rather those of the common good.

Three policy recommendations may be inferred from King's review. He saw a need to integrate immigrants into the public school system, avoiding as far as possible the provision of separate schools. He feared that too heavy an emphasis on Christian doctrine in public schools would cause the Jewish people to demand their own schools, and he sympathised with Italians who, left to their own devices, would have chosen public schools, but had been directed by their priests to support separate Catholic schools. The other recommendations were for the provision of better housing and the prevention of geographical segregation.

But neither better housing nor geographical intermixing was ever probable given the ideology of late-Victorian liberalism. As long as the housing market was unconstrained and housing provision remained the domain of private landlords, there was little prospect of either good-quality housing for new arrivals or their rapid dispersal across the city. As experience in Britain had already demonstrated, a public-health approach to housing, banning nuisances, closing and clearing unfit housing, but making no new provision, merely served to exacerbate problems, forcing the poor into a diminishing stock of housing that was just good enough to avoid condemnation, but which quickly became unfit once it was the only housing available for the poor. All that happened was that it, in turn, became overcrowded, and its landlords were enabled to charge higher rents—as happened in Toronto, where rents doubled during the decade following King's articles.[13] Moreover, as rents increased, so did capital values, encouraging landlords to cash in their capital gain, selling to sitting tenants or better-off new immigrants who aspired to owner-occupation. The logic behind this "disinvestment" by private landlords was the fear of a future collapse of rents and capital values, as had occurred in the 1890s, and the attraction of alternative, less risky forms of investment, such as mortgages, stocks, and bonds. But the consequence was to restrict further the supply of cheap housing to rent to poorer families.[14]

Nor was it easy to prevent segregation. Even if explicit discrimination—"No Jews need apply"—had been outlawed, it was impossible to change the way in which information on housing flowed between landlords, their existing tenants and newly arrived migrants. So the acquisition of property by immigrants, which King regarded positively as a sign of their becoming established as part of host society, was also a way in which immigrants became geographically concentrated. If Italians acquired much of Elm Street (table 6), it was not surprising if Italian immigrants became the tenants.[15]

As "The Ward"—the part of St. John's Ward delineated by Queen, Yonge, and College Streets and University Avenue—became ever more "foreign," so immigration attracted an increasingly critical press. By 1911, when Toronto's Medical Health Officer, Charles Hastings, produced an important investigation of "slum districts," the city's population had reached 377,000, of whom 13.6 per cent were of non-British ethnic origin, and approximately 9 per cent "foreign-born" (born outside either the British Isles or Canada).[16] Among indicators of "slum conditions," Hastings enumerated the "foreign-born" in three of six districts investigated by his staff. By cross-referencing from one part of the report to another, it is possible to compare these three districts with one another, and with the aggregate of the remaining three districts not separately discussed by Hastings (see table 7). It is clear that, outside "The Ward," only a small proportion of slum families were "foreign," while inside "The Ward," the principal problems were the large numbers of lodging houses and tenement houses, and the resultant high density of population. In many respects, conditions in "The Ward" were, at least statistically, no worse and sometimes better than those in

Table 7. Statistics Calculated from the Report of the Medical Health Officer (1911)

District	No. of families	% families "foreign"	% families Hebrew	% families Italian	% families Polish	% families German	% families French	% families Macedonian	% families Russian
Central or City Hall	2,051	72.0	58.8	8.8	1.6	1.2	0.3	0.1	–
Eastern Avenue	851	12.9	2.8	0.2	0.2	0.7	2.4	4.9	0.7
Niagara Street	809	10.9	1.9	0.6	4.7	0.5	0.1	0.5	1.2
Other areas	1,671	6.8	1.3	0.5	0.2	0.5	1.0	0.2	1.7

District	Population	No. of houses	% houses "unfit"	% houses with lodgers	% houses "rear houses"	% houses with "over-crowded rooms"	% houses with no drains	% houses with baths	% houses with indoor w-c
Central	11,645	1,653	6.5	17.8	5.9	2.5	37.4	36.8	49.3
Eastern Ave	4,892	828	9.3	4.6	6.3	5.4	21.1	23.3	40.7
Niagara St	2,253	731	1.2	1.6	0.8	1.6	21.2	38.3	36.3
Other areas	7,623	1,484	13.3	4.1	6.1	0.7	26.1	35.0	56.2

Source: Hastings, *Report of the Medical Health Officer* (1911)
Note: "Central or City Hall District": bounded by College, Queen and Yonge Streets, and University Avenue
"Eastern Avenue District": from River Don west to Parliament Street, and from Lake Ontario north to Queen Street
"Niagara Street District": from Bathurst west to Shaw Street, and from Lake Ontario north to Queen Street
"Other areas": from Parliament Street to the Don, between Queen and Wilton Avenue (now Dundas); from Bathurst to Bellwoods
Avenue, between Queen and Arthur (now Dundas); from Spadina to Bathurst, between Front and King

the other "slum districts" with much lower proportions of "foreign" residents.

But the impression provided by the arrangement and ordering of the statistics in the report was that slums were closely associated with (if not caused by) the foreign population. This impression was reinforced in the section of the report devoted to common lodging houses, where the emphasis was on "overcrowded, unsanitary lodging houses, where from 10 to 30 foreign men are crowded into a small house. . . . Our inspectors have some evidence that certain small hotels and old and roomy houses are about to undergo the dangerous transformation into foreign lodging houses." It was not that these immigrant men were poor; they were in receipt of "good wages"—$2 to $3 per day (though this was a "good wage" only if you did not have a family to support, and if you could rely on secure employment, earning $2–3 day in, day out, throughout the year). The implication was that they should expect to spend more on housing (and therefore save less, and therefore take much longer before they could be reunited with families still in Europe, or before they could become property-owners themselves). Critically, "their ideas of sanitation are not ours." This relates back to the earlier point about how space was occupied: there was a "pre-urban approach to the use of city space,"[17] which gave the impression of being disorderly, from which it was assumed that it must also have been unsanitary.

Attitudes toward "foreign nationalities" were also indicated by their positioning in Hastings's report—after a listing of the numbers of families with tuberculosis, the numbers of unsanitary houses, and various indicators of crowding, and before "The Lodging House Evil" and "The Tenement House Problem." Note also that the need for *sanitary* inspection of lodging houses appeared to depend on the presence of *non-English speaking* and *recently arrived immigrants*. Generously, we might suppose that Hastings was viewing them as *victims* who needed extra help because they were non-English speaking and recently arrived, and therefore unable to complain for themselves or ignorant of how to complain, or to whom. But the impression remains that they were being blamed for being at least part of the cause of the problem.

This interpretation is reinforced by a reading of the Bureau of Municipal Research's report of 1918, *What Is "The Ward" Going To Do With Toronto?* Reviewing the physical conditions in "The Ward," the Bureau concluded, "The obvious inference is that the standard of living of the tenant is largely determined by the standard set by the property owner in the way he maintains the building."[18] This would seem to absolve the immigrant residents of blame, except that, by 1918, most property in "The Ward" was owned by "foreign," especially Jewish, landlords.[19]

"However," the Bureau report continued, "it is only fair to concede that there are many exceptions to this statement, especially where the tenants are recently arrived immigrants whose ignorance of the first principles of sanitation and whose careless personal habits create more problems than the best-intentioned landlord or most active sanitary officer can solve."[20]

Indeed, the obstinacy of immigrants in the face of official sanctions could be blamed for worsening conditions: "Apparently the residents, who are mostly poor and of foreign birth or parentage, and with but a superficial knowledge of our laws and standard of living, when forced by circumstances to vacate their dwellings, do not always leave the district, but manage to crowd into some other dwelling in the vicinity." And so, claimed the Bureau, the number of persons per occupied dwelling had increased from six in 1909 to eight in 1916, and even this was thought to be an underestimate, since "Where lodgers are kept, the foreigners cannot always be relied upon to give accurately the number of occupants in the house, fearing that this will mean increased assessment, increased rent, and possibly investigation by the Health Department."[21]

Following these almost incidental observations, the report went on to focus on the foreign-born residents of "The Ward," estimating that the area's population was now 68 per cent Jewish, 12 per cent Italian, and 20 per cent "other nationalities," and enumerating a series of "family histories," "not generally typical, but representative of certain types." These included a family of Russian Jews, the father working as a peddler and literate in English, but his wife and four children graded variously as "low-grade imbecile," "idiot," or—at best—"borderline case." Other histories recorded Jewish and Italian families with fathers who deserted them from time to time, threatened and abused their wives, or whiled away their time at "cards in ice-cream parlors"; criminal children; "very delicate" children; and an army of the chronically sick, "mentally defective," and "feebleminded." Not *every* case involved non-British immigrants, but most did; and a statistical analysis of "feeble-mindedness" concluded that "the foreign element, or 9.19 per cent of the city's population, produces 23.6 per cent of the feeble-minded and insane persons."[23]

Moreover, the tenor of the report was to suggest that the problems of "The Ward" were spreading, infecting adjacent neighbourhoods.

Slums, and their constituent conditions, including their immigrant populations, were a kind of plague: hence the strange title *What Is "The Ward" Going To Do With Toronto?*

Nonetheless, the solution was not to ban immigration, but to improve education. "Each community suffers politically, socially and financially, in times of peace and war, by neglecting its immigrants instead of making valuable assets of them." Immigrants should be taught English, "for mutual understanding, to avoid handicap in getting employment, to protect themselves from professional exploiters, and to adjust themselves to new social and economic conditions." They should be issued with guide books, and receive night classes in technical training and health and sanitary advice. "Immigrants arrive with an active desire for knowledge, but since there is practically no organization to show them where this desire may be satisfied, it is allowed to die away" and they resort to old, bad habits.[23]

Despite these conciliatory words, it is hard not to sense a changing attitude between Mackenzie King's articles in 1897 and the reports of the 1910s. What the *Mail and Empire* headline writer had taken a week to convert from "Another Phase of the Great City Problem" to "A Worthy Class, by Whose Presence Toronto, If Wisely Guided, May Greatly Prosper" was back to being a *problem* again. The racism that was evident in King's treatment of the Syrians, and that he condemned in his contemporaries' attitudes toward the "Coloured" population, was more generally evident once the geographical focus was narrowed to concentrate on the city's major "slum"—"The Ward." And by the 1910s, it was easier to narrow the focus, as non-British immigrants became more concentrated, in part because of the success of "foreign" landlords in acquiring property which they then let to more recently arrived immigrants. This concentration reflected the emptiness of the bold sentiments expressed by progressive liberals in the 1890s before the massive population growth of the 1900s took off. And it was a concentration that made it even easier for anti-immigrant sentiments to be expressed during the difficult decades of the 1920s and 1930s.

> When my parents came to Toronto [after World War II], they saw that most of their fellow immigrants settled in the same downtown district: a rough square of streets from Spadina to Bathurst, Dundas to College, with waves of the more established rippling northward towards Bloor Street. My father would not make the same mistake. "They wouldn't even have the trouble of rounding us up."[24]

King's assimilation—and that of Hastings and the Bureau of Municipal Research—involved a no-nonsense conversion to "our ways": no cultural melting-pot, and certainly no multicultural celebration of diversity. Perhaps that was the only realistic policy in 1897, and acceptable given King's later role in differentiating Canada from Britain; but geographical segregation—as most multiculturalism is in practice—continues to carry threats of stereotyping and stigmatization.

Notes

1. Information on Mackenzie King is from H. Ferns and B. Ostry, *The Age of Mackenzie King* (Toronto J. Lorimer, 1976), and R. M. Dawson, *William Lyon Mackenzie King: A Political Biography 1874–1923* (Toronto: University of Toronto Press, 1958).
2. For a more socially theorized approach, see R. Dennis, "Property and Propriety: Jewish Landlordism in Early Twentieth-Century Toronto," *Transactions of the Institute of British Geographers*, NS 22 (1997): 377–97.
3. *Daily Mail and Empire*, 25 September 1897. Unless stated otherwise, all quotations by Mackenzie King are from either this or the subsequent (2 October) article.
4. D. Ward, *Poverty, Ethnicity, and the American City, 1840–1925: Changing Conceptions of the Slum and the Ghetto* (Cambridge: Cambridge University Press, 1989).
5. Note that in 1897 the population of Chicago was approximately 1,500,000; that of Winnipeg, 32,000. But King was foreshadowing Winnipeg's growth through the 1900s and the publicity subsequently afforded by J. S. Woodsworth in *Strangers Within Our Gates* (Toronto, 1909) and *My Neighbor* (Toronto, 1911), both written while he was superintendent of All Peoples' Mission, Winnipeg.
6. It is surprising that King identified this small group for particular attention, but it seems that they had only recently arrived in Toronto, so their presence was still a novelty. Their origins were in what is now Lebanon. See S. Gadon, "The Syrian Religious Experience in Toronto, 1896–1920s," *Polyphony: The Bulletin of the Multicultural History Society of Ontario* 6, no. 1 (Spring/Summer 1984): 65–7.
7. Census figures summarized in J. M. S. Careless, *Toronto to 1918* (Toronto: J. Lorimer & Co., 1984), 202.
8. "The Chinese in Toronto," *Toronto Saturday Night*, 23 December 1905, 11.
9. R. F. Harney, "Chiaroscuro: Italians in Toronto, 1885–1915," *Polyphony:*

The Bulletin of the Multicultural History Society of Ontario 6, no. 1 (Spring/ Summer 1984): 46.

10. J. E. Zucchi, *Italians in Toronto: Development of a National Identity, 1875– 1935* (Kingston: McGill-Queen's University Press, 1988), 34–48.

11. A. Bridle, "Etchings in the Ward," *Toronto Saturday Night*, 12 August 1905, 7.

12. Information from City of Toronto Assessment Rolls, City of Toronto Archives.

13. On British housing, see J. Burnett, *A Social History of Housing, 1815–1985* (London: Methuen, 1986); on rents in Toronto, see E. J. Chambers, "A New Measure of the Rental Cost of Housing in the Toronto Market, 1890– 1914," *Histoire sociale/Social History*, 17 (1984): 165–74. Chambers calculated that if the rent index for a typical six-room house was set at 100 in 1900, the index declined from 97 in 1890 to only 77 in 1897, then increased to 185 in 1907 and 224 in 1913. James Mavor, professor of economics at the University of Toronto and a former teacher of King's, also calculated that rents doubled between 1897 and 1907; see James Mavor Papers, University of Toronto, MS Collection 119, Box 70, file ARe, "Rents and Housing in Toronto."

14. R. Dennis, "Landlords and Housing in Depression," *Housing Studies* 10 (1995): 305–24; idem, "Private Landlords and Redevelopment: 'The Ward' in Toronto, 1890–1920," *Urban History Review/Revue d'histoire urbaine* 24 (1995): 21–35.

15. On processes of residential clustering among Italians and Jews, see Zucchi, *Italians in Toronto*, 34–67; S. A. Speisman, *The Jews of Toronto: A History to 1937* (Toronto: McClelland and Stewart, 1979).

16. Careless, *Toronto to 1918*, 201–2; C. P. Hastings, *Report of the Medical Health Officer Dealing With the Recent Investigation of Slum Conditions in Toronto ...* (Toronto, 1911), City of Toronto Archives.

17. R.F. Harney and H. Troper, *Immigrants: A Portrait of the Urban Experience 1890–1930* (Toronto: Van Nostrand Reinhold, 1975), 40.

18. Bureau of Municipal Research (BMR), *What Is "The Ward" Going To Do With Toronto?* (Toronto, 1918), City of Toronto Archives.

19. Dennis, "Property and Propriety," 381.

20. BMR, *What Is "The Ward,"* 31.

21. Ibid., 32.

22. Ibid., 37–58.

23. Ibid., 55.

24. Anne Michaels, *Fugitive Pieces* (London: Bloomsbury, 1997), 243.

Irish Emigration to Canada in the 1950s

Tracey Connolly

THE 1950S SAW A DECLINE IN THE POPULATION OF IRELAND. IN 1951, the total population was 2.96 million; it fell to 2.82 million by 1961.[1] The paradox of these figures is that both natural increase and marriage rates were high during the period, although the average age at marriage was older. The population drop was due to the high rate of emigration throughout the 1950s. This decade witnessed the heaviest outflow of people in twentieth-century Irish history; in fact, it was the highest outflow since the 1880s. The greatest emigration of the 1950s occurred in the second half of the decade. So great was the exodus that in the year following June 1957, emigration superseded death as the major cause of population decline.[2] The year 1958 witnessed the highest losses, as 58,000 left the country.[3] The majority of emigrants who left in the 1950s were aged 15 to 30 years. A third of those in this age group in 1951 had emigrated by 1961.[4] For every 100 children aged 15 years in 1951, 43 had emigrated over the following 10 years.[5] Between 1951 and 1961, for every three persons added to the population by birth, two others left by emigrating.[6]

The most popular destinations for emigrants leaving Ireland in the 1950s were Britain, the United States, Canada, and Australia. Britain had been the main destination for Irish emigrants since the 1930s. The Wall Street crash and subsequent depression in the United States were instrumental in the decision to emigrate eastward rather than westward. Throughout the Second World War, employment opportunities in Britain were a major incentive for Irish emigrants, coupled with Irish networks established in the 1930s. When the war ended, Britain continued to be the favoured destination for Irish emigrants; however, the flow to America and Canada resumed at a more substantial rate than had been the case since the 1930s. As a result, the 1950s heralded changes in the destinations chosen, increasing the popularity of the United States, Canada, and Australia among Irish emigrants.

It appears that Canada became a more popular destination for those emigrating from the Republic of Ireland as the decade progressed. In the 1951 Canadian census, 24,110 persons enumerated themselves as being from the 26 counties, whereas in the year 1957 alone, the total number of persons arriving with Irish Republic passports was 7,500.[7] Of this figure, 5,000 had emigrated directly from Ireland, while the remaining 2,500 had left from Britain. According to a memorandum from the Irish Department of External Affairs, between 1951 and 1957, a total of 14,392 Irish emigrated directly from Ireland to Canada. It is important to note that it was common for Irish emigrants already in Britain to emigrate some years later from Britain to the United States or Canada. Rarely did Irish emigrants in the United States or Canada move on to Britain.

Despite a worldwide economic boom in the 1950s, Ireland experienced a recession. The major problem in the Irish economy involved the balance of payments and over-reliance on agriculture as the main source of income. Ireland's economy was the worst in Western Europe throughout this period. From 1951 to 1958, the cumulative decline in employment was over 12 per cent.[8] The unemployment rate in building and construction was over 19 per cent and the rate in non-agricultural work was 9 per cent.[9] The agricultural sector lost 59 per cent of its workforce between 1946 and 1966.[10] The increase in farm machinery greatly contributed to the unemployment of farm labourers in the post-war period. Rural electrification also reduced the demand for farm labourers. Between 1948 and 1961, the number of rural households with electricity had risen by 41 per cent.[11] A newspaper article in 1950 emphasized the repercussions of mechanisation: "Since in the future more, and not less machines will be put on the land, the problem of finding jobs for those who are displaced will become more critical."[12] In a society so dependent on agriculture, these structural changes had major implications in employment terms.

It appears that the main cause of emigration was economic necessity and advancement. Unemployment peaked in 1957, when 59,000 were listed on the unemployment register.[13] Such unemployment figures were unprecedented in twentieth-century Irish history. Public outcry was deep-felt, resulting in marches and demonstrations in Dublin. The only visible solution to unemployment was emigration, as one writer aptly summed up: "The unemployment marches on Leinster House [Irish Government buildings] of the mid 50s made America more glamorous."[14] The areas of unemployment were very similar to the employment that emigrants entered, which suggests a correlation between unemployment and the decision to emigrate. Construction work can be taken as an example, which saw large employment losses in Ireland; of the emigrants entering Canada from the Republic of Ireland in 1957, 36 per cent were employed in the building and construction industry. Among those who left for economic reasons were excess siblings and relatives from rural areas, who would not inherit the family farm.

There were, of course, social motivations for emigrating. Wanderlust and social advancement were other reasons to leave Ireland. In the case of women, it was felt that there were better marriage prospects abroad. In rural areas, farmers' sons tended to put marriage on hold until they inherited the farm, at which stage they were middle-aged. Impatient women were therefore more likely to emigrate.

While unemployment at home was a push factor, the economy abroad was a pull factor. During this period, ample employment opportunities existed in the countries to which the Irish were emigrating. Historically, Irish emigration has been high when the economy abroad is good, and low in times of depression abroad.

Irish immigrants to Canada in the 1950s appear to have been young. In 1958, for example, 28 per cent of the Irish who immigrated to Canada were under 20 years of age, of whom 22 per cent were classified as children, which indicates that families immigrated. The 20–34-year-old group comprised 53 per cent of the total, while those aged 34–49 comprised 13 per cent and the remaining 6 per cent were 50 years old and over.[15] It must be noted, however, given the distance from Ireland to Canada, that young single people were more likely to emigrate than older people. Of the Irish who immigrated to Canada in 1958, females accounted for 57 per cent of the total. This was quite typical, for throughout the decade more Irish females than males left Ireland. Female emigrants were typically better educated than males, particularly as the decade progressed and nursing opportunities abroad increased.

Irish emigrants have tended to settle in urban centres. Those who immigrated to Canada in the 1950s resided principally in the provinces of Ontario, Quebec, and British Columbia. Of those who went to England and Wales in the same period, a third were living in the Greater London area, while two-fifths of those who went to Scotland settled in

Glasgow. This suggests that the Irish emigrated largely for economic reasons, given that they went to urban areas, where employment opportunities were greater.

A growing number of middle-class emigrants left Ireland in the 1950s, though they remained a minority of the total migrants. The findings of a study by the Southern Ireland Faculty of the College of General Practitioners revealed that 60 per cent of the 408 doctors who graduated from University College Cork between 1945 and 1954 had emigrated by 1964.[16] Whether they left shortly after graduating or in the early 1950s is impossible to say. However, it is more probable that they emigrated soon after graduating, when they were most likely still single and consequently free of the constraints of family ties. An estimated 10 per cent of the Irish emigrants who went to the United States in the 1950s were middle class,[17] and 20 per cent of Irish males going to Britain during the period belonged to the professional, intermediate, and skilled non-manual worker category.[18] It is important to note here that the working class emigrate in vast numbers when the economic situation is bad at home, whereas the middle class leave during such times as well, but also when they are employed. Their reason for emigrating more commonly relates to career advancement and experience. In the context of Irish emigration to Canada in the 1950s, a remarkably high proportion of the emigrants were middle class. Taking the occupations of the Irish who arrived in Canada in 1957 as an example, manufacturing, mechanical, and construction work was the greatest employer, engaging 36 per cent of the total number of newly arrived immigrants. As in other countries, Irish immigrants were most represented in this industry. The next highest sector was clerical work, which employed 16 per cent, closely followed by civil engineers, nurses, and teachers who comprised 12 per cent—quite a high proportion. Eight per cent were occupied in finance and administration. Only 14 per cent were employed in agriculture and as labourers.[19] These figures make it very plain that the Irish who immigrated to Canada were more educated and skilled than were their counterparts headed for other countries. According to one Irish visitor to Canada in the 1950s, "The social and educational standards of the recent [Irish] immigrants . . . is above average emigration standards: and which may be illustrated by my experience in cities of Canada which I have had the occasion to visit: that one never comes across Irish maids in hotels, while the receptionist staff is as likely as not to include Irish employees."[20]

Evidence suggests that Irish immigrants in Canada assimilated well into their adopted country. According to one writer in the 1950s, "the non-existence of any Irish-interest weekly or monthly publication, provides a partial explanation for their assimilation."[21] It appears that Irish communities were not established in Canada. In other countries, such as Britain, the United States, and Australia, Irish communities were widespread. This made Irish emigration to Canada unique. An Irish visitor in Canada during the 1950s noted that "the Irish immigrants to Canada have shown no tendency to want to meet each other in social groups."[22] In other countries, Irish immigrants had very close ties, tended to live in one area, work together and socialise together.

In 1954, a book entitled *The Vanishing Irish* dealt (rather sensationally) with Irish emigration and the decline of the Irish population. The author warned, "If the past century's rate of decline continues for another century, the Irish will virtually disappear as a nation."[23] In 1948, the Irish government set up a Commission on Emigration to "investigate the causes and consequences of the present level" of emigration and "in particular, the social and economic effects."[24] The publication of this report marked a milestone in official attitudes toward emigration, raising awareness about the extent of the problem. It was published at a time when a more critical appraisal of Ireland's economic performance was beginning to emerge. Despite its comprehensive coverage and practical recommendations, no policy on emigration or population followed its publication in 1954. The importance of the Commission was overshadowed by the publication of *Economic Development* in 1958, which was to guide economic progress in Ireland up to the early 1970s. Overall, the 1950s had been a decade of economic gloom in Ireland, with unemployment and emigration rates unprecedented in twentieth-century Irish history. Radical changes in the economy were vital. Such changes occurred largely because of greater emphasis on industry than solely on agriculture. A reversal of mass emigration in the 1950s resulted from the upturn in the economy in the 1960s, which brought major changes in Ireland's social and economic life. *Economic Development* achieved positive results and elevated the cloud of doom which had prevailed for so long.

Notes

1. J. J. Lee, *Ireland 1912–1985* (Cambridge: Cambridge University Press, 1989), 360.

2. Kieran Kennedy and Brendan Dowling, *Economic Growth of Ireland: Experience Since 1947* (Dublin: Gill & Macmillan, 1975), 222.
3. National Economic and Social Council 90. *The Economic and Social Implications of Emigration* (March 1991), 56.
4. J. J. Sexton, "Employment, Unemployment and Emigration," in Kieran Kennedy, ed., *Ireland in Transition* (Cork: Mercier Press, 1986), 31.
5. Brendan Walsh, *Ireland's Changing Demographic Structure* (Dublin: Gill & Macmillan, 1985), 10.
6. Desmond Gillmor, *Economic Activities in the Republic of Ireland: Geographical Perspectives* (Dublin: Gill & Macmillan, 1985), 26.
7. National Archives, S16325 B, "The Irish in Canada."
8. Kieran Kennedy, Thomas Giblin, and Deirdre McHugh, *The Economic Development of Ireland in the Twentieth Century* (London: Routledge, 1988), 62.
9. Ibid.
10. R. Kennedy, *The Irish: Emigration, Marriage and Fertility* (Berkeley: University of California Press, 1973), 109.
11. Ibid., 96.
12. *Sceala Eireann.* 25 October 1950.
13. National Economic and Social Council, *Economic and Social Implications,* 56.
14. John Healy, *No One Shouted Stop!* (Achill: The House of Healy, 1988), 47.
15. National Archives. S16325 B. Department of External Affairs Letter. June 1959.
16. Richard Lynn, *The Irish Brain Drain,* Paper No. 43 (Dublin: Economic and Social Research Institute, November 1968).
17. Gerard Hanlon, "Graduate emigration: A continuation or a break with the past?" in Patrick O'Sullivan, ed., *The Irish World Wide Vol.1. Patterns of Migration* (Leicester: Leicester University Press, 1992), 185.
18. J. A. Jackson, *The Irish in Britain.* (London: Routledge & Paul, 1963), 130.
19. All statistics from National Library S16325 B.
20. Ibid.
21. Ibid.
22. Ibid.
23. John O'Brien. *The Vanishing Irish: The Enigma of the Modern World* (London: H. Allen, 1954.)
24. *Commission on Emigration and Other Population Problems 1948–1954. Reports,* 1.

Disrupting Mexican Refugee Constructs: Women, Gays and Lesbians in 1990s Canada

Sebastián Escalante

M AINSTREAM DISCOURSE OFTEN ASSERTS THAT ECONOMIC DETERMI-
nants and an abuse of the refugee system are the major causes for
Mexican refugees in Canada. An effort to mould these refugees into
economic or labour migrants is fundamentally apparent in such discourse. The refugees are seen as similar to the economic migrants from
Mexico to the United States. From these debates, the term "refugee" can
be read as "economic migrant." Yet Mexican refugees in Canada are not
economic migrants or tourists, as they have been portrayed. This economic discourse is not new at all. It calls to mind the "refugee crisis"
debates of the late 1980s, arising from an increase in the number of
refugee admissions to Canada. This polemic alleged that the large
number of fraudulent claims had undermined Canada's "flexible" refugee system and led to the dismissal of human-rights concerns as a basis
for determining refugee status. As this paper will reveal, the principal,
but not exclusive, grounds reported in these refugee claims was persecution based on sexual orientation or domestic violence. In this regard,
Canadian refugee law has evolved to include the claims of refugees
belonging to particular social groups, such as gays and lesbians, and
women's claims of gender-oriented persecution, particularly domestic
violence. The evolution of human rights has a direct impact on the
definition of the term "refugee."

In Mexico, human-rights violations and patriarchal elements in
society are key factors which have led to the persecution of certain
social groups. These two factors are used as evidence to support the
authenticity of claims by Mexican nationals in Canada. It is often assumed that in Mexico, human-rights violations due to sexual orientation and domestic violence are nonexistent, and therefore not valid

grounds to claim refugee status. The Mexican state believes that Canada is overly flexible in its determination of refugees. Until recently, the Mexican government did not address gender issues in its social policies. Mexico has reformed some of its laws specifically to deal with women's rights as human rights, in accordance with its commitments to the Beijing Conference. Mexico has also signed international covenants to protect women. However, this has not necessarily ensured the enforcement of these laws or brought about any major changes in the core patriarchal structure of Mexican society. In the case of gay and lesbian rights, homosexuality in Mexico has never been considered a criminal act. Yet this does not imply an open tolerance of sexual minorities,[1] or the absence of human-rights violations against them. Rural-urban dichotomies and determinants such as race, class, and gender are central to an understanding of persecution related to sexual orientation and domestic violence in Mexico.

Canada has adopted a progressive interpretation of human rights, particularly where the refugee system is involved. The Canadian Immigration and Refugee Board (IRB) has adopted specific guidelines on refugees fleeing gender-related persecution, and also accepts refugees who claim that they fear persecution due to their membership in a particular social group. This can be seen as a positive measure not just for women, but also for gay and lesbian individuals, who may fear persecution and thus become refugee claimants. These initiatives by the IRB constitute a watershed for refugee law and its jurisprudence.

Dealing with Mexican Refugees: Refugee Constructs and Migration Assumptions

With the North American Free Trade Agreement (NAFTA), it has been assumed that migration within North America is limited to highly skilled and professional individuals. This view is partial because it fails to consider unskilled, illegal, or undocumented migrants, or refugees. Most analyses of North American migration centre on the Mexican-American experience and do not address the Canadian factor at all.[2] However, the importance of migration linkages between Mexico and Canada, particularly as they relate to the increasing number of Mexicans who come to Canada claiming refugee status, must be emphasized.[3] General discussions on migration mobility in North America assume that Mexican migration is mainly directed to the United States, guided by economic and labour determinants. Thus, the United States has been typified as a more common destination for emigrants from Latin America and the Caribbean than Canada.[4]

Interest has been directed to the phenomenon of Mexican temporary migrant workers in Canada, which is viewed as a reproduction of the previously existing Bracero Program with the United States.[5] Indeed, the evaluation of migration between Mexico and Canada has overlooked migration movements unrelated to labour.[6] At the same time, Mexico is also described as a bridge to be crossed by migrants en route to the United States, or as a refugee haven for Central American refugees, such as those from Guatemala or El Salvador, particularly during the 1980s, when armed strife and violence were rampant in the region.[7] This fabricated impression has been legitimated by events at which naturalization certificates and acknowledgements are distributed. Such symbolic recognition endorses the efficiency of certain governmental initiatives.[8]

However, migration is not just related to these phenomena. Scholars such as Alan Simmons have suggested that, after NAFTA and the advance of significant economic exchanges, one unresolved concern relates to the impact of social and human-rights practices. The increasing integration of Mexico into a North American regional economy raises issues outside the realm of labour.[9] Democratic practices and social justice within Mexico are concerns that cannot be discarded. However, a fundamental trend has focused, instead, on regional economic exchanges and international co-operation concerns. From this vantage point, these factors are seen as a key catalyst for economic integration and political development. Consequently, this view affirms that migration and other related obstacles based upon regional inequality will be eliminated.[10] Therefore, this supposes that the impact of these mechanisms will diminish international migration.

Mexican migration analysis believes that a labour or economic determinant prevails, and has never accepted the existence of other migration, such as that of refugees. Mexico has not been characterized as a country that creates refugees.[11] An extensive violation of human rights and a lack of protection of essential rights by the Mexican state have led Mexican nationals to seek international protection. Political analysts, such as Sergio Aguayo, have declared that Latin America, despite its peculiar political developments and democratic transitions, has not been, in general, a refugee producer.[12] Today, this assertion is subject to challenge.

Recognition of refugees is also problematic due to the refugee's delicate and controversial situation. Refugees are often perceived as a symbol of a state's failure to protect its citizens. No government likes to recognize that its nationals have felt constrained to leave their own country.[13] Therefore, any attempt to recognize Mexican refugees in Canada has been compromised by the state's failure to accept the fact that critical human-rights violations are occurring in the country. A basic fear of persecution has led these individuals to seek asylum elsewhere. Yet the state, in this case the Mexican state, chooses not to recognize individuals leaving the country as refugees because of human-rights violations. Rather, the Mexican government has declared that there is a "real motive"—that these refugee claims might be based on economic reasons.[14] When the Mexican government describes these refugees as economic migrants, it argues that the refugee system accepting them is not efficient, and thus reduces the problem to a mere institutional failure. The receiving systems are depicted as being flexible, non-restrictive, and operating in a wide-open-door fashion, which is obviously not the case.[15] This construction of economic migrants versus refugees has been a traditional response during times of "refugee crisis" and a source of disagreement between governments. In Canada, this discourse is not new at all.[16] The former Canadian Ambassador to Mexico, Marc Perron, stated in a 1997 press interview that Mexican refugees to Canada were basically tourists who were abusing the refugee system and taking advantage of the welfare benefits offered to "real" refugees:

> They go to Canada and declare themselves political refugees. Mexicans are intelligent, astute. They know that there are ways to remain in the country because the Constitution of Canada has an obligation to protect refugees. . . . Mexicans do not require a visa to remain in the country. It is a good deal for them, and they can visit the country for free.[17]

Therefore, these refugees lack recognition and at the same time are permanently portrayed as system abusers, economic migrants, and even tourists.

Unravelling Refugeehood: Domestic Violence and Sexual Orientation as Grounds for Persecution

Domestic violence and sexual orientation[18] were the main grounds of persecution presented by Mexican refugee claimants in Canada in 1996 and 1997. This does not mean that no other reasons for persecution are given, but simply that these are the most common. This affirmation stems from two Canadian sources: first, a review of the available hearings of Mexican refugees. These hearings can be consulted at the Documentation, Information and Research Branch of the IRB. This division collects information about country conditions as they pertain to the requirements of the Convention Refugee Determination Division (CRDD), a body that determines the status of Convention refugees for Canada.[19] The IRB does not keep track of the number of claims based on gender persecution (i.e., domestic violence) or sexual-oriented persecution.[20] However, refugee claims are published in *RefLex*, which compiles certain cases and provides an update on legal issues and jurisprudence.[21] Second, other evidence can be confirmed through information requests, which are available to the public. A considerable number of information requests dealing with domestic violence and sexual-oriented human rights violations have been released by CRDD.[22] Press reports and interviews with immigration attorneys in Canada have also confirmed a rise in Mexican refugee cases based on both grounds of persecution. [23]

Canada was the first country to adopt comprehensive gender guidelines to address refugee women.[24] In March 1993, the IRB issued the *Guidelines on Women Refugee Claimants Fleeing Gender-Related Persecution*, intended to recognize different forms of persecution experienced by women.[25] It also recognized the special needs and concerns of women refugee claimants during the refugee process.[26] The Canadian Guidelines were created for use within the IRB, not within the broader Canadian legal apparatus.[27] However, they are the first regulations that address gender exclusion as an enumerated basis for refugee status.[28] Before the *Gender Guidelines* took effect, a "refugee" had been commonly portrayed as a male seeking protection from other states. This has been the refugee model, despite that fact that refugee women and girls comprise an average of 80 percent of refugees worldwide.[29] The jurisprudence on persecution and refugees has been concerned mainly with the experiences of men. Women have been treated as if they were victims of the same types of persecution as those experienced by men.[30] The regulation of female infanticide, genital circumcision, bride burning, forced marriage, abortion, prostitution, compulsory sterilization, and domestic violence are examples of female-specific claims which have been unattended until recent years.[31]

Countries such as the United States have followed Canada's lead and have also issued guidelines that admit rape, domestic violence, and other forms of violence against women as possible grounds of persecution.[32] Mexico is not the only country that has reported refugee cases based on domestic violence.[33] Domestic violence is a main cause of women's migration.[34]

The United Nations High Commissioner for Refugees (UNHCR) has long held that refugee claims based on homosexuality are another form of gender-related persecution because they challenge the "roles that men and women are expected to play in society."[35] Sexual minorities, in general, have been denied basic rights through government action and/or inaction, and have often faced large-scale violence and murder.[36] Many countries target lesbians and gay men for persecution based on their sexual and gendered identity. Police forces and state representatives often pursue formal and informal policies of harassment, violence, and repression against sexual minorities.[37] In some countries, homosexuality is treated as a disease that can be cured with medication and electro-shock therapy. This may also entail "involuntary medical treatment."[38] In other countries, sodomy laws and the death penalty still prevail.[39] Canada and other countries, such as the United States, Australia, New Zealand, Germany, Finland, Belgium, and the Netherlands, provide refugee status to persecuted gay men and lesbians from states that disapprove of sexual "diversity."[40] In Canada, one of the first reported cases based upon sexual orientation, the Inaudi case, was heard in 1992, when a gay man from Argentina who had been battered and raped by the police successfully acquired refugee status.

It is necessary to emphasize that the *1951 Geneva Convention* and the *1967 Protocol related to the Status of Refugees* offer a universal definition of the term "refugee." Article 1A(2) of the Convention identifies "persecuted individuals on the grounds of race, religion, nationality, membership in a particular social group or political opinion, as the central basis for refugee claim."[41] The Convention restricts the scope of persecution to these five grounds, but its member states have adjusted what has been understood to constitute a refugee in their jurisdictions by shaping fundamental developments, or limiting them, in terms of refugee law.[42] A continuous evolution of the definition and perception of "refugee" in world-wide jurisprudence keeps the refugee system functioning. International customary law and domestic legislation are fundamental in defining the term "refugee."[43] From this viewpoint, the concept of refugee has been constantly evolving as a result of particular developments and interpretations in other states. Canada, acting as a member of the Convention and Protocol on Refugees, heeds this universal definition of the term "refugee" and also interprets these developments.

Countries that follow these instruments have each adopted a specific jurisprudence on refugeeism.[44] In international refugee law, the idea of persecution is fundamental. However, this notion is not the single condition for refugeeism. Authors such as Andrew Schacknove indicate that the unwillingness or inability of a state to protect basic rights might also determine international protection.[45] The law specifies that individuals whose state cannot protect their basic needs might request that protection externally.[46] Hathaway claims that "there is a failure of protection where a government is *unwilling* to defend citizens against private harm, as well as in situations of objective *inability* to provide meaningful protection."[47] This non-protection is based on a clear opposition by the state's authorities to stifle basic human rights violations.[48] Moreover, the interpretation of a "particular social group" within refugee law is essential for this study because it illustrates how the concept of social group has been expanded to include gender and sexual-oriented refugee claims.

The definition of social group, as understood in the Convention, has been forged by legal interpretation. Legal scholars such as Grahl-Madsen believe that this social category was created to afford protection to those persecuted by unforeseen causes. Race, nationality, religion, and ethnic background were more specific, and a concept that "clarified" the definition of refugee was required.[49] Maryellen Fullerton, quoting Guy G. Goodwin-Gill, concludes that a strict definition of social group is impossible, and that the concept should be "open-ended" to include different groups that might suffer persecution.[50] However, legal academics agree that a social group requires similar and particular bonds that establish a certain *commonality*, not simply a demographic characteristic.[51]

In Canada, the interpretation of a particular social group was delineated by the Supreme Court after the *Ward* judgement in 1993.[52] This case delineated three categories that would constitute a "particular social group." It was stated that those individuals fearing persecution on bases such as gender, linguistic background, or sexual orientation were designated as a social group due to their *immutable* characteristic.[53] This common or innate characteristic might be similar to sexual, race, or kinship ties and does not imply an open-door policy for anyone who simply discloses his or her sexual orientation or demonstrates grounds for gender persecution. Numerous refugee claims since this case have interpreted homosexual men and women as members of a "particular social group." For example, an IRB panel accepted that "persons infected by the HIV virus in Poland"[54] could be seen as members of a particular social group.[55] Therefore, human-rights violations due to sexual orientation are comparable to those based on racism, sexism, and other possible forms of persecution. Sexual orientation is a fundamental right that is also linked with personhood, liberty, equality, freedom of conscience, expression, and association.[56] In the Canadian context, sexual orientation has been treated as an "immutable personal characteristic" by which a particular social group can be defined for the purposes of Canadian refugee law.[57] Therefore, sexual minorities might establish a "well founded fear of persecution" based on one of the five designated categories stated in the Convention—that is, their membership in a "particular social group."[58]

Some legal academics indicate that membership in a particular social group alone is insufficient ground for an asylum claim. There must be a bond either to race, religion, nationality, or political opinion. The magnitude of "particular social group" is unique compared to other grounds.[59] However, not every claimant would necessarily belong to a particular social group merely by virtue of common victimization.[60] Some IRB panels have found that certain women lacking protection in their country of origin do not necessarily constitute a particular social group.[61] As in the case of some negative refugee determinations involving Mexican homosexual claimants, discrimination does not constitute an automatic cause for refugee status. It must be established that the claimant fears discrimination that amounts to persecution.[62]

This progress does not eliminate certain factors during refugee hearings, which veil the particular experiences of refugee claimants, or how these policies are regulated through numerical quotas. Other processes that form the so-called global apartheid are also restructuring the original idea of refugeehood and humanitarianism.[63] Comments have also been made against HIV-positive refugee claimants because they were seen as an extra burden on Canada's strained health-care system.[64] A newspaper note states that at least seven HIV-positive refugee claimants have been determined as refugees since mid-1995. Mexico, Chile, and countries from the Caribbean and Africa are mentioned.[65]

In Canada, further data based on interviews with immigration attorneys across the country show that at least 160 people were con-

Table 1. Total Number of Refugees to Canada

Year	Positive determinations	Negative determinations	Withdrawn or finalized by other means
1997	10,031	9,107	5,805
1996	9,541	7,037	5,225

Source: Immigration and Refugee Board, *Country of Persecution Analysis Report*, Standards, Analysis and Monitoring. Statistics for 1996 and 1997 (released in January 1997 and February 1998).

ceded refugee status in Canada based on their sexual orientation.[66] In comparison, since 1994 when the United States recognized persecution based on sexual orientation as a feasible cause for seeking asylum, around 60 foreigners received asylum on this basis.[67] Washington received approximately 17 refugee claims from Mexican gays and lesbians in less than six months during 1997.[68]

Reviewing Numbers: Mexican Refugees in Canada

In Canada, the total number of refugee claims reported in 1996 was 26,120 cases according to statistics from the IRB. A total of 9,541 cases were granted, while about 7,000 were determined as negative and over 5,000 were withdrawn or finalized by other means. In 1997, 22,584 cases were referred to the IRB; just over 10,000 were determined as positive refugee claims, just over 9,000 were determined as negative, and almost 6,000 cases were withdrawn or finalized in another form (see table 1). [69]

The number of Mexican refugees in Canada has been escalating since 1995. In 1994, 247 Mexican claims were referred to a hearing, but in 1995, 548 were presented. In 1996, 951 Mexican claims were registered by the IRB. In 1996, Mexico placed ninth (after Somalia), and was the second leading country in the American continent (after Chile) with respect to the number of refugee claims. During 1997, Mexico was the principal country in the hemisphere presenting refugee claims in Canada. A total of 926 refugee claims were presented from Mexican nationals, data that situated Mexico as sixth among countries presenting refugee claims at the national level, after Pakistan and before China (see table 2). The IRB granted refugee status to 40 Mexicans in 1995, and to 106 in 1996. In 1997, 159 Mexicans were accepted as Convention refugees, which implies that Mexico has the most positive refugee determina-

Table 2. Top Ten Countries as Sources for Refugee Claims in
Canada, 1996–97

1996		1997	
1) Sri Lanka	2,946	1) Sri Lanka	2,665
2) Chile	1,224	2) Czech Rep.	1,216
3) Iran	1,728	3) Iran	1,210
4) India	1,367	4) India	1,166
5) Israel	1,270	5) Pakistan	1,047
6) Zaire	1,127	**6) Mexico**	**926**
7) Pakistan	1,105	7) China	900
8) Somalia	962	8) Algeria	857
9) Mexico	**951**	9) Congo	767
10) China	929	10) Somalia	689

Source: Immigration and Refugee Board, *Country of Persecution
Analysis Report*, Standards, Analysis and Monitoring. Statistics for 1996
and 1997 (released in January 1997 and February 1998).

Table 3. Total Number of Mexican Refugees in Canada (1994–97)

Year	Claims referred	Positive determinations	Negative determinations	Withdrawn or finalized by other means
1997	926	159	314	351
1996	951	106	76	165
1995	548	40	65	102
1994	247	35	140	66

Source: Immigration and Refugee Board, *Country of Persecution Analysis Report*,
Standards, Analysis and Monitoring.

Table 4. Top Five Latin American Countries with Positive Inland
Refugee Determinations in Canada, 1996–97

1996		1997	
1) Peru	152	**1) Mexico**	**159**
2) Venezuela	120	2) Cuba	129
3) Guatemala	110	3) Venezuela	116
4) Mexico	**106**	4) Peru	115
5) Cuba	89	5) Guatemala	55

Source: Immigration and Refugee Board, *Country of Persecution
Analysis Report*, Standards, Analysis and Monitoring. Statistics for 1996
and 1997 (released in January 1997 and February 1998).

tions in Canada within Latin American countries (see tables 3 and 4).[70] In December 1997, there were 1,266 Mexican claims still awaiting a hearing.[71] This number of pending refugee claims has been highlighted by the Canadian press, mentioning that Mexican refugee cases are partly responsible for the refugee backlog.[72] At present, Quebec is the province which accepts most Mexican refugees and with the largest number of positive resolutions of refugee status. Vancouver is the second leading place where Mexican refugees have been accepted, and Toronto is third.[73]

Nevertheless, it is essential that our understanding of the relevance of migration not be limited to large numbers of migrants coming and going from one place to another. An evaluation of migration as a whole, based on numbers and statistical analysis, must weigh the relevance of existing international protection: refugees are necessarily escaping from war and violent strife, or form part of mass movements of people. In the case of refugees, we cannot allow numbers to monopolize our attention, but rather, the existence of a legal remedy and a shelter provision for those persecuted individuals who need external assistance.

The basic premise of this paper has been to reveal, contrary to mainstream perceptions, that Mexican migration is not based solely on economic or labour determinants. Migration based on human-rights violations and persecution also has to be acknowledged. This affirmation implies that serious recognition must be given to the current trend of Mexican refugees migrating to Canada in the 1990s. In general, human-rights concerns and social justice have been ignored for the benefit of market and state interests. The perspectives of the market and the state have interpreted migration as a homogeneous process, interrelated with labour or development. Such a perspective disregards the presence of refugees. Thus, it becomes necessary to emphasize that refugees should not be confused in any way with any other migrant categories.

However, certain states have interpreted refugees as economic migrants as a tactic to hide their failure to protect the basic rights of their citizens. Mexican refugees to Canada have been explained as economic refugees who migrate to find better employment opportunities. They have been also described as tourists who travel to Canada and abuse the Canadian refugee system by taking advantage of the available welfare benefits. However, to deny refugees legitimacy by reducing their movement to economic motivations implies the nonexistence of human rights violations. This affirmation also supposes that the refugee determination system—in this case the Canadian system—is inefficient and abused by all migrants. From this perspective, Mexican refugees going to Canada are an important focus in the study of migration in North America. Mexican refugees challenge assumptions on migration movements in North America. The existence of refugees within this geographical area proves that meaningful socio-political disparities and human rights violations persist.

The consideration of gender in Canadian refugee law, an enactment of gender guidelines, or the interpretation of immutability for those refugee claims grounded on sexual orientation are essential facts in this dynamic. In Mexico, legislation that prosecutes domestic violence at the national level has not been in existence for very long; it is thus still uncertain how this legislation will be enforced in practice. Legal instruments and international conventions adopted by the state do not necessarily guarantee their real applicability.

The persecution of certain individuals based on their sexual orientation is a complex issue that is not often accepted by governments. The relationship between refugeehood and sexual-oriented persecution might still be perceived as non-legitimate by many people. It might be asserted that sexual minorities should not have basic rights endorsed on the basis of sexual choice or deviance, nor should they have the opportunity to be considered refugees in North America. However, a review of international law, and of Canadian refugee law in particular, shows that sexual orientation *has* been positively considered as an immutable characteristic that can lead to the persecution of individuals. Homophobic attitudes and social prejudice have often coincided with the unwillingness or deficiency of the state to protect sexual minorities from human rights violations. In this regard, refugee law does not interpret mere harassment or social prejudice as valid grounds for persecution. One cannot present a valid refugee claim *unless* it is proven that harassment or prejudice comprise justifiable grounds for persecution in the eyes of the refugee-board panelists.

From this perspective, some of the Mexican cases that were positively determined as refugees are central. Some of the available cases involve lesbians who lived in small Mexican cities such as Aguascalientes, showing that not only persecuted male homosexuals have gained refugee status. The case of claimants who disclosed HIV-positive status as another determinant for persecution is also interesting in terms of the new scope of refugee law and human rights treatment in Canada. In this regard, the traditional notion of refugees that reduces them to the human fall-out of violent strife and war, or their description as mass movements of people, has had to be reconsidered. However, these interpretations are further narrowed by the existence of generalized restrictions on refugee admittance, presented through numerical quotas and other limitations. For instance, in 1998, the IRB proposed establishing a significantly different functionality of the overall refugee and immigration system.[74] In summary, looking at these two particular grounds of persecution is necessary to an understanding of why certain Mexican individuals seek refugee status in Canada. It is hoped that the evidence presented has broken down common assumptions about refugees as "economic migrants" or "tourists." Social justice and the implementation of human rights are fundamental processes that should be integrated with the current initiatives of trade and investment interests promoted by the dynamics of liberal capitalism. Further ties between Mexico and Canada should recognize the importance of a multi-level relationship. The understanding of a framework based on social justice and human rights concerns is as important as promoting major economic exchanges between Mexico and Canada.

Notes

1. Wilets defines "sexual minorities" as "those individuals that have been distinguished by societies because of their sexual orientation, inclination, behaviour, or gender identity." James D. Wilets, "International Human Rights Law and Sexual Orientation," *Hastings International and Comparative Law Review* 18, no. 1 (Fall 1994): 4.
2. The actual academic narrative focuses primarily on labour-supply factors, the formation of transnational communities, and migration networks (social capital chains). There is also a vast literature on world systems theory and migration showing the importance of the movement of people and its relation to the global economy and service industries. It is necessary to look at the xenophobic attitudes ("new nativism"), the role of the media, and the state policies that permeate the rules for the inclusion and exclusion of migrants in North America.
3. In Canada, the Immigration Act recognizes two types of refugees: 1) Convention refugees are those who meet the definition of the Geneva

Convention and are outside their country of nationality; and 2) overseas selected refugees, individuals who are selected at post or refugee camps abroad, following a quota and a selection process based on resettlement. Library of Parliament, *Canada's Immigration Program* (Canada, 1996), 9–11.
4. Hania Zlotnik, "Policies and Migration Trends in the North American System," in Alan B. Simmons, ed., *International Migration, Refugee Flows and Human Rights in North America. The Impact of Trade and Restructuring* (New York: Centre for Migration Studies, 1996), 86. This geographical proximity has been primarily related to labour migration. For example, "While Canada is now an established destination for hemispheric migrants for the Caribbean and a few Central American and South American countries where refugee flight is or has been important, it is not as yet an important destination for Mexicans. Given the strong historically developed migration links between Mexico and the United States, it does not seem likely that NAFTA will have much direct influence on the flow of Mexicans to Canada. Modest numbers of Mexican farm workers, however, have been coming to Canada on work visas for some years. Just as this eventually led to larger flows in the case of the United States, these modest flows and other contacts facilitated by NAFTA, could lead to an expansion of migration between Mexico and Canada." Ibid., 100.
5. Mexican temporary workers in Canada are on the rise. In 1992, 4,778 workers came to work primarily in the agricultural sector (vegetables and tobacco) in Ontario, Quebec, Alberta, and Manitoba. In 1997, a total of 5,647 workers came under this program. Only 67 women were contracted in 1997. These workers came mainly from Tlaxcala, México, and Guanajuato states. Subsecretaría del Trabajo y Previsión Social, Subsecretaría "B," Dirección General de Empleo. *Programa de Trabajadores Agrícolas Migratorios Temporales Mexicanos con Canadá* (Mexico, mimeo, 1997).
6. See Department of Foreign Affairs and International Trade, *Declaration of Objectives for the Canada-Mexico Relationship* (Ottawa: June 12, 1996 mimeo).
7. The Mexican Migration Commissioner declared that Mexico receives around 8 million migrants every year. He also declared that an average of 7,000 naturalization certificates have been issued in recent years. See "Llegó José Saramago; Confía Migración en que *respete la ley,*" *La Jornada,* March 8, 1998; "Corriente Migratoria Centroamericana a México," *Asuntos Migratorios en México,* Coordinación de Planeación e Investigación del Instituto Nacional de Migración (Mexico, 1996).
8. The intention is to show the existence of a traditional policy of asylum, while at the same time the state is disregarding the human rights concerns of indigenous peasants and transmigrants at the Mexican–

Guatemalan border. In a recent ceremony, 393 naturalization certificates were distributed to Guatemalan individuals who acquired Mexican nationality. See "Zedillo: Vigente, la Tradición del Asilo," *La Jornada*, December 12, 1997. Charles Keely and Sharon Russell declared,

> Mexico also has a long and important tradition of exile reception. Though strained by the movements from Central America, this tradition is an important part of the political culture and defining characteristics of Mexico. . . . In North America the first concern is with reinforcing economic growth in Mexico. Among many other beneficial results, the presumption is that this will lead, with a lag time, to lower Mexican migration. (C. Keely and S. Russell, "Asylum Policies in Developed Countries: National Security Concerns and Regional Issues," in Simmons, *International Migration*, 240.)

9. Alan B. Simmons, "Research and Policy Issues in the Field of International Migration and North American Economic Integration," in Simmons, *International Migration*, 1996 pp.3-6

10. Ibid., 23.

11. In comparison to Canada, in the early 1990s, only a few hundred Mexicans applied for asylum in the United States—claims that were habitually denied. In 1994, the number of requests increased to more than 6,000. However, only 5 reported cases were granted. In 1995, 9,304 applications for political asylum were presented, but only 54 were conceded. Between October 1995 and September 1996, the United States government had accumulated a total of 128,000 refugee claims from all over the world: 63,000 from El Salvador, 9,000 from Guatemala, 7,820 from Mexico, and 4,000 from India. These data show three main points. First, they confirm the existence of refugees not only in Canada, but also in the United States. Second, they reveal how Canada has a higher level of refugee acceptance compared to the United States; third, they show that these refugees reaffirm that their claims are not based on economic factors, as they have been mainly described. See "Asilo EU a 43 Mexicanos entre 1995 y 1996," *La Jornada* (Mexico, December 8, 1997); "Diez Mil Mexicanos Solicitaron Asilo en EU en 1996," *El Excelsior* (Mexico, August 6, 1997); *Latin America Weekly Report*, Dec.14, 1995.

12. Aristide R. Zolberg, Astri Suhrke, and Sergio Aguayo, *Escape from Violence. Conflict and the Refugee Crisis in the Developing World* (New York: Oxford University Press, 1989), 27.

13. United Nations High Commissioner for Refugees, *The State of the World's Refugees 1995* (New York: Oxford University Press, 1995), 245.

14. "Diez Mil Mexicanos."

15. Daniel Stoffman, "Open Door Travesty," *Saturday Night* (November 1994), 52–60.

16. See Tanya Basok, "Canadian Refugee Policy: Globalization, Radical Challenge or State Control?" *Studies in Political Economy,* 50 (1995): 133–66; Jennifer Hyndman, "International Responses to Human Displacement: Neo-liberalism and Post-Cold War Geopolitics," *Refuge* 15, no. 3 (1996): 5–39; Gillian Creese, "Politics of Refugees in Canada," in Vic Satzewich, ed., *Deconstructing a Nation: Immigration, Racism and Multiculturalism in 90s Canada* (Halifax: Fernwood Publishing, 1992), 127.

17. "The Refugees go on Vacation," *Ottawa Citizen*, October 11, 1997, B4.

18. Sexual orientation is defined as an "erotic and/or affectional attraction to members of the same or opposite gender; from biological sex; gender identity (psychological sense of being male or female) and social sex roles (adherence to the culturally created behaviours and attitudes that are deemed appropriate for males or females)." Taken from Suzanne B. Goldberg, "Give Me Liberty or Give me Death: Political Asylum and the Global Persecution of Lesbians and Gay Men," *Cornell International Law Journal* 26, no. 3 (1993): 613.

19. This documentation branch is fundamental because it has a body of researchers that produce trustworthy and evidence-based work, used not only by CRDD members, but also by refugee claimants and counsellors. Some of the works produced by the branch are Country Profiles, The Question and Answer Series Papers, Responses to Information Requests (*REFQUEST*), and the Weekly Media Reviews. See Gerald H. Stobo, "The Canadian Refugee Determination System," *Texas International Law Journal* 29, no. 3 (1994): 385–7.

20. The CRDD is required to provide written reasons for negative refugee decisions. This is not required in the case of positive determinations; therefore, very few positive decisions are written. Almost all positive decisions are orally terminated, and most of the CRDD jurisprudence that is available to the IRB and to the public is negative. See Stobo, "The Canadian Refugee," 391.

21. The Legal Services Department of the IRB has particular criteria to track cases which are uncertain. However, this is the only way to access some refugee decisions. These cases, even if they are not necessarily representative of all claims, constitute fundamental evidence of refugee cases. *RefLex* is available in hard copy (a set of binders) and also can be accessed on the Web at www.irb.gc.ca/en/decisions/reflex.

22. See, for domestic violence in particular, MEX 27953.E (October 1997);

MEX 27356.E (August 1997); MEX 25619.E (November 1996); MEX 24723.E (November 1996); MEX 24984.E (September 1996); MEX 24516.E (July 1996); MEX 23317.E (April 1996); MEX 20856.E (June 1995); MEX 26407.E (March 1997). *Refquest Database*, on line at http:// www.cisr.gc. ca/reserc_e.stm

23. This assumption stemmed from personal interviews with immigration attorneys in Vancouver, Montreal, and Toronto, and during a workshop on sexual orientation and refugees. *Workshop on Sexual Orientation as a Basis for Refugee Status*, organized by Vigil Toronto and sponsored by the Toronto Lesbian and Gay Community Appeal, November 23, 1997.

24. The United Nations High Commissioner for Refugees (UNHCR) adopted in 1991 the *Guidelines on the Protection of Refugee Women*. In this manual, the UNHCR encouraged the need to recognize claims made by women as gender-related grounds of persecution. In Canada, the IRB had previous denials of women's refugee claims during 1992–93. The *"Nada"* case (April 1991) constituted a watershed. This case involved a Saudi Arabian woman who fled to Canada after being punished and having her life threatened for her feminist beliefs. Her claim was neglected, and later she was allowed to remain in Canada on humanitarian and compassionate grounds. However, her case opened the consideration of gender in refugee determinations. See Valerie I. Oosterveld, "The Canadian Guidelines on Gender Related Persecution: An Evaluation," *International Journal of Refugee Law* 8, no. 4 (1996): 574–5; Library of Parliament, *Gender Related Refugee Claims* (Ministry of Supply and Services, 1994), 2; Hélène Lambert, "Seeking Asylum on Gender Grounds," *International Journal of Discrimination and the Law* 1 (1995): 173–4.

25. In 1994, 47% of all refugees resettled from abroad were female, higher than the 42–43% of other years. In 1994, 195 women were granted refugee status in Canada under these guidelines. Other findings show that between March 1993 and January 1995, the IRB identified 650 gender-related claims. Citizenship and Immigration reveals that between 1981 and 1991 fewer than half of admitted women were Convention refugees. See Oosterveld, "The Canadian Guidelines," 595. See also data in Pamela Foster, "Gender and Refugees In Canada. In Between Self and Other," M.A. research essay (Norman Paterson School of International Affairs, Carleton University, 1996), 102, 114.

26. Some women's experiences are difficult for them to express during the hearing; this required that refugee hearing personnel be trained. The Rape Trauma and Battered Woman's syndromes are constraining factors for a credible hearing. See Oosterveld, "The Canadian Guidelines."

27. Kristine M. Fox, "Gender Persecution: Canadian Guidelines Offer a Model for Refugee Determination in the United States," *Arizona Journal of International and Comparative Law* 11, no. 1 (1994), 119.

28. France was the first "Western" nation to establish female genital circumcision as a form of persecution within the United Nations Convention of Refugee Status. The Canadian guidelines make it the first country to grant such a status as part of its conventional refugee procedure. See Kris A. Moussette, "Female Genital Mutilation and Refugee Status in the United States: A Step in the Right Direction," *Boston College International and Comparative Law Review* 19, no. 2 (1996): 353.

29. Women and children represent over 80% of the world's 27 million refugees and displaced people. See *Rebuilding the Future Together: II UNHCR and Refugee Women* (Geneva: UNHCR, 1997), 32.

30. See Jacqueline Bhabba and Sue Shutter, "A Well Founded Fear of Exclusion: The Legal Problems of Women Refugees," in Jacqueline Bhabba and Sue Shutter, eds., *Women's Movement: Women under Immigration, Nationality and Refugee Law* (London: Trentham Books, 1994), 229–57.

31. Judith Ramírez, "The Canadian Guidelines on Women Refugee Claimants Fearing Gender Related Persecution," *Refuge* 14, no. 7 (December 1994): 4; Oosterveld, "The Canadian Guidelines," 578.

32. The U.S. Gender Guidelines were approved on May 26, 1995. See *Migration News* 2, no. 6 (June 1995); see http://migration.ucdavis.edu/Archive/MN_95/jun_95-05.html.

33. See some of the available cases grounded in domestic violence from the Dominican Republic (CRDD M96-11828 Nov. 1997; A95-00400 Nov. 1996); Venezuela (T95-03276, T95-03277 Apr. 1997; and T95-05227, T95-05228 Nov. 1996); Jamaica (T95-04279 Dec. 1997); Brazil (U95-04594 Nov. 1996); Guyana (T96-02397 Apr. 1997); Ecuador (U94-04509 Jan. 1997; U95-04292 Oct. 1996); Grenada (U96-03524 Aug. 1997); Barbados (T96-00112 Aug. 1997); India (U96-03318 June 1997); Iraq (T96-03638 June 1997); Bangladesh (U96-01850, U9601851, U9601852, U9601853 in Sept. 1997).

34. Domestic violence is one of the leading causes of Mexican women's migration to the United States. A report from the Office of Asylum Affairs from the State Department in the United States states, "Occasional claims are received from women who allege they are members of a particular social class consisting of women who were abused by husbands or boyfriends, forced into prostitution, or otherwise abused or mistreated in Mexico. Although the Constitution provides for equality between the sexes, neither the authorities nor society in general respect this in practice. The most pervasive violations involve domestic and sexual violence,

which is believed to be widespread and vastly underreported." See U.S. Department of State, Office of Asylum Affairs, Democracy, Human Rights and Labour, *Mexico. Profile of Asylum Claims and Country Conditions* (Washington, May 1996), 5.

35. See Office of the United Nations High Commissioner for Refugees, *The State of the World's Refugees 1997–98* (Oxford: Oxford University Press, 1997), 196–7.

36. Ibid., 26.

37. See Goldberg, "Give me Liberty," 620.

38. Ryan Goodman, "The Incorporation of International Human Rights Standards into Sexual Orientation Asylum Claims: Cases of Involuntary Medical Intervention," *Yale Law Journal* 105 (1995): 255–89.

39. Some scholars, framing a cultural relativist and social construction of "gay" and "lesbian" arguments, assert that sodomy laws do not violate universally accepted human rights because their regulation would impose Western standards of morality on other areas of the world. However, since 1991, Amnesty International considers persons arrested for their homosexual identity or for engaging in homosexual activities as prisoners of conscience. See Amnesty International, *Breaking The Silence: Human Rights Violations Based in Sexual Orientation* (London: Amnesty International, 1997); Laurence R. Helfer and Alice M. Miller, "Sexual Orientation and Human Rights: Toward a United States and Transnational Jurisprudence," *Harvard Human Rights Journal* 9 (Spring 1996): 90.

40. The International Gay and Lesbian Human Rights Commission (IGLHRC) has reported more than 650 asylum cases worldwide. See Nicole LaViolette, "The Immutable Refugees: Sexual Orientation in *Canada (A.G.) v. Ward*," *University of Toronto Faculty of Law Review* 55, no. 1 (1997): 3.

41. The Convention states that a refugee is an individual who, owing "to a well founded fear of being persecuted for reasons of race, religion, nationality, membership in a particular social group or political opinion, is outside the country of his nationality and is unable or, owing to such a fear, is unwilling to avail himself of the protection of that country." See Guy S. Goodwin-Gill, *The Refugee In International Refugee Law* (Oxford: Clarendon, 1996), 394 and appendix.

42. James Hathaway, *The Law of Refugee Status* (Toronto: Butterworths, 1991), 11.

43. Goodwin-Gill explains how basic human rights obtain their significance from customary international law. Conventions are not the only source of international law. This is the case for the interpretation concerning emergent "social groups," a category that was broadly defined by the Refugee

Convention to encompass groups without a specific enumeration. See Goodwin-Gill, *The Refugee*, 358–9.

44. Andrew E. Shacknove, "Who is a Refugee," *Ethics*, no. 95 (January 1985): 275.

45. In "Who is a Refugee," p. 277, Schacknove states, "[P]ersecution is but one manifestation of a broader phenomenon: the absence of state protection of the citizen's basic needs. It is this absence of state protection which constitutes the full and complete negation of society and the basis of refugeehood."

46. Ibid., 281.

47. Hathaway, *The Law of Refugee Status*, 127.

48. Ibid., 123.

49. Goodwin-Gill, *The Refugee*, 515.

50. Maryellen Fullerton, "A Comparative Look at Refugee Status Based on Persecution due to Membership in a Particular Social Group," *Cornell International Law Journal* 26, no. 3, (1993): 518.

51. Persecution related to a person's gender or sexual orientation is not explicitly mentioned in the Convention and Protocol on refugees. However, there has been an increased recognition in worldwide jurisprudence to include gender in the concept of persecution. Grahl-Madsen asserted that "shared interests, values, or background" of a social group are likely to combine qualities over which individuals have no control with matters that they can control. Goodwin-Gill also emphasizes the importance of societal attitudes toward subsets within that society, noting that widely shared perceptions often indicate the existence of a persecuted social group; see Fullerton, "A Comparative Look," 517.

52. The *Ward* case concerned a member of the Irish National Liberation Army (INLA) who sought refugee status in Canada after defecting from this terrorist organization. The claimant, after becoming a member of the INLA, was assigned to guard two hostages who were later sentenced to death. The asylum seeker helped the hostages escape, for which he was sentenced to death by the INLA. He then sought asylum in Canada. This case was related not to sexual-orientation or gender claims, but it had relevance as jurisprudence due to the interpretation of "social group." Hence, in this case, three categories of social group were defined: 1) the existence of an innate or unchangeable characteristic; 2) a voluntary association for reasons so fundamental to their human dignity that they should not be forced to forsake the association; and 3) the association by a former voluntary status, unalterable due to its historical permanence. See

Fullerton, "A Comparative Look," 536; Goodwin-Gill, *The Refugee*, 360–2; Hélène Lambert, "Seeking Asylum on Gender Grounds," *International Journal of Discrimination and the Law* 1 (1995): 161.

53. Ramírez, "The Canadian Guidelines," 6.54. See LaViolette, "The Immutable Refugees," 931.
55. See IRB M92-01550, Mar.24/94 quoted in "Asylum Project Quotes," *International Gay and Lesbian Human Rights Commission*, http://www.iglhrc.org/asylum/
56. See Helfer and Miller, "Sexual Orientation," 86.
57. Donald G. Casswell, *Lesbians, Gay Men and Canadian Law* (Toronto: Emond Montgomery Publications, 1996), 590–1.
58. Ibid., 586–7.
59. LaViolette, "The Immutable Refugees," 9.
60. Library of Parliament, *Gender Related Refugee Claims*, 15.
61. Social group has been interpreted as "single women living in a Muslim country without the protection of a male relative," "young Tamil women in Sri Lanka," "women and girls who do not conform to Islamic fundamentalist norms," "unprotected Zimbabwean women or girls subject to wife abuse." See Rebecca M.M. Wallace, "Men, Their Rights and Nothing More; Women, Their Rights and Nothing Less," *Saskatchewan Law Review*, 58 (1994), 222–3.
62. Donald G. Casswell, *Lesbians, Gay Men and Canadian Law* (Toronto: Emond Montgomery Publications, 1996), 590–1.
63. Peter C. Godfrey, "Defining the Social Group in Asylum Proceedings: The Expansion of the Social Group to Include a Broader Class of Refugees," *Journal of Law and Policy*, 3 (1994), 262.
64. "The Nation Refugee Status in HIV Case Defended," *The Globe and Mail*, February 21, 1995, A1, A4.
65. "7 with HIV let into Canada," *Toronto Sun*, October 31, 1997, 19.
66. "Safe Haven for Sexual Refugees," *Ottawa Citizen*, July 14, 1997, A1-A2.
67. See "Expanding Access to Asylum," *Migration News* 4, no. 1 (January 1997) (URL: migration.ucdavis.edu/mn/index.html); William Branigin, "More than 60 Homosexuals Claiming Persecution Have Been Granted Asylum in US," *Washington Post*, December 17, 1996.
68. "Diez Mil Mexicanos Solicitaron."
69. See Immigration and Refugee Board, *Country of Persecution Analysis Report*, Standard, Analysis and Monitoring (IRB), Statistics for 1996 and 1997. Released in January 1997 and February 1998.
70. In comparison, in 1997, Cuba obtained a total of 129 positive refugee

determinations, Venezuela 116, Peru 115, Guatemala 55, Nicaragua 52, and Chile 46. See Immigration and Refugee Board, *Country of Persecution Analysis Report.*

71. Ibid. The backlog of refugee cases has increased by about 75%. Canada processes about 20,000 asylum applications each year. See "Canada: Immigration Up," *Migration News*, 4, no. 5 (May 1997); "Refugee claims jump 75 percent," *Toronto Sun*, February 10, 1997.

72. "Refugee-Claims Backlog Soars: Hopefuls From Chile and Mexico Push Total Past 30,000," *The Province* (Vancouver), February 11, 1997, A14; see also "Refugee System a Mess; Auditor General Cites Backlog, Failure to Deport," *Toronto Sun*, December 3, 1997, 4.

73. In 1996, Montreal accepted 72 Mexican refugees; Vancouver, 25; Toronto, 4; Ottawa, 3; and Calgary, 2. In 1997, Montreal determined 108 Mexican refugee claims as positive; Toronto, 34; Vancouver, 14; and Ottawa, 3. See Immigration and Refugee Board, *Country of Persecution Analysis Report.*

74. See *Not Just Numbers: A Canadian Framework for Future Immigration*, Minister of Citizenship and Immigration (January 1998). On line at http:cicnet.ci.gc.ca/ legrev/final/email.html.

International and Interregional Migration in North America: The Role of Returns to Skill

Gary L. Hunt and Richard E. Mueller

Introduction

I N THIS PAPER, WE EMPLOY THE NOTION THAT MIGRATION IS MOTIVATED by individuals who, in seeking to maximize utility, may choose to migrate from their region of birth and take up residence in another area, or even another country. It is well known that economic incentives play a significant role in internal migration[1] and in international migration.[2] Treating migration as a human capital investment decision,[3] an individual is predicted to migrate if the present value of additional lifetime labour-market earnings attained through migration exceeds the present value of migration costs. Migration in such cases increases the value of an individual's human capital, similar to investments in human capital through formal education or experience. Given a population in which skills differ among individuals, migration would be expected to increase the human capital value of some individuals and decrease its value for others. The likelihood of migration by the former group of individuals should exceed that of the latter.[4] In other words, we would expect that migration is selective of those who benefit from it. A number of studies have found support for such self-selection behaviour in internal migration[5] and international migration.[6]

Borjas, Bronars, and Trejo[7] utilize a Roy-style model of self-selection[8] to provide additional evidence on the nature of the selection process. In their version of the Roy model, regions within the United States have different wage-generating characteristics. Some areas have relatively high average wages but relatively low returns to skill, so that these areas have wage distributions with relatively high means but relatively low variances. Other areas have relatively low means and relatively high variances. Therefore, across regions in the United States, wage distributions differ in their means and in their returns to skills (variances). Borjas and his colleagues find evidence that higher-skilled individuals self-select into regions with higher returns to skill and that lower-skilled individuals self-select into regions with lower returns to skill. They conclude that the selection process in migration in the United States not only influences the aggregate amount of migration between regions but also the skill mix.

Our main objective in this paper is to determine whether immigration within North America follows this self-selection process and the role of returns to skill in this process. A secondary objective is to investigate the Canadian "brain drain" to the United States. This issue is of policy relevance in Canada, where there is renewed concern that some of the country's best minds are leaving for the greener wage-earning pastures of the United States. This has led some to question the role of publicly funded universities that train individuals who may migrate south after graduation. And it has left government officials pondering the implications of years of cutbacks to publicly financed medical care and research programs, also blamed for driving competent professionals south of the border, where skills tend to be rewarded more handsomely.

Theoretical Considerations

Because of its suitability in analyzing migrant self-selectivity by skill, we have employed a Roy model framework for our analysis. Roy's original work addressed occupational choice. He asserted that there were only two vocations that an individual could select, rabbit hunting and trout fishing, and the choice made would be based on individual-specific skills. Roy noted,

> The rabbits are plentiful and stupid and even the less skilled man can ensnare a fair number in a year's hunting while the exercise of a quite appreciable degree of skill does not enable the better hunters to catch many more. The trout, on the other hand, are particularly wily and fight hard, so that many men would undoubtedly starve if they had to eat only what they themselves caught; but nevertheless the real fisherman can obtain very big catches in a year's fishing, although such catches are pretty rare occurrences.[9]

Thus, even a relatively unskilled hunter could sustain himself, whereas a skilled fisherman would be wasting his talents hunting since these would be better rewarded by fishing.

This occupational-choice model can be adapted easily to the study of interregional and international migration in North America. For current purposes, we assume that migration is based solely on the ability to increase one's lifetime income. Of course, this is a limiting assumption since we know that migrants respond to non-monetary factors (or compensating differentials) in making migration decisions.[10] For example, if individuals have preferences for certain climate amenities (e.g., warmth versus cold), then equilibrium wages will be lower in regions characterized by more of the climatic amenity. The lower regional wages do not imply lower utility because the lower wages are *compensating* for the attractive climate amenity. Work-in-progress addresses these non-monetary factors.

An important difference in our approach compared to that of Borjas et al. is that we include international as well as interregional migrants. We expect that this will be important because of the fundamental theoretical basis of comparative advantage underpinning the Roy model. In Roy, self-selection into an *occupation* depends on two basic factors: the mean earnings and the variance of earnings around the mean that characterize an occupation, and the skill characteristics of individuals vis-à-vis the occupation. The first factor depends on market conditions that influence the price of output produced by an occupation and on production conditions that influence the costs of output. The community's preferences for rabbit or fish impact upon the wages of hunters and fishers through their effect on the relative output price. The relative difficulty of catching rabbits compared to fish influences relative costs. The second factor depends on how an individual's skills translate into prowess in hunting and fishing. Some individuals may have skills that make them relatively good hunters, while others may have skills that make them relatively better fishers. Some skills may be useful in both hunting and fishing.

Translating this model into an interregional migration context requires that regions vary in one of two ways. Regions could vary in their returns to skills *in general*, with some regions having lower returns to skill *in general* (i.e., a more compressed wage distribution) and others having greater returns to skills *in general* (i.e., a less compressed wage distribution).[11] In this case, Roy selection would lead higher-skilled individuals to migrate to regions with higher returns to skills and lower-skilled individuals to migrate to regions with lower returns to skills, other things being equal. This is because highly skilled individuals would be rewarded for their superior skills in a region with high returns to skills, whereas those less talented would have their incomes protected in areas with low returns to skills. Alternatively, regions could vary in the specific skills that were more or less productive. In this case, skills would be as "region-specific" as they are "occupation specific" in Roy.[12] We make the former assumption in this paper. Given the structural similarities between the American and Canadian economies, this assumption seems reasonable.

In particular, we assume that each individual has a certain set of skills and that these skills are transferable between regions. Thus, a highly skilled person in (say) Alberta would also be a highly skilled person in (say) Florida. What may differ between regions, however, is the return to these skills, and this may be the motivation for migration between two regions. This skilled person in Alberta may therefore wish to migrate to Florida if the return to his or her skills is higher there.

Consequently, we are assuming that migration does not change an individual's skill level. Returns to migration are generated by regional variations in mean wages and the returns to skill. Reasons for variations in mean wages and returns to skills across regions include differences in stocks of complementary inputs (e.g., natural resources, physical capital) relative to labour, aggregate regional economic conditions, differences in relative output prices of goods in which regions specialize and trade, and amenities.

Thus, we have individual wages in each area being determined by two components. The first of these is the average wage in the region. The second is the way in which skills differing from the average skills level are either rewarded (in the case of higher-than-normal skills) or penalized (in the case of below-normal skills).[13]

Regional wage differences (and hence wage distributions) are thus determined by differences in skill levels among the individuals in the region, and also by differences in returns to these skills. It is the product of skills and returns to skills that determines the wage rate for any individual. For example, computer programmers may be highly paid in Silicon Valley compared to the Ottawa Valley. But this difference may be due to the fact that programmers in the region are more highly skilled, or are rewarded more handsomely for these skills, or a combination of these two factors.

Since we are interested in individual choices of destinations and

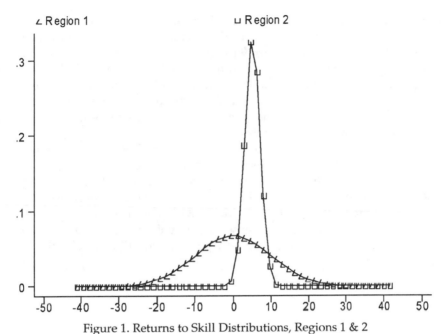

Figure 1. Returns to Skill Distributions, Regions 1 & 2

the varying returns to skills that drive the migration phenomenon according to our theory, we need to remove variations in the interregional wage distribution that result from differences in skill mix. This is achieved by using a standardized skill distribution.[14] We then use this distribution to determine the differences in returns to skills between regions.

Figure 1 illustrates two hypothetical returns to skill distributions (i.e., probability density functions) for two regions. The horizontal axis shows the returns to skill. To the right of the zero, individuals have superior skills and are rewarded for them. To the left, individuals have inferior skills and are penalized for them. We have assumed that skills are perfectly correlated between regions. In other words, if individuals have superior (inferior) skills in one region, they will also have superior (inferior) skills in the other region. The vertical axis shows the probability of observing these returns in either of the regions. Returns in both regions follow a normal distribution, although means and variances differ. In region 1, the mean return to skills is relatively low, but the dispersion of returns is wide. By contrast, the mean return in region 2 is high but the dispersion is low. Thus, the individual with high skills will be rewarded more by locating in region 2 than in region 1. Conversely, low-skilled individuals will prefer region 2 since lower returns to skills are not penalized as heavily. Although we have only included two regions in this figure, the results could easily be expanded to include any number of regions. The point is that individuals will migrate to those locations where returns to their skills are the highest (or where penalties for low skill are the lowest).

In terms of the Roy selection process outlined above, mean wages increase the well-being of all individuals, and therefore should increase the probability of selection of the area by all individuals, other things being equal. A larger dispersion in returns to skills should increase (decrease) the well-being of individuals with higher (lower) skills, and therefore should increase (decrease) the probability of selection of that area by individuals with positive (negative) skill differentials, all else being equal.

Data

Data on individuals are taken from the 1990 United States Census of Population and Housing and the 1991 Canadian Population Census. The subsample selected includes males[15] in 48 U.S. states (excluding Alaska and Hawaii) and Washington, D.C., and the 10 Canadian provinces who meet the following criteria: individuals 25 to 64 years of age who are not in school or the military and are not self-employed, and who worked positive weeks and hours and had positive wage and salary earnings in the prior year (1989 for individuals from the United States census and 1990 for individuals from the Canadian census).

In addition to the usual array of socio-economic characteristics, these census data include information on the current state/province of residence, as well as the location of the respondent five years previous to the date of the census. If an individual resided in one of the 48 U.S. states in 1985, or one of the 10 Canadian provinces in 1986, then the corresponding area is the individual's origin. If an individual resided in one of the 48 U.S. states in 1990, or one of the 10 Canadian provinces in 1991, then this area is the individual's destination. The individual is a migrant during the period 1985–90 in the United States data or 1986–91 in the Canadian data if his origin and destination are not the same area.

Table 1. Averages of Estimated State/Provincial Wages

	U.S.A.	Canada
Number of states/provinces	49	10
Average wage (natural logarithm)	6.2069	6.2116
Standard deviation	0.1187	0.0886
Average wage (US $ per week)	499.70	500.28
Standard deviation	61.99	44.51

There are a total of 59 origins and destinations (i.e., 48 states plus the District of Columbia, and 10 Canadian provinces).

Since we are concerned with both average wages within regions and the distribution of these wages, we must construct the appropriate variables.[16] As mentioned above, wages for each individual are a combination of the skills that individuals have, as well as the returns to the skills in each area. Since we hypothesize that it is returns to these skills that drive the migration process, we must control for the fact that the average *quantity* of individual skills between regions can differ. We do this by using a *standardized* skill distribution.[17] In this way, we are able to "net out" the differences in returns to skills between regions. Finally, we calculate the skill level of each individual and how this compares to the group mean, since we hypothesize that those with above-average skills will migrate to regions with the highest returns to these skills.

Due to computational limitations, the number of individuals in the sample is 15,576, but these figures are weighted accordingly so that some 43.46 million males (3.85 million in Canada and 39.61 million in the United States) are represented by these data.

Results

Table 1 presents simple national averages of state/provincial estimated average weekly wages, along with the standard deviations of these measures. Two points are worthy of consideration and germane to the current work. First, the average estimated log wage in the United States is about the same as that in Canada (once the latter is adjusted for price-level and exchange-rate differentials). In the United States, the average estimated log wage is 6.2069, compared to the Canadian average of 6.2116. This translates into an average weekly wage of about U.S. $500 in both countries. The difference is not statistically significant. By contrast, the average value of the standard deviation is higher in the United States than in Canada, and this difference is statistically significant at the 1 per cent level. As we expected, this is indicative of the wider distribution of returns to skill in the United States (since we have controlled for differences in skill mix).

To test the validity of the Roy model outlined above, we tabulate simple correlation coefficients. These coefficients have a range between −1 (perfect negative correlation) and 1 (perfect positive correlation). A value of 0 would suggest that there is no relationship between the two variables. For example, although not presented here, the correlation between an individual moving and his or her age is −.1251, suggesting that older individuals are less likely to relocate. This is a common result in the literature.

More specifically, the variable MOVE denotes an individual who has relocated from his state or province of residence five years prior to the census (the origin) if this location differs from his location at the time of the census (the destination). The variable MEAN WAGE is the estimated mean wage in the destination state/province. We have hypothesized above that the individuals will be more willing to move to areas with higher mean wages. Finally, the variable SD*RRTS is a composite variable calculated as the product of the skill differential of the individual relative to the sample mean (SD) and the relative variance of returns to skill in the destination area of the respondent (RRTS). According to the theory, we would expect this number to be positively correlated with relocation. The logic is that individuals with high skills will be more handsomely rewarded for these skills (in the form of higher wages) in areas that have a wider (i.e., less equal) distribution of returns to these skills and thus will be more likely to migrate to these areas.

Table 2 shows these results. Numbers in bold indicate that they are significantly different from zero at the 5 per cent level. The first panel shows the results for the entire sample of Canadians and Americans. These data include all persons who did not move, who moved between provinces or states in the previous five-year period, as well as those who migrated between countries during the same period. The correlation coefficient between MOVE and MEAN WAGE is −.0304 and significant, suggesting that individuals are slightly less likely to move to areas with higher mean area wages. The correlation between MOVE and SD*RRTS is positive but insignificant. This fails to confirm that individuals with higher skills are more likely to move to regions with

Table 2. Correlation Coefficients, Destination United States and Canada

	Entire Sample		
	(sample size = 15,576)		
	MOVE	SD*RRTS	MEAN WAGE
MOVE	1.0000		
D*RRTS	0.0107	1.0000	
MEAN WAGE	**−0.0304**	**0.0538**	1.0000

	Destination – United States		
	(sample size = 8,853)		
	MOVE	SD*RRTS	MEAN WAGE
MOVE	1.0000		
SD*RRTS	0.0094	1.0000	
MEAN WAGE	**−0.0282**	**0.0578**	1.0000

	Destination – Canada		
	(sample size = 6,723)		
	MOVE	SD*RRTS	MEAN WAGE
MOVE	1.0000		
SD*RRTS	−0.0416	1.0000	
MEAN WAGE	**0.0249**	**0.0395**	1.0000

Notes: 1 SD = skill differential, RRTS = relative (variance) of returns to skill.
  2 Bolded numbers indicate statistical significance at the 5% level.

returns to skill distribution that is wider. Similarly, these data fail to reflect that those with below-average skills are less likely to migrate to these areas.

The second panel limits the sample to include only those who had the United States as their destination. This includes all individuals who lived in the United States in 1990. Five years prior to the census, they may have lived in Canada, another state, or the same state (although they may have moved between locations within the state). Similarly, the third panel is for those who lived in Canada on the date of the census in 1991, although they may have lived in another Canadian province or in the United States in the five years before.

Disaggregating the sample in this manner exposes two interesting results. First, in the U.S. sample, MOVE and MEAN WAGE are negatively correlated, whereas these two variables are positively correlated in the Canadian sample. This implies that those who move to or within the United States are slightly more likely to move to areas with lower average wages. In Canada, by contrast, the correlation between these two variables is positive. Second, there is a positive correlation between MOVE and SD*RRTS in the U.S. case, but a negative correlation in the Canadian data. In neither case, however, is this result statistically important, although more sophisticated techniques reveal the significance of these variables.[18] This is an interesting result and shows that more skilled individuals move to those areas in the United States with the highest returns to skills. In Canada, however, more skilled individuals are less likely to move to these areas. Given the more narrow distribution of returns to skill in Canada, this result is not surprising.

These results imply that those who move to either the United States or Canada have different factors related to their destination choice. For movers with the United States as a final destination, the more dispersed returns to skill appear to be important, whereas the mean wage in the area is not as important. This is the type of result we would expect, since only those with superior skills would tend to migrate to these areas, and these individuals, expecting to be rewarded for their skills, would not be motivated by the mean wage of the area. In Canada, the area mean wage appears to be relatively more important than are the returns to skill distribution. This could be because the wage compression across provinces in Canada causes migrants to be more interested in high mean wages, since they are apt to be lower-skilled migrants moving within Canada or from the United States. Stated differently, it is lower-skilled individuals who will be less penalized in Canada. These results support the Roy model.

The secondary goal of this paper is to attempt to find empirical support for the migration of talented (i.e., highly skilled) Canadians to the United States. To do this, we break down the sample into skill deciles (i.e., into ten same-sized groups) in which the first decile contains the 10 per cent of the population with the lowest estimated skills, the second decile the second lowest 10 per cent, and so on. The tenth decile will have the 10 per cent of individuals with the highest estimated skills. Figures 2 and 3 show the decile positions of individuals in the standardized skill distribution in the Canadian and U.S. data. These are further broken down into individuals who did change state or province of residence in the five-year period before each national census, those who moved internally, and those who came from the other

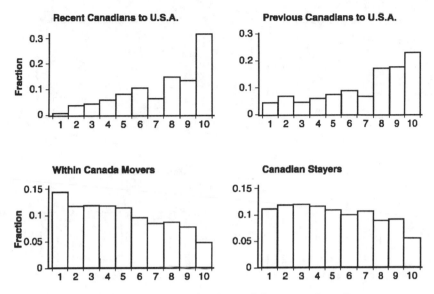

Figure 2. Skill Distribution by Mobility type, Canadians.

country. This latter group is further broken down into those who arrived in the other country sometime in the five-year period before the census date, and those who arrived more than five years before the census.

Figure 2 shows the data for Canadian-born males. The most recent wave of Canadian immigrants to the United States is clearly congregated in the upper deciles of the standardized skill distribution. In fact, some 30 per cent of recent arrivals are in the tenth decile. This result is as expected since presumably this group went to the United States (at least in part) to reap the higher rewards to these skills in the United States. Previous Canadian immigrants to the United States are also heavily concentrated in these upper deciles. By contrast, those who stay in Canada are slightly more likely to have lower skills. Those who relocate within Canada are particularly concentrated in the lower tail of the skills distribution. This, along with the results presented above, implies that those with lower-than-average skills may migrate within Canada to regions with high average wages, as any deficiency in skills will be protected. This is suggestive of a brain drain to the United States.

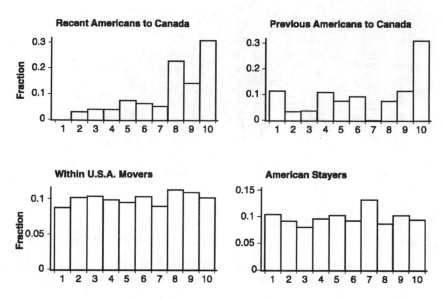

Figure 3. Skill Distribution by Mobility Type, Americans.

Figure 3 presents comparable information for American-born males. What is striking about these figures is the concentration of American immigrants to Canada in the upper deciles. This is contrary to our expectations and shows that even the most highly skilled Americans come to Canada although we would expect that they would be rewarded more in the United States. This underlines the importance of factors other than income in determining migration patterns between the two countries. As with the Canadian data, Americans who remained in the United States are more uniformly distributed throughout the skills deciles. Movers within the United States, however, are more likely than are their Canadian counterparts to have superior skills.

The pattern of immigrants being concentrated in the upper tail of the skill distribution is especially pronounced for Canadians in the United States. Given the wider distribution of income in the United States, this supports the Roy model as we do expect these types of self-selection biases among Canadian immigrants in the United States. The Roy model, by contrast, suggests that Americans in Canada should be concentrated in the lower deciles. This is hardly the case, as we find highly skilled Americans residing in Canada.

Conclusion

We have used the Roy self-selection model to attempt to explain the migration flows between, and also within, Canada and the United States. In our context, the Roy model basically asserts that individuals will choose to locate in the destination that maximizes their well-being. This is influenced by many factors, including climate (heat, humidity, snowfall, etc.), distance from family and friends, and so on. Also of importance, however, is the relative wage which an individual can be expected to earn in the new location. This expected wage is influenced by the mean wages in the area, as well as by the returns to skill distribution and how an individual's skills compare to others. It is this latter motivation for relocation on which we have focused.

Using Canadian and United States census data and simple analysis, we do find some empirical support for the Roy model. Highly skilled individuals do tend to move to areas with higher returns to skill and do not appear to be motivated by area mean wages. This is the result of individuals having sufficient skill that they expect to earn wages above the average so that this average is not important in their migration decision. By contrast, individuals with lower skills tend to move to areas with high mean wages and lower returns to skill. This too makes sense in terms of the theory, since those with low skills will have their wages protected in such areas. We also find evidence of an exodus of Canadians with superior skills to the United States. However, we also find that highly skilled Americans have been coming to Canada. The latter result suggests the importance of accounting for non-wage factors in determining the factors behind migration. Our current work addresses a number of these factors.

Notes

1. See Michael J. Greenwood, "Research on Internal Migration in the United States: A Survey," *Journal of Economic Literature* 13 (1975): 397–433; idem, "Human Migration: Theory, Models, and Empirical Studies," *Journal of Regional Science* 25 (1985): 521–44.
2. See George J. Borjas, "The Economics of Immigration," *Journal of Economic Literature* 32 (1994): 1667–1717.
3. Larry A. Sjaastad, "The Costs and Returns of Human Migration," *Journal of Political Economy* 70, Supplement (1962): 80–93.

4. Over a sufficiently long decision interval, individuals whose migration decisions reduce the value of their human capital can potentially reverse this negative consequence by return migration. See Greenwood, "Research on Internal Migration"; E. K. Grant and J. Vanderkamp, "Repeat Migration and Disappointment," *Canadian Journal of Regional Science* 9 (1986): 299–322.

5. Robert A. Nakosteen and Michael Zimmer, "Migration and Income: The Question of Self-Selection," *Southern Economic Journal* 46 (1980): 840–51; idem, "The Effects on Earnings of Interregional and Interindustry Migration," *Journal of Regional Science* 22 (1982): 325–41; Chris Robinson and Nigel Tomes, "Self-selection and Interprovincial Migration in Canada," *Canadian Journal of Economics* 15 (1982): 474–502; K. B. Newbold, "Income, Self-selection, and Return and Onward Interprovincial Migration in Canada," *Environment and Planning A* 28 (1996): 1019–34.

6. George J. Borjas, "Self-Selection and the Earnings of Immigrants," *American EconomicReview* 77 (1987): 531–53; idem, "The Economics of Immigration."

7. George J. Borjas, Stephen G. Bronars, and Stephen J. Trejo, "Self-Selection and Internal Migration in the United States," *Journal of Urban Economics* 32 (1992): 159–85.

8. A. D. Roy, "Some Thoughts on the Distribution of Earnings," *Oxford Economic Papers* 3 (1951): 135–46.

9. Ibid., 137–8.

10. Greenwood, "Human Migration"; Kathleen M. Day, "Interprovincial Migration and Local Public Goods," *Canadian Journal of Economics* 25 (1992): 123–144; Gary L. Hunt, "Equilibrium and Disequilibrium in Migration Modelling," *Regional Studies* 27 (1993): 341–9.

11. In this case, skills are unidimensional. A person is more or less skilled, in general, if she or he has a higher or lower value of the unidimensional skill index. Areas offering higher returns to skill in general generate higher wages for individuals with more skills. An individual's skill index is perfectly correlated across all regions because skills are unidimensional, and therefore the individual has the same skill level regardless of the region where she or he is employed.

12. In this case, skills are multidimensional. A person is more or less skilled in a particular region, or occupation, if he or she has a higher or lower value of the skill index in that region or occupation. Even with interregionally invariant returns to skills of a particular type, individuals have incentives to work in regions where their skill mix is most productive and therefore generates the highest wages. In this case, an individual's skill

index is not perfectly correlated across all regions. In fact, positive or negative or zero pairwise correlations between regions for an individual can occur.

13. Mathematically this can be expressed as

$$w_{ij} = \mu_j + \phi_j[\upsilon_i - \upsilon],$$

where w_{ij} is the expected value of the of the wage for individual i in region j, μ_j is the average wage in region j, υ is the average skill level across all individuals, υ_i is the skill level of individual i, and ϕ_j is the region-specific returns to skills. Thus, if an individual in area j has above (below) average skills, then $\upsilon_i > (<) \upsilon$. In such cases, the mean of the wage distribution will differ across areas due to both interregional differences in average skills (i.e., $\upsilon_i - \upsilon$), and the values of μ_j and ϕ_j.

14. Technically, this is done by OLS estimation of a log wage equation using the entire sample. The mean values for the entire sample are then used to simulate the average skill level (in terms of the log wage). Next, values of individual-specific human capital variables are included to obtain an individual-specific skill level. The difference between this estimate and the average skill level determines whether the individual is more or less skilled than is the average individual in the sample.

15. Work in progress also addresses female migration.

16. To ensure consistency between Canadian and U.S. wages, the 1990 Canadian wages are first deflated by the 1990 Canadian CPI (4.8 per cent) and then converted to U.S. dollars using the 1989 U.S./Canadian dollar exchange rate (1.184).

17. Technically, we estimate a log wage equation for each of the 59 areas using the individuals in that area and their usual human capital and demographic characteristics (e.g., education, potential experience, marital status, industry, occupation, etc.). We then use the estimated coefficients from these log wage equations to simulate wages in the area if the average individual in this area had the same characteristics as the average individual in the entire sample. This gives us a standardized average wage and also a standardized wage distribution. Full details of this procedure can be found in Gary L. Hunt and Richard E. Mueller, "An Empirical Model of Interregional and International Migration: Canada and the United States," unpublished paper (1998).

18. It should be noted that MEAN WAGE and SD*RRTS are significantly correlated in both the Canadian and the U.S. samples. For this reason, it is difficult to disentangle these effects and determine how each influences the migration decision of an individual in this type of analysis. More

sophisticated analysis (not presented here), which allows us to separate the influence of each of these factors, does in fact show that both MEAN WAGE and SD*RRTS are individually significant. In particular, estimating simple probit equations separately on the U.S. and Canadian data (i.e., MOVE as the dependent variable with MEAN WAGE and SD*RRTS as the independent variables) results in the same-signed coefficients as in table 2, but all coefficients are significant at the 1 per cent level.

Migrant Imaginings and Atlantic Canadian Regionalisms

Christopher J. Armstrong

"NATION" AND "MOBILITY" SEEM INCOMPATIBLE CONCEPTS. "NATION" is commonly understood as having to do with place and essence, and hence it appears to be an inherently static concept. What, after all, are the prominent icons of any nation but landscape, industry, and urban skylines? From literature and the popular imagination come narratives of typical, essential ways of life—static, folk, or folkish visions of "home." These images and stories find common ground in the idea of rootedness, which itself occupies an important place in definitions of the concept of "culture"—in the sense of "cultivation."[1] This paradigm of nation and culture valorizes spatial permanence, temporal continuity, and psychical emplacement. And it is accompanied by the belief that such conditions of stability are crucial for culture to develop and find expression—and hence for the nation to come into being.

Yet if, as we are often told, nations are modern inventions and their cultural traditions recent codifications, we are justified in asking whether modern conditions of mobility have anything to do with nation and nationality. We have not far to look for confirmation. Consider a salient example. What better fastens in our minds as a graspable and durable image of the *Canadian* nation than the speeding aerial camera greeting us at the opening and closing of every television broadcasting day, the camera which, to the booming strains of "O Canada," crosses the Atlantic coastline, St. Lawrence seaway, prairie seas of grain, piercing Rockies, and lush Pacific forests in under ten seconds? The mobile camera not only provides a series of concise, essential images of the nation, but is a crucial condition of the nation's possibility as an imaginary unity. We could work our way backwards in history and find other means by which the nation is constructed (by technology and its discourses, in institutions of national publishing and literary criticism, in networks of trade and commerce, and so on). But the point, for our purposes, is that we need not confine ourselves to nations here. For colonies, regions, or locales are also so constructed.

This paper is concerned with another kind of mobility, within a single region of Canada, and with the theme of mobility as captured by the "lens" of fiction. Specifically, I will discuss the importance of migration in the cultural imaginary of Atlantic Canada, and indicate briefly the shaping of that experience in works of fiction written during the postwar "modernization" of the region. Let us begin with some definitions and historical background.

"Cultural imaginary" refers to a matrix of images and ideas, symbols, and stories whose shape is codified in relatively distinct discursive form at specific historical moments to suit specific social needs. More of these particular needs shortly. For now, we will designate those historical actors who work on and within a cultural imaginary following Benedict Anderson's inclusive, anthropologically oriented definition of nationalism as "imagined community." According to Anderson, this entity is composed of all those people who, although perhaps never to meet, claim a communal belonging to a bounded collectivity[2]—to the "Maritimes" those who call themselves and their fellows "Maritimers"; to "Newfoundland" or "the Rock" those who call themselves "Newfoundlanders"; or simply to "Atlantic Canada" those who call themselves "Atlantic Canadians": such imagined communities name an important identification of self and other that, in popular and official varieties, is both celebrated and denounced as regionalism.

We should be careful about social position, especially what regionalism is often said to exclude: identities of class, gender, and race, as well as the unequal distribution of education across these and other social groups. For while all who imagine themselves members of this community have a role to play in its construction, a distinct group called "cultural intellectuals" have considerable power in controlling access to the means of representation. Moreover, they collect the dividends of cultural capital returned by their intellectual labour. This is not to limit the discussion to intellectuals in the traditional sense, or to imply that all such cultural activity can be understood in exclusively liberatory humanistic terms. Following John Frow,[3] we include workers in the institutions of education, politics, and various print and electronic media (which includes literature—and the university literature department, which is its key venue). And taking Frow's Foucauldian and Gramscian lead, we understand "cultural intellectuals" as engaging in social regulation: creating and maintaining values as well as securing consent for them in the community. The region, like the nation, is an imaginary (although not unreal or necessarily untrue) construction. It is the product of a complex interplay of media representation, historical experience, and popular consent, its image and attributes legitimated as common-sense resources of personal identity.

Migration is an important enabling condition and a key theme of the regionalism of Atlantic Canada, where, since the last decades of the nineteenth century, it has been the subject of familial remembrance and expectation, and, more recently, of government policy and scholarly interest. This paper focuses on the literary and historical dimensions of the postwar period. In the 1950s, at the height of postwar optimism and amid the considerable social and political institution-building of the "Atlantic Revolution," some 82,000 people left the region.[4] While these rates declined in the 1960s—another decade of intense region-building and social equalization—a considerable share of the young and the educated continued to leave.[5] Through the 1970s, rates of out-migration rose to equal almost half the provincial rates of natural population increase.[6]

In response to such trends, social science scholars of migration (who are not excluded from the category of "cultural intellectuals" defined above) have attempted to discover factors determining the quantity and quality of the flows of out-migrants across time and space. Patricia A. Thornton points out that "costs, inertia, distance, migration laws or inadequate information channels" have an important influence on these flows, and that two sets of economic forces operate here: "push" and "pull."[7] Adversity may "push" people from their homes en masse. By contrast, the promise of work or success elsewhere may "pull" the young, the educated, or the highly skilled toward cities or other centres of work. Migration, then, varies in its selectivity of skills and social groups. Moreover, its selection depends to a large extent on the conditions at the points of origin and of destination.

Does this—albeit crude—account of migration theory tell us much about the literary representations? Do literary texts shed light on theory? Migration theory tells us about the broad social and economic factors which determine migration. It does not allow us a glimpse into the personal dimensions of this experience—namely, what other factors of "push" or "pull" beside economic ones might determine out-migration or what attitudes might bear on one's decision to remain despite economic disadvantage. It needs to be pointed out that works of fiction have an exemplary role to play. Fiction can serve three related functions in this regard: security, adaptability, and intelligibility. The first may be seen as a variant on what Anthony Giddens calls "ontological security"[8]: through whatever means available, fiction tells that all is well in the world as it is; that we have a secure place in it. Closely related to this somewhat passive notion is what we might call fiction's adaptive function, an especially modern social need that it serves. By identifying and transmitting experience as story, fiction sharpens our ability to respond to an inherently dynamic modern scene. Hence, in adverse conditions, we can feel relatively "at home" in the world. Finally, fiction provides resources of identity—of ourselves and others. It tells us who or what we are and are not. This latter act of meaning-making conforms to what Adorno calls the "logic of identity."[9] It is a gesture of exclusion, the achievement of community by means of a criticism or rejection of an imagined "other."

What follows is an outline of two uses that the region's cultural intellectuals make of the migration experience. First, the migration experience is useful as a vehicle of social critique. Most often directed at what does not conform to one's cherished idea of "home" or "being at home," it is an act of binding that relies on exclusion or negation. Second, the migration experience serves as the occasion for evoking nostalgia, a lament for severed bonds of family and place that constitute a characteristically *modern anti-modernism*. These uses of migration experience can most profitably be viewed in the context of the region's coming to grips with modernization—namely, the forces of urbanization, commercialization, rising living and education standards, and social and physical mobility. In the first part of this paper, I survey a number of works which are notable for the stability of voice and value that informs the stance of either critique or lament. I then take a close look at a novel, Paul Bowdring's *The Roncesvalles Pass*,[10] in which such stability of distinction is lacking. In accounting for its absence in the novel, I hope to shed some light on questions of regionalism, nationalism, and cosmopolitanism in recent times.

Standing at the beginning of the period in question is Ernest Buckler's 1952 novel *The Mountain and the Valley*.[11] We are already at the centre of a modern paradox. We detect in Buckler's sensitive intellectual hero, David Canaan, all the rhetorical uses of migration experience. David is alternately nourished by the closeness and comfort of farm life in rural Nova Scotia and frustrated by its inane and ignorant culture.

He also displays a strong sense of estrangement from his compatriots, a sense of distance and difference in even the most tranquil of moments. What is most perplexing is that David has never left his rural home. As Glenn Willmott has persuasively argued, this paradox stems from the fact that urban centres—within and outside regions—extend their influence into the hinterlands, creating "invisible cities" in the countryside and in this case working in David a "double repulsion" from both "City" and "Country." David dislikes the city because, as Willmott puts it, the city is "founded on the inauthenticity of the commodity"; yet David has little patience for the country because it is characterized by a "poverty of self-reflection."[12]

To be sure, such conditions effect a symbolic and material displacement of local relations of power—a key notion for understanding the sense of political and cultural subordination that regionalism is sometimes meant to signify. Curiously, a number of the texts that I shall examine reveal that modernization need not be assumed to make things better. And even such liberatory humanist activities as reading and education become subtle, insidious means by which local (or regional) values are both symbolically and materially displaced. The region's cultural intellectuals and their fictional alter egos are implicated in this paradox in particularly conflicted ways. The educated David, for example, shares the city-dweller's consciousness, but both critically and painfully recognizes the differences between these worlds of country and city.

> He knew from the way she smiled and spoke that they were city people. . . . This was a bigger car than any of the town cars. These were the people the town people tried to imitate. . . . That automatic ease. . . . They took little bites out of whatever they looked at, lazily, without tasting.[13]

Moving ahead some twenty years, we find another Nova Scotian, Alistair MacLeod, paying attention to the experience of the migrant labourer as well as that of the educated intellectual and marking out the boundaries of geography and value that divide city from country, those who go and those who stay. Two stories from his 1976 collection *The Lost Salt Gift of Blood* deserve brief attention.[14] In "The Vastness of the Dark," the young adult narrator resolves to leave the exhausted coal mines of his Cape Breton home. His leaving is tied up with sexual maturation and boredom as well as economic determinants. But while speeding out of the region with a fast-talking Ontario salesman, he realizes that the car in which he is travelling is the symbol of a cruel reduction of the permanence and continuity of his community. A quick roadside stop allows for reflection, and suddenly the young narrator feels as if he were "in a sort of movable red and glass showcase,"[15] a figure that recalls MacLeod's frequent equation of modernity, commercialization, and sterility. "I am overwhelmed," he continues, "by the awfulness of oversimplification. For I realize that I have been guilty of it through this long and burning day but also through most of my yet young life."[16]

In the collection's title story, "The Lost Salt Gift of Blood," a young academic returns to the Newfoundland outport where his young son is being raised by grandparents. The narrator believes that the urban milieu in which he now makes his living is sterile, an unsuitable place for raising children. Here, a lament for the severed father–son bond is expressed in a literary parody of the conventions of tradition of Celtic balladry, one that nonetheless inscribes the modern experience in a long history of migrations and displacements: "And perhaps now I should go and say, oh son of my *summa cum laude* loins, come away from the lonely gulls and the silver trout and I will take you to the land of the Tastee Freeze where you may sleep till ten of nine."[17] There is a sense of nostalgia and bitterness here—of self-reproach and guilt as well.

If guilt is generated in those who *leave* the region in the work of MacLeod, there is an attitude of hostility for those who *return* in the work of New Brunswick writer David Adams Richards. Education is again a key theme. In the Miramichi communities of such novels as *Nights Below Station Street* (1988), *Evening Snow Will Bring Such Peace* (1990), and *For Those Who Hunt the Wounded Down* (1993),[18] the returning educated are often the sowers of discord. They possess the social and cultural capital of education (if not also of urban values), perhaps also government jobs; they hatch plans for instituting change—all seen to be disruptive of the local values of the community. Richards's heroes, by contrast, are rooted, intuitive, and spontaneous (mostly employed in labouring tasks). They seek change, if at all, in modest ways. And it is the conflict of a socially acceptable intellectual violence, usually legitimated by urban, educated values, and a physical violence or criminality that is played out in his novels.

Tensions evoked among return migrants and their former communities are also evident in the work of M. T. Dohaney. The heroine of Dohaney's 1992 novel *To Scatter Stones*,[19] Tess Corrigan, returns to her native Newfoundland to run as a candidate in a provincial by-election. The conflicts that arise here are not only those of a professional woman breaking with traditional roles and negotiating the public and private spheres of party politics and romance, but also the nativist suspicion of one who has been away too long.

What all of the foregoing works of fiction share is a certainty of voice and values. As well, all possess a sense of clear boundaries and differences between home and "away," between city and country: in short, sense of self and sense of place are relatively strong. We will now turn to an example of a novel of migration whose central consciousness is a deterritorialized intellectual dwelling in the metropolis. It has special importance in its representation of migration and a corollary significance for regional identity in the urgent late-twentieth-century context of nationalism and globalism.

Paul Bowdring's *Roncesvalles Pass* is a book about the urban exile of a group of Newfoundland migrants. Its setting is Toronto, probably during the economic boom of the early 1980s. Its narrator, Hugh Myers, is intelligent and well-read. He possesses a sense of irony tinged with melancholy, and his mind harbours an imagination that can evoke terror out of ordinary events. Myers guides us through a few days of his life—days in which he loses an unrewarding night watchman's job, broods on the fate of a troubled relationship, frequents the haunts of his fellow exiles, and finds a new job in a second-hand bookstore, all the while casting an artist's keen eye on his urban milieu.

It is a slim volume, perhaps not at all the "novel" its back-cover promotion claims it to be. Its "chapters" have the feel of the sketch or the vignette. A few appeared separately in the Newfoundland literary magazine *TickleAce* as many as four years prior to the novel's appearance in 1989 in the lists of Breakwater Books of St. John's. At a glance, it appears to be a highly structured work, with a prologue and an epilogue, three main sections identified with titles and roman numerals, and thirty "chapters," each titled and identified with arabic numerals.

What becomes quite clear after only a few chapters is that scrutinizing the minutiae of the urban environment is the novel's central interest. The ironies and significances of otherwise banal occurrences are offered up regularly; minute patchworks of allusion, wordplay, and symbol are constructed out of the insipid detritus of the urban landscape. Frequently, they are juxtaposed with memories of Newfoundland life, dreams or nightmares of some future or of some "elsewhere" of the imagination: the worlds of literature, film, music, history. Of the strategy of evocative detail, the novel's prologue is a case in point. Myers takes his old, brown-suede shoes (symbol of the migrant's interminable pavement-pounding) to a shop for repair; his right shoe has been making an inexplicable creaking noise. The shoe repairman, himself a Polish immigrant, offers a poetic, almost metaphysical discourse on shoes. "The noise is in the sole," he confirms, intimating the spiritual disquiet that haunts Myers and his fellow exiles.[20] As he continues his discourse, Myers senses a message of import; it flickers but then is gone, and the prologue ends in the banal but evocative. Myers buys some baked goods in the shop upstairs: "She folded the top closed with a quick wringing motion. The bag lay on the counter as I paid the girl at the cash register, the paper crackling in an effort to unfold itself."[21]

It may be significant that this prologue in fact prologues nothing of grand thematic significance—the notion of spiritual disquiet and the imminent "unfolding" of the tale are only verbal glimmers here. This suggests perhaps that the novel's structure of beginning (prologue), middle, and end (epilogue) is a ruse. Indeed, it is true that narration is somewhat of a problem in this novel, for what stands out in contrast to the novel's rich poetic moments is Myers's clumsy handling of aspects of narration that call for explanations of causality and larger complexes of social meaning. Narrative tasks are not handled with the deftness or intensity of the ironic observation. It is not that social meanings are inexplicable. Rather, such aspects come off sounding like narrative chores, things he would rather not have to labour at.

Paul Bowdring, who as author takes credit for the imaginary creations in this text, is a poet, the novel his first. These facts might explain the brilliant handling of the evocative detail marred by a clumsy narrativization of the experiential and social diversity of the city. But whatever the actuality, it can be argued that the novel is the product of a happy convergence of artistic talents and interests, deliberate writing strategies, and the nature of the urban environment itself. The urban environment rewards a sensibility attuned to odd mixture and juxtaposition, to playfulness and novelty, to jarring contrasts; it rewards Bowdring the lyric poet as well as his artistically minded protagonist, offering a panoply of strange sights and sounds, confounding and upsetting certainties and conventions. Some examples: a garishly dressed country-and-western singer in the subway, from whom "fringes hung . . . like strands of dried moss from the limbs of some dead ancient tree."[22] On a city streetcar, Myers eyes an old woman "muttering to herself in Italian. Her veined, liver-spotted hands clutch a black missal with a gold cross on the cover. Over her head, a telephone company ad said, 'Talk is cheap. Even cheaper on Sundays.'"[23] A distant figure in a window wiping condensation from the pane of glass mistaken by Myers for someone greeting him recalls an enigmatic remark by Stéphane Mallarmé.[24] The shoe shop to which Myers takes his protesting right shoe is, he notes, "oddly situated" beneath a bakery.[25] The effect is a curious mixture of the smells of leather and baked bread, Myers tells us.[26]

A recognition of the topsy-turvy requires a sense of order, a norm that is violated. And if baked bread recalls "home" (and, of course, "woman"), we have found one measure by which the disarray of the city can be gauged by this Newfoundland exile. Myers's Maritimes-born girlfriend, Claire, provides one such measure of value. Perhaps most telling is Claire's repudiation of fashion—that exemplary urban sign. She proudly wears clothes that Myers takes to be old-fashioned. She is not one for the cheap products of the city either: while buying a cup of coffee at a park-side kiosk, Myers recalls that Claire is not the kind of person who would ever drink from a styrofoam cup.[27] Significantly, Claire and Myers's relationship is on the rocks, in some zone of undecidability, and Claire herself is absent throughout the novel. That their relationship is troubled is confirmed for Myers by the arrival of a greeting card from her. On its cover is a reproduction of de Chirico's "Nostalgia of the Infinite." Strikingly unlike past cards—featuring "commonplace images," "no hidden messages or meanings"—this one throws Myers into interpretive vertigo. What is to be made of the two tiny silhouetted figures in the painting? he wonders. "Were they sharing some intimate secret? Meeting after a long absence? Or exchanging a last farewell?"[28] Symbolically, it seems, the regional standards of value that "woman" and "home" represent for Myers are absent.

As in other works of migration fiction—especially in Buckler and MacLeod—a critique of urban life and urban values is here. In Bowdring's novel, however, the critical tone ranges widely and uncertainly from the quietly ironic to the apocalyptic. At the apocalyptic end of the spectrum are references to Canadian poet Archibald Lampman's famous "The City of the End of Things." The poem seems to be meaningful to Bowdring's work not for its nineteenth-century moral outrage at the urban milieu, but for its apocalyptic imagery alone. Late-twentieth-century metropolitan massification, like its nineteenth-century counterpart, produces the apocalyptic daily, but fascination and imaginative response are what set Myers apart from Lampman. Just off a wearying night shift, Myers spies a headline that reads "165 expected to die this

Victoria weekend" and finds it "easy" on the crowded subway "to imagine that some great tragedy had already happened, and we had been the unfortunate ones."[29]

In the city, to be sure, there is plenty of grist for the embittered migrant's mill, for the regionalist dreaming of "home." And what better target than the excesses of the urban avant-garde? But once again, there is indecision. Myers and friends spend an afternoon visiting art galleries. At one installation, Myers tells us,

> I stood before a large roped off area of concrete floor that was littered with what looked like smashed pieces of pottery. This the catalogue informed me, was "the residue of a performance in which the artist had broken loose from a body shield of fired clay to reveal the imperfect female form beneath the idealized shell. The broken bits and pieces of this armour record the struggle to discover and accept one's individual identity."[30]

What is perhaps most striking here is that there is both irony and earnestness in this passage. One gets the impression that Myers assumes this catalogue entry parodies itself—that it is a self-caricature of the "artsy-fartsy." On the other hand, the self-reflexive quest for identity and belonging evoked here resonates strongly with the habitual brooding of Myers's mind. Myers (and Bowdring), I would suggest, cannot make the break from one or the other attitude.

Indeed, from even these brief glimpses into Bowdring's text, we can conclude that the novel is unsure of the response that it should make to the social and cultural scene of the late-twentieth-century city. This may be a strength—for uncertainty of response may imply an ethical stance against totalization; it may also portend an authentic encounter with an experiential-historical novelty. Yet such uncertainty may also be merely the sign of a stagnation in literary response to the city. In this connection, Italian critic Franco Moretti has entertained the hypothesis that compelling literary imaginings of urban life both began and ended in the nineteenth century. Even in the modernist "masters"—those agitated cosmopolitans Joyce, Eliot, Kafka, Borges, Pynchon—he insists,

> We find no new convention, but rather a hollowing out of former conventions. It is as if the developments of the literary image of the city were strictly of a negative and critical character: a model exists

which must be mangled and enervated, treated with irony, further and further removed—but never abandoned once and for all.[31]

It helps us little that Myers's points of reference are almost entirely high-modernist cultural intellectuals, whether in direct reference or in similarity of technique: E. J. Pratt, Mallarmé, Eliot, Baudelaire, and Joyce. There are other possibilities, of course. For one, the facts may be rooted in the peculiar desires that drive what we might call an "intellectual migrant economy." It is plausible, following Moretti, that the artistic migrant may have social needs whose satisfaction the city has readily met since the inception of city's modern form. Let us sketch some of the forces of "push" and "pull" on this educated, artistically inclined migrant in order to shed light on this peculiar economy.

Like the hero of Percy Janes's 1970 novel *House of Hate*, Juju Stone, Hugh Myers and his fellow exiles view their native Newfoundland as a place lacking in intellectual nourishment. During the course of narrating a dream, Myers recalls that the *Home Medical Guide* and the Bible were the only books he ever saw in his home: "Comprehensive maintenance manuals," he tells us, "for the life of the body and the soul. . . . The mind was left to forage for itself."[32] And those who leave inspire compulsive imaginings of escape in those who stay. Myers recalls also the story of his uncle Iv, who left when he was nineteen: "Growing up on an island within an island, walking along the rough beach in the evenings and staring out to sea, one mainland visible, the other only in my imagination, I thought often of Iv's departure. . . . I would clasp the consoling certainty of it while quietly planning my escape."[33]

Among Myers's circle of friends is Francis Wats Watson, poet-in-residence at the group's watering hole. In Wats, education has played a formative role that has all the unaccountability of a fall from grace. Wats confesses to Myers that he also wanted to get away from Newfoundland as a youth. Leaving was connected with learning. "Some asshole teachers who'd been to university and come back to the Bay with their two-bit summer school teaching certificates had filled my head with a lot of garbage."[34] Despite the ambivalence, perhaps even resentment, surrounding education, the places that facilitate pursuits of the mind most embody "home" for Wats. He recalls how he had once hitch-hiked as far as Wolfville, Nova Scotia, and then stumbled drunk and singing around the campus of the university: "I'll tell you," he says, "As I strolled around that leafy, manicured intellectual Garden of Eden, that gloomy old nostalgia really got to me right then and there. I felt an awful longing for those golden, peaceful fifties college days. Now how did I get all that shit in my head? I must have only been in elementary school by then."[35] The idea of the university as an intellectual garden of Eden to which one can always return remains a source of comfort. "Now I guess the place is just an ace-in-the-hole—as long as I know it's still there waiting, I feel all right."[36]

Paradise deferred indeed. Added to that is Wats's and Myers's confession that prolonged residence in the city has worked feelings of comfort: "The place is almost beginning to feel like home."[37] And this despite the fact that intellectual talent and employment opportunities find no convergence for these migrants. "There are two boring jobs for every person in this city," Wats announces,[38] resolving never again to be a "wageslave." This complaint, however, is no Marxist critique of capitalist exploitation. Rather, it is a plea for the intellectual autonomy that characters such as Wats feel that they deserve: freedom to cogitate and create in leisure. Indeed, the problem is that at the metropole, a surplus of jobs keeps one on call to employment officers. "How can you get any work done," Wats complains, "when they keep offering you these boring fucking jobs. You can't be unemployed for any more than a week and your mailbox is stogged with appointment cards."[39]

The artistic migrant economy is relatively clear. Clear also is the fact that it incorporates other attitudes suiting its world view. A scorn of materialism and a workingman's distrust of the officialese of government converge in Wats. He tells Myers that a turn-around in economic circumstances threatens to take him home to Newfoundland at the call of his father, who, because of a government grant, has given up fishing and moved into berry farming.

> He wrote me a letter "inquiring as to whether"—can you imagine my old man saying something like that!—inquiring as to whether I'd like to go into business with him. Sounds like he's developing some sort of dementia lingua—probably the result of exchanging too many letters with the government. Anyway he's got a big fish on the line—maybe a $50,000 grant from Rural Development—and he's about to become an EMPLOYER himself.[40]

If we were to subscribe to the idea of a Hegelian progression of consciousness, it would surely be worth suggesting that a new historical consciousness about "being" and "moving" in the world has arisen here, and that modifications in the meanings and values of "home" and "away" have taken shape before us. After all, this book is important for what it can no longer accept in the conventions of novels of country-to-city migration: moral outrage, the assumption of rural authenticity or virtue, clear boundaries of value between "home" and "away." The novel's consciousness is enthralled by urban society's strange sights, sudden illuminations—those things that the city produces daily—as now alienating, now fascinating spectacle. A new perspective on "being as moving" in the world then? Perhaps it is an old one. The novel's epigraph from Hugo of St. Victor suggests much:

> The man who finds his homeland sweet is still a tender beginning; he to whom every soil is as his native one is already strong; but he is perfect to whom the entire world is a foreign land.

Yet it would be wrong to herald as general the stoic cosmopolitanism that this passage implies. We are not all at home in the wide-world, not all "perfect"-because-estranged urban exiles, crossing borders, residing in-between. To be attentive to the staggering diversity of migrant experience is one of the cautions raised in *At Home in the World: Cosmopolitanism Now*, Timothy Brennan's recent critique of the current discourse of cosmopolitanism.[41] Intellectuals are frequently enjoined, says Brennan, to expose the inauthenticity of national or regional cultures and ethnic or religious particularisms and to celebrate cosmopolitan mobility in this era of globalism. Brennan not only ponders such unthinkable questions as the shared interests of the transnational corporation and the cosmopolitan intellectual, but also chides the latter for ignoring the crude and blatant discourses of global power. Moreover, he calls for continued attention to other economies of migration—those of migrant labourers, political exiles, refugees, victims of sexual abuse and identity persecution—that continue to be quotidian realities. He reminds us that older responses to the city remain: the condemnation of the excesses of the city (absence of community, "the decadent West"), maudlin expressions of nostalgia, and idealized counter-visions of home. These are historical expressions that have real force in the lives of migrants. Alongside such accounts, Bowdring's novel—which, although a "literary" response to the city, is cognizant of and relativized by these other experiences—is important for laying bare aspects of the artistic economy of migration. It is important also for suggesting the shifting relations between Canadian regional-national and global contexts.

Let me suggest some tentative conclusions in the latter area. First, in this age of intensified global mobility, we might be inclined to herald not only the end of the nation-state but also that of its subordinate regions. Region-and-nation has been, after all, a mutually defining tension in Canadian history, politics, and literature. On the evidence of Bowdring's novel, the idea of the Canadian city as an exclusively regional metropole has been replaced with the image of the multicultural world city. Myers and company are regional exiles who move through an urban landscape alongside migrants and exiles from around the globe. Second, identity—regional and national—seems also to be shifting: in Bowdring's novel, "home" has become less able to supply resources of personal identity that are relevant to the dynamism of modernity. We might, however, want to temper such conclusions given the artistic migrant economy that informs the vision here: how representative is Bowdring's vision or the attitudes of either Myers or Wats? Indeed, if globalism boils down to the problem of nations, regions, and communities making good nationalists, good regionalists, or just plain good neighbours, then one can expect that, in social, political, and cultural discourses, there will not be a further dissolution of identities but a reactionary solidification of these categories. Anxious about selling their souls to the transnational corporation and national and regional governments, their cultural intellectuals will invest in shoring up those identities now inserted into the shifting and dynamic global networks of trade and information. Manuel Castells, for one, has recently noted that contemporary societies are reconfiguring around "a bipolar opposition" of global networks and "historically rooted, particularistic identities."[42] Similarly, Jocelyn Létourneau has dubbed this "postnational," "postkeynesian" global world order "the migrant economy," arguing that both people and capital can be understood in terms of the new socio-economic categories of *"migrants"* and *"enracinés."*[43]

The consequences of the question "Should I stay or should I go?" have never been more pressing or complex. As for the writers and artists, they are, in the end, easily satisfied with the one or the other. To return to our tale, Myers has found a sort of home at the novel's end, one that provides a modicum of comfort, some mild satisfaction of his ideal community. He works in a used-book store. Curiously, it is an establishment that is made to sound more like a refugee shelter for migrant books than a business—let alone a profitable one. There are "so many books coming into the shop and so few going out," Myers says. But we continue "to buy and stamp" and try "to find a home for them" near where they belong.[44] Myers and Mr Umani, the store's owner, share a connection with books which seems to be a key to their exile identities: "He was an immigrant on a street full of immigrants, in a city of displaced persons; but the nature of his exile seemed to be of a different sort altogether. He had the look of a man without a homeland— a man who would have felt like an exile even in his native land."[45]

Wherever they are, the bookish types—the artists—are united by their outsider status. The same goes for Wats, who by contrast is on the move, this time to Iceland, "poet's paradise." He is pursuing an impossible, imaginary "community of imagination." In Iceland, "Writers are actually paid to write, no questions asked," he tells Myers. "They read and write and publish more books than anywhere on earth." The exaggeration here is proportional to the magnitude of the desire to belong that underlies Wats's sarcasm: In Iceland "everyone writes," he insists, and "[t]hey worry about those who don't."[46]

Notes

1. Raymond Williams, *Keywords: A Vocabulary of Culture and Society*, rev. ed. (New York: Oxford University Press, 1983), 87.
2. Benedict Anderson, *Imagined Communities: Reflections on the Origins and Spread of Nationalism*, rev. ed. (London and New York: Verso, 1991), 6–7.
3. John Frow, *Cultural Studies and Cultural Value* (Oxford: Oxford University Press, 1995).
4. E. R. Forbes and D. A. Muise, eds., *The Atlantic Provinces in Confederation* (Toronto: University of Toronto Press/Fredericton: Acadiensis Press, 1993), 384.
5. Ibid., 458.
6. Ibid., 461.
7. Patricia A. Thornton, "The Problem of Out-Migration from Atlantic Canada, 1871–1921." *Acadiensis* 15, no. 1 (Autumn 1985): 10.
8. Anthony Giddens, *The Consequences of Modernity* (Cambridge: Polity Press, 1990), 92.
9. Theodor Adorno, *Negative Dialectics*, trans. E. B. Ashton (New York: Continuum, 1973).
10. Paul Bowdring, *The Roncesvalles Pass* (St. John's, Nfld.: Breakwater Books, 1989).
11. Ernest Buckler, *The Mountain and the Valley* (1952) (Toronto: McClelland and Stewart, 1970).

12. Glenn Willmott, "On Postcolonial Modernism: The Invisible City," *The Mountain and the Valley*. *American Review of Canadian Studies* 25, no. 2–3 (Summer/Autumn 1995): 301.
13. Buckler, *Mountain*, 167.
14. Alistair MacLeod, *The Lost Salt Gift of Blood* (Toronto: McClelland and Stewart, 1976).
15. Ibid., 48.
16. Ibid., 49.
17. Ibid., 69.
18. David Adams Richards, *Evening Snow Will Bring Such Peace* (Toronto: McClelland and Stewart, 1990); idem, *For Those Who Hunt the Wounded Down* (Toronto: McClelland and Stewart, 1993); idem, *Nights Below Station Street* (Toronto: McClelland and Stewart, 1988).
19. M. T. Dohaney, *To Scatter Stones* (Charlottetown: Ragweed Press, 1992).
20. Bowdring, *Roncevalles Pass*, 10.
21. Ibid.
22. Ibid., 35
23. Ibid., 55.
24. Ibid., 71–2.
25. Ibid., 9.
26. Ibid., 10.
27. Ibid., 14.
28. Ibid., 70.
29. Ibid., 15.
30. Ibid., 52.
31. Franco Moretti, "Homo Palpitans: Balzac's Novels and Urban Personality," in *Signs Taken for Wonders: Essays in the Sociology of Literary Forms*, trans. Susan Fischer, David Forgacs, and David Miller (London and New York: Verso, 1988), 128–9.
32. Bowdring, *Roncevalles Pass*, 56.
33. Ibid., 24.
34. Ibid., 49.
35. Ibid., 49–50.
36. Ibid., 50.
37. Ibid., 48.
38. Ibid., 47.
39. Ibid., 48.
40. Ibid.
41. Timothy Brennan, *At Home in the World: Cosmopolitanism Now* (Cambridge and London: Harvard University Press, 1997).

42. Manuel Castells, *The Rise of Network Society* (London: Blackwell, 1996), 3.

43. Jocelyn Létourneau, *Les années sans guide: Le Canada à l'ère de l'économie migrante* (Quebec City: Boréal, 1996).

44. Bowdring, *Roncevalles Pass*, 112.

45. Ibid., 113.

46. Ibid., 125.

Songs of Love and Longing: Songs of Migration

Karen Clavelle

I'm leaving Loch Leven
I'm leaving this heaven
I'm going to a foreign shore
My fortune for to seek.[1]

SONGS, LIKE POETRY, WRITTEN FOR A VARIETY OF REASONS, EXPRESS AND often poignantly expose sentiments held close to the heart. For some of us, songs speak the unspeakable—express the desires or heartache that we are otherwise perhaps unwilling to acknowledge even to ourselves, never mind reveal to others. Perhaps history should begin with the voices of the people who, one by one, together, form a chorus of what becomes history. We tend to read, or in the past have read and generally accepted, history as a litany of big events or discoveries: military, scientific, medical, technological, and political. We have encountered battles won and lost, named famous people living and dead, reported events in the lives of tyrants, saviours, saints, and sinners. But every one of those "discoveries," without exception, arises out of the lives of ordinary people. Those common people, whose lives are hidden, become part of the collective stories that they helped to shape through their expressions of love and loss, joy and pain. It is to their experience that we now turn.

The words that introduced this paper, *I'm leaving Loch Leven*, express a sentiment surely felt by thousands upon thousands of immigrants, wrapped in little more than hope, as they bid tearful farewell to their homeland. Although most of those who left would never again return home, neither would they ever forget their ties to the homeland, as many of these songs indicate.[2]

Why people would leave home is a complex question to which there are myriad answers: the pursuit of adventure or employment, fear of persecution, avoidance of political troubles, family problems, love or pursuit of it, and combinations of these. What begs an answer is: how do they feel upon arriving in a new place? What about those they left behind? How do people cope with feelings of love and longing, joy and grief? What do the very simple lyrics of some of their poetry and melodies reveal?

The approach of this paper is literary, rather than ethnological or historical; its primary concern is to identify the position of the speaker and the emotions revealed in the text of each piece. The appendix to this paper contains the words to all the songs cited. Speculation about the songs, and the people behind them, has also been included.

The issue of who writes the songs and for what reasons—to express loss, hope, or a sense of being relatively "okay"—relates to the experience of being exiles, emigrants, or expatriates. These categories are important because the element of choice, which informs the distinctions, has a great deal to do with one's happiness or potential happiness abroad. Table 1 names in two ways the songs examined, and allows us to begin classifying. The categories, for our purposes, are defined as follows:

Exiles: those forced to leave their homes for reasons beyond their control; in a position of assent as opposed to consent. They are forced to leave and to resettle. *If their skills are inadequate in the new world, they have little choice but to adapt.* Returning is not an option.

Emigrants: those who choose to leave and resettle, possibly for political or economic reasons which are a factor in whether they return; the position is one of consent. *If their skills are inadequate they adapt, perhaps banking on returning home at some point.*

Expatriates: those who chose freely to leave, and may as freely return. *If their skills are inadequate they adapt; if they are unhappy, they leave.*

Table 2 attempts a loose classification of the pieces as love songs or laments; speculates on whether they were written for entertainment or historical purposes; and infers the gender, age, and impulse behind each song.

We begin an examination of the songs with *Charming Sally Greer*, a mid-nineteenth-century tale of a young Ulster Scot turned out of his parents' home and sent to America to seek his fortune in an apparently unveiled attempt to force him away from his sweetheart. This is a case of exile. Although the lad leaves home over love, he clearly gets adventure in the bargain. En route to Quebec, he spends twelve days ship-

Table 1a

Position	Exile	Immigrant	Expatriate
Left behind	– Red River Valley – The Eviction of the Highlanders	– There in Windsor	
Happy to Leave Happy to Stay		– I'm Leaving Loch Leven – Mamma, Mamma – The Wilno Boys	– Your Country Is Love
Happy to leave Unhappy to arrive	– Farewell My Homeland	– Song of America	
Unhappy to leave Happy to stay		– I'm Leaving Loch Leven	
Unhappy to leave Unhappy to arrive	– The Gloomy Forest – On the Other Side of the Atlantic – Un Canadien Errant	– I Remember That Morning – Scarborough Settler's Lament	
Unhappy to leave Happy to return	Charming Sally Greer	– The Wind Does Blow – Oh Canada, Oh Oh Canada – Song for Valparaiso	

Table 1b

	Loss/nostalgia	Hope	Contentment
Exile	– Farewell My Homeland – The Eviction of the Highlanders – Un Canadien Errant	I'm Leaving Loch Leven	
Immigrant	– Oh Canada, Oh Canada – Song of America – On the Other Side of the Atlantic – I Remember That Morning – Scarborough Settler's Lament	– The Wilno Boys	– Mamma, Mamma – Rent Money
Expatriate			– Song for Val- paraiso Your Country Is Love

Table 2. Songs of love and longing: Songs of migration

Song Title Narrator:	Sex	Age	Time	Voice	Loss	Hope	Comfort
Canadian Boat Song	M	M,	10+	WE	EXILE		
Charming Sally Greer LO/LA/EN	M	Y	1YR	I /WE	EXILE		
Eviction of the Highlanders H/LA	M	M	N/A	WE	EXILE		
Farewell My Homeland LA	M/F	Y-M	N/A	I	EXILE		
The Gloomy Forest LA	M	M	–1YR	I /WE	EXILE		
I'm Leaving Loch Leven EN	M	Y	N/A	I /WE		EMIG	EXPAT
I Remember that Morning LA	F	M	10+	I	EMIG		
Mamma, Mamma EN	M	Y	N/A	I	N/A		
Many Are Strong among Strangers	M	M	10+	I	EMIG		
Oh Canada, Oh Canada LA	M	Y-M	1+	I	EMIG		
On the Other Side of the Atlantic	F	M	N/A	I	EMIG		
Red River Valley EN	M/F	Y-M	N/A	I	N/A		
Rent Money EN	F/M	Y-M	N/A	I /WE			EMIG
Scarborough Settler's Lament EN	M	M	10+	I /WE	EMIG		
Song of America LA	M	M	10+	I	EMIG		
Song for Valparaiso LO	M	Y-M	–5	I	EMIG		EXPAT
There in Windsor H	M	Y-M	N/A	I	EMIG		
The Wilno Boys EN	M	Y	N/A	I /WE		EMIG	
The Wind Does Blow LA	M	Y-M	N/A	I		EMIG	
Un Canadien Errant	EN/LA	M	Y	N/A	N/A	EXILE	
Whether I Walk or Stand	F	Y-M	N/A	I /WE		EMIG	
Your Country Is Love EN/LO	M	Y	–5	I		EXPAT	

Key

Age: Y–M: young to mature (assumed)
Time: Length of time away from home (assumed, in years)
N/A: songs assumed to represent people left behind or planning to leave

Purpose of song:
LO: love song
EN: entertainment
LA: lament
H: history

Voice: I/WE indicates whether the speaker speaks alone or on others' behalf
Loss/Hope/Comfort (in combination with exile, emigrant or expatriate) indicates the impulse and/or position out of which the song is assumed to have been written

Exile: one who assents to leave
Expat: Expatriate, one who chooses freely to come and go
Emig: Emigrant, one who consents to leave

wrecked on the Island of St Paul north of Cape Breton Island. Four of the eighteen immigrants on board the *Rose of Aberdeen* from Belfast have drowned; the survivors are left with no more than the clothes on their backs. But in this tale of true love, experience seems only to have strengthened the narrator's resolve to return to his sweetheart. The narrator, despite leaving her behind, and despite being shipwrecked, losing all his possessions and money, and spending twelve days out in the open on an uninhabited island in the Gulf of St. Lawrence, writes a surprisingly good-humoured song. *Charming Sally Greer* includes signs that mark the narrator's departure, such as the reference to *verdant Ireland; my heart was with my girl;* and *I'm in hopes to be back . . . in the arms of my charming Sally Greer*:

> *Charming Sally Greer*
> *Good people all both old and young, my age is twenty-three,*
> *My parents turned me from their door unto A-mer-I-cay,*
>
> *All from that verdant Ireland where first my breath I drew,*
> *They forced me to A-mer-I-cay my fortune to pursue.* [K 8–9]

Although the song may appear to be the expression of a single voice, that of a young male narrator in love, it comes to represent, at least in part, other young men who may have left sweethearts behind. Sally Greer comes to represent, in some readings at least, those to whose arms they long to return.

Sally Greer, lucky Sally, has a sweetheart, but the following song, in translation from an older Lithuanian dialect, addresses the age-old problem of women, who, for whatever reason, do not. In this song, the speaker urges her "sisters" to abandon their unhappiness and head for the new world, where, she dreams, awaiting them are bachelors who live in happiness and abundance. As in the earlier example, the narrator apparently speaks for herself, but in addressing her sisters, who may as easily be figurative as biological, she may be voicing common concerns. The voice at the end of the song makes a collective suggestion: "Let's talk [things] over. . . ."

> *Whether I walk or stand, lie down or get up, I always find myself thinking*
> *About the problems of the girls in Lithuania.*
>
> *What a state they are in . . . how many troubles girls have to suffer.*

They have to stand a lot of gossip, plenty of ridicule,
Still unmarried, they suddenly notice that they are getting old.

One buys the big books and prepares herself for a holy life,
But there isn't a thing to do—it's so hard to get a husband.

Overseas, at the far side of the world there are plenty of bachelors,
Who live in happiness and await us.

So, let's talk it over, sisters, and travel to them,
When there, each one might get a husband. [K 20]

Though being in exile is hardly an issue in this song, as no one has yet gone anywhere, the position of the narrator is close to that of an emigrant. If she is to leave, it will be for the express purpose of getting a husband, a reason closely concerned with economics. Clearly, the act of leaving evokes thoughts of loss on both sides of the ocean for various reasons.

For some, embarking on the voyage brings its own pain. *Adiey mayn Faterland* reveals an almost untouchable depth of sorrow, as it evokes a tremendous sense of loss in lyric and melody alike. For the narrator, these are the only the words emotions will permit:

Lang, lang, bin ich geshtanen,
Bey dem beg fun yam.
Die shiff geyt op fun danen
Adiey mayn faterland.
Adiey, adiey, adiey, adiey,
Adiey mayn faterland. (x2) [K 7]

For a long time, the narrator says, *I waited at the ocean's edge. The boat is now departing. Farewell, my homeland.* It is undoubtedly a fact that Canada has been, in no small part, settled by many emigrant people in exile, who, God knows, would have preferred never to have left home in the first place. We can hear lamentation, too, in the following translation:

I have left my country, my dear, lovely Hungary. As I looked back halfway through my journey, from my eyes the tears were falling. Sorrow's my lunch, sorrow's my dinner, unhappy is my every hour, I look up at the starry sky, I cry underneath it enough. Oh my God, please provide shelter, I've grown tired always hiding in strange lands, my restless living, night and day, my endless weeping. [K 22]

Laments, though, are by no means exclusive to Eastern Europeans.[3] Based on the melody of *Lord Lovat's Lament*, the words of *Fuadach nan Gàidheal* (*The Eviction of the Highlanders*), by Henry Whyte, tell what it was like in the Highlands after the evictions that took place in the aftermath of "The Forty-Five."[4] Speaking on behalf of the people left behind, the narrator, who keenly feels the impact of the departures, poignantly expresses in the final verse how lonely it is in the aftermath:

High in the heavens the lark trills its tuneful song,
With not a soul to listen as it soars ever upwards;
Those light-hearted generous people will never, never return
They have been scattered forever like chaff in a day of wind. [K 28–9]

Thoughts of leaving home, for whatever reason, are not always entertained with sorrow, however. Most likely "writing" for entertainment, in *Mamma, Mamma*, the narrator light-heartedly plays with the idea of emigration.

Mamma, Mamma dammi cento lire
Che in America voglio andar. (x2)

Cento lire ti voglio dare
All'America non vi andare
Cento lire te gli darei
Non America voglio andar [K 12].

Mamma, Mamma, the speaker begs, *give me a hundred lire/For to America I want to go.* And she replies: *A hundred lire I can give you/But in America, I don't want you to go!* If the narrator in the above song were to leave, he would most likely set out alone, as was quite common at the turn of the century. Men frequently left, intending to send for their sweethearts or their wives and families at a later date, or to return home having made their fortune. Indeed, many of them did return, but, undoubtedly, problems were occasioned by the separations. The following humorous account of leaving a wife behind touches on the serious problem of how relationships could be strained by separation. But it is not just that: *Viter Vîye* (*The Wind Does Blow*) addresses the prospects of being remembered, and ultimately returning home. While the narrator obviously speaks for himself, he also speaks for everyone who has left a lover behind:

> *The wind does blow, the wind does blow,*
> *and rustles up the blackthorn;*
> *In whose care, oh friend,*
> *shall I leave my wife?*
> *Leave, oh, comrade,*
> *leave her in my care,*
> *I'll look after her*
> *even better than you.*
> *Do so, oh comrade,*
> *Do look after my wife;*
> *When I return from Canada,*
> *We'll drink up and celebrate with whisky.* [K 44]

Until the middle of this century, to travel from many parts of the world meant having little or no communication with those left at home. *Oh Canada, Canada* expresses the touching despair of someone on the move, able neither to send mail nor to receive it. The comic element in this song serves to offset the poignant and sad truth expressed in longing for news from home:

> *Somewhere my beloved is writing letters to me;*
> *She writes and writes in very small letters,*
> *And when I read it I shed bitter tears.*
> *I would write a letter but I have no paper*
> *I would take it to the Post Office, but I don't know the way.*
> *I might find the way, but I don't speak the language,*
> *Oh, God, dear God, what am I to do?*
> *I shall write a letter but in fine script*
> *I shall send it with the mighty wind.*
> *I stood on the bridge for one month and an hour*
> *I was waiting for a letter from my beloved family.* [K 47–8]

Although many songs clearly express regret over leaving home, none are so bitter as *The Gloomy Forest*, composed by the Scots bard John McLean in about 1819. The eighteen stanzas of the song address many of the problems confronting new immigrants. We should probably be thankful that McLean did not have today's media at his disposal; if he had, emigrants would never have left home! McLean's is a cautionary tale warning against the false promises and deceit practised by colonial agents and describing the hardships he endured. But he had a handicap much larger, perhaps, than did other emigrants. He himself may have been the greatest impediment to his own ability to accept the place in which he had arrived. He was obviously alone and evidently, at least at the time of writing, short of both physical and inner strength, and possibly even of the desire required to keep "body and soul" together. McLean bemoans the fact that his poetic talents have forsaken him, that he cannot express himself fully. He is right. Of course he would lose his language, or at the very least, find it altered in some way. He arrives in Canada with a language that does not fit. In *The Journals of Susanna Moodie*, Margaret Atwood's Susanna Moodie addresses exactly this disparity. Is *here* really contrary to nature (and *there* not?) or is it that McLean's (or Moodie's) expectations have been informed by another place?[5]

In 1819, land clearances would likely have been the primary reason for McLean's migration, and, consequently, would have had some bearing also on his willingness to embrace a new place. And what about grief and feelings of loss of place, of identity? This was a man in exile, physically and spiritually, something that Atwood addresses: "A person who is 'here' but would rather be somewhere else is an exile or a prisoner; a person who is 'here' but *thinks* he is somewhere else is insane."[6] Although McLean comes to love Canada, at the point of writing, he *is* clearly an exile. Here are his words in translation from the Gaelic:

> *I am alone in the dreary forest*
> *My thoughts are anxious, my heart downcast;*
> *I have found this place so contrary to nature*
> *That all my poetic talents have forsaken me.*
> *It prevents me from fashioning my songs*
> *My Gaelic is no longer as fluent as it once was*
> *In the old country across the sea.*[7]

The alien nature of this new land, he claims, prevents him from writing his song. It does not entirely succeed in discouraging him, however, for he is still able to write seventeen more verses of this lament, although these will suffice here:

It's no wonder that I am sad
Living here on the far side of the mountains
In the middle of a wilderness by Barney's River
Where only potatoes are made to grow;
Before I will have succeeded in planting and raising a crop
And clearing the terrible wood
By the strength of my own arms only
My health will have failed while my children are still young.

. . . .When winter comes and dark dismal weather
The snow piles up as high as the branches of trees
And thick and deep it comes past your knees. . . .

When summer comes and the month of May
The sun's heat leaves me faint;
But it revives all the animals
Which lie dormant in their dens;
The fierce bears rise out and do great damage to the herd,
And the biting black fly exuding venom
Wounds me repeatedly with its sharp pointed lance. [K 56–8]

The voice in the next song provides considerable contrast to the one we hear in *The Gloomy Forest*. In the 1860s, Wilno, Ontario, became the site of the first Polish settlement in Canada. For the Polish writer of *The Wilno Boys*, who, unlike McLean, is not alone, the conditions would have been no less vigorous or trying: cold winters, hot summers, black-flies, and longing for friends. Two crucial differences emerge, however: first, the men from Wilno were well fed at the farm, which McLean may not have been (remember his comment about growing potatoes?); second, camaraderie goes a long way in times of duress. The men of Wilno had each other; McLean was arguably alone. With hardship in mind, then, consider the words to *The Wilno Boys*, an adaptation of an Ottawa Valley lumbering song, *The Chapeau Boys*. A word of explanation: the turkey in the song is the bandanna tied to a stick used to carry shanty boys' belongings. In a song that appears to have been written for personal enjoyment, as well as perhaps entertainment, the narrator speaks with pleasant familiarity ("you know my name") and in a style that is inclusive of both the Wilno boys and the audience, possibly people in his home community. This narrator, evidently a healthy, energetic, good-humoured young man, speaks from the position of someone who is both immigrant to and, as seasonal worker, migrant within Canada. His absence from home is arguably voluntary, as much as having to work away from home can be said to be voluntary, but he is not an exile, and that may, at least in part, figure in the overall tone of his song. This is a person who is comfortable where he is; he has a good time while he works, but he looks forward to going home.

The language of the song, "Polish English," with a charm all its own, lends a particularly interesting flavour. The song begins with a single-voice "I," but quickly switches to "we." The verb tenses and the use of pronouns are wild in their wobbling, and beg a closer look. Consider these lines:

> *Now when on your patience* **I** *[singular subject]* **beg** *[present tense] to intrude*
> *We [plural subject]* **hired** *[past tense] with Fitzgerald, he was agent for Booth . . .*
> *We* **packed** *[past tense] up our turkeys on [the] first of July*
> *Bronas Raczkowski, Joe Shalla and I;*
> *On the straightway to Pembroke our luggage we* **take**, *[present tense]*
> *There we* **boarded** *[past tense] the Empress and* **sailed** *up the lake.*

The Wilno Boys stands out from the others in this collection, in part because it has such character and charm. It also provides a nice counter to so many more melancholy laments.

> *The Wilno Boys*
> *I'm a jolly old fella, you know my name,*
> *I live at Wilno the village of fame;*
> *For singing and dancing and all kinds of fun,*
> *Sure the boys from Wilno they can't be outdone.*
>
> *When the drive will be over, I wish it was soon,*
> *So we'd intend to go home on the first week of June;*
> *And if God spares our lives to get home in the spring,*
> *And we'll make our hall at Wilno to ring.* [K60–2]

Whereas "the Wilno boys" expressed no complaints about the conditions they faced, the speaker in a Yiddish piece, to which we now turn, grouses good-naturedly about lack of money—one of the past, and continuing, motivating forces in the settlement of Canada. We could all take a lesson from *Rent Money* on how to deflect a little of the stress in our own lives, by perhaps remembering the laughter that comes from music itself. Part of the appeal of this piece lies in the irrepressible spirit of the Klezmer-like melody.

> *Rent Money*
> *Rent money, oy, oy, oy, oy,*
> *Rent money we must pay*
> *Rent money, a policeman!*
> *We must pay rent money.*
>
> *The superintendent arrives*
> *And takes off his hat to you*
> *But if you don't pay your rent,*
> *He hangs out a sign "To Let."*
>
> *The landlord comes in*
> *With his thick cane,*
> *But if you don't have your rent to pay,*
> *He puts your beds out on the street.*
>
> *Why should I pay him the rent*
> *If the kitchen is in disrepair?*
> *Why should I pay him the rent*
> *If I don't have what to cook on?* [K 78–80][8]

The remaining songs are primarily expressions of nostalgia, longing for friends and family, but longing, perhaps equally, for a lost sense of place. If we have never emigrated, can we ever know what it is like to leave home? The Lithuanian song *On the Other Side of the Atlantic* does not tell of physical difficulty, but reveals the narrator's tremendous sense of being out of place. This song catalogues a more personal account of the emigrant's feeling of loss, particularly of a language that is not understood in the new place. *Here,* [she writes] *I have no friends of mine/ Nor do I hear the songs I used to sing,/And even if I sang them, who would understand?/ When my heart aches, who would feel for me?* [K 105–6] Another Lithuanian song, *I Remember that Morning,* holds a memory of the narrator's childhood, of a time in which she recalls her mother speaking: *Overseas,*[she said] *a land of gold, / Where no one knows, no one sees the hardships.* The narrator continues:

"Tell us, dear Mother, tell us, Old One
Where are the mountains of gold; where is this happiness?" (x2)
"Dear Daughter mine, my beloved,
In Lithuania, in the homeland, there is true happiness." (x2) [K 113–14]

The mother's view is opposed to the one expressed in an alternative version of the previously cited Italian song, in which the mother disputes the myth of "unlimited" prosperity in the new world: *Don't tell me,* [she says] *that there they eat fish in the sea.*

Ieremia Fîrtàiasu, the writer of *Many Are Strong Among Strangers,* comments about his song as follows: *I wrote it in 1917, in a forest. Nobody knows it . . . . Oh, yes, I sang it many times, when we had parties, mostly the old people. The young ones don't know about heartaches. They didn't leave behind brothers, parents . . .* [K 123]. Anyone who emigrates knows about heartache. Children and grandchildren born to immigrants may know more about loss of place than we might guess. The first and second generations, those born in the new place, are also somewhat out of place. They live in a world of conflicting cultures, quite different from the world of the ancestral family, and quite apart from it. If the immigrants leave parents, brothers, and sisters behind, then their children enjoy no extended family. They have to struggle in their own way to develop a sense of place, something which is unlikely to have been an issue at all for the generation who left home in the first place.

With few exceptions, then, these emigrant songs are not those of "high culture." They are not "composed" songs meant for silent audiences in auditoriums or concert halls—or lecture halls, either, for that matter. They are not particularly literary, nor do they attempt to present themselves as such. These are songs of the people who shared them, for whatever reasons. They are songs of experience, almost completely without guile. Whatever lack of literary merit they might reveal, they do provide insight for those of us who have not had the experience of immigration, and strike chords for those of us who have.

This paper will close, then, with the lines to a poem, *The Canadian Boat Song,*[8] first printed in *Blackwood's Magazine* in 1829 and attributed to John Galt. The narrator speaks for all emigrants in his poignant expression of longing for home, the feeling stressed in the simple and quietly objecting chorus which finishes each stanza. Fair is this world, it says, but this is not home:

Listen to me, as when ye heard our father

Sing long ago the song of other shores—
Listen to me, and then in chorus gather
All your deep voices as ye pull your oars:
Fair these broad meads—these hoary woods are grand;
But we are exiles from our father's land.

From the lone sheiling of the misty island
Mountains divide us, and the waste of seas—
Yet still the blood is strong, the heart is Highland,
And we in dreams behold the Hebrides:
Fair these broad meads—these hoary woods are grand;
But we are exiles from our father's land.

We ne'er shall tread the fancy-haunted valley
Where 'tween the dark hills creeps the small clear stream,
In arms round the patriarch banner rally,
Nor see the moon on royal tombstones gleam:
Fair these broad meads—these hoary woods are grand;
But we are exiles from our father's land.

Appendix

Note: The source for songs with asterisks is Fowke, *The Penguin Book of Canadian Folk Songs* (see note 2); the source for all other songs is Karp, *Many are Strong* (see note 1).

Charming Sally Greer
Dear people all both old and young, my age is twenty-three,
My parents turned me from their door unto A-mer-I-cay,
All from that verdant Ireland where first my breath I drew,
They forced me to A-mer-I-cay my fortune to pursue.

The reason they transported me I intend to let you hear,
'Twas because I would not break the vow from the girl I love so dear,
'Twas because I would not break the vow from the girl I love so dear,
That girl I love so tenderly, that charming Sally Greer.

'Twas on board the Rose of Aberdeen from Belfast we bore down,
With eighteen immigrants on board, 'twas to Quebec we were bound,

We were long time on the ocean but no danger did I fear,
For my heart was with my girl I left, my charming Sally Greer.

Whether I Walk or Stand

Whether I walk or stand, lie down or get up, I always find myself thinking about the
problems of the girls in Lithuania. What a state they are in . . . how many troubles
girls have to suffer. They have to stand a lot of gossip, plenty of ridicule, still unmar-
ried, they suddenly notice that they are getting old. One buys the big books and
prepares herself for a holy life, but there isn't a thing to do, it's so hard to get a
husband. Overseas, at the far side of the world there are plenty of bachelors, who live
in happiness and await us. So, let's talk it over, sisters, and travel to them. When
there, each one might get a husband.

I Have Left My Country

I have left my country, my dear, lovely Hungary. As I looked back halfway through
my journey, from my eyes the tears were falling. Sorrow's my lunch, sorrow's my
dinner, unhappy is my every hour, I look up at the starry sky, I cry underneath it
enough. Oh my God, please provide shelter, I've grown tired always hiding in
strange lands, my restless living, night and day, my endless weeping.

The Eviction of the Highlanders

How sad I am lamenting the fate of the country,
And the old solid stock of courage and renown;
Landlords have evicted them far across the seas,
Their land has been taken from them and been given up to the deer.

What a shameful thing it is, to see a strong race
"Being expelled across the ocean like useless human rejects,"
White deer now roam over that once beautiful land
Nettles dominate gardens and grass hides the ruined dwellings.

Where once many men lived with their wives and families,
Today you can find in their place only cheviot;
By the cattlefold you see no milkmaid carrying her cow-fetter
And no fair-haired youth tending the white-shouldered cattle.

High in the heavens the lark trills its tuneful song,
With not a soul to listen as it soars ever upwards;

Those light-hearted generous people will never, never return
They have been scattered forever like chaff in a day of wind.

Farewell, My Homeland
For a long time I waited at the ocean's edge.
The boat is now departing.
Farewell, my homeland

The Scarborough Settler's Lament*
Away wi' Canada's muddy creeks and Canada's fields of pine!
Your land of wheat is goodly land, but ah! it isna mine!
The healthy hill, the grassy dale, the daisy-spangled lea
The purling crag and craggy linn, auld Scotia's glens, gie me.

Oh I wad like again to hear the lark on Tinny's hill,
And see the wee bit gowany that blooms beside the rill.
Like banished Swiss who views afar his Alps wi' longing e'e
I gaze upon the morning star that shines on my countrie.

Nae mair I'll win by Eskdale Pen, or Pentland's craggy cone
The days can ne'er come back again of thirty years that's gone
But fancy oft at midnight hour will steal across the sea
Yestreen amid a pleasant dream I saw the auld countries.

Each well known scene that met my view brought childhood's joys to mind,
The blackbird sang on Tushy Linn the song he sang lang syne
But like a dream time flies away, again the morning came,
And I awoke in Canada, three thousand miles "frae hame."

Mamma, Mamma
Mamma, Mamma dammi cento lire
Che in America voglio andar. (x2)

Cento lire ti voglio dare
All'America non vi andare
Cento lire te gli darei
Non America voglio andar.

There in Windsor
There in Windsor in the valley (2x)
Comes a choompa with wagons (2x)
Comes a choompa with a whistle (2x)
I climb it singing
My parents remain crying.

The saloons are empty (2x)
As the young fellows left. (2x)

Because of the problems, let the fire eat them (2x)
I left my village and place (2x)

Because of the problems, let the fire eat them (2x)
I left my place, my country. (2x)

The Wind Is Blowing
The wind does blow, the wind does blow,
and rustles up the blackthorn;
In whose care, oh friend,
shall I leave my wife?
Leave, oh, comrade,
leave her in my care,
I'll look after her
even better than you.
Do so, oh comrade,
Do look after my wife;
When I return from Canada,
We'll drink up and celebrate with whiskey.

Oh Canada, Oh Canada
Oh Canada, you are so deceitful,
For you have separated many a husband from his wife;
Separated him from his wife, and his small children, too,
How sad it is for me to live in Canada.
I wander through Canada and I count all the miles
And wherever darkness finds me, there I spend the night.
On the mountain grows the grass which the wind does not sway

Somewhere my beloved is writing letters to me;
She writes and writes in very small letters,
And when I read it I shed bitter tears.

I would write a letter but I have no paper
I would take it to the Post Office, but I don't know the way.
I might find the way, but I don't speak the language,
Oh, God, dear God, what am I to do?
I shall write a letter but in fine script
I shall send it with the mighty wind.
I stood on the bridge for one month and an hour
I was waiting for a letter from my beloved family.
Many fish did swim under the bridge,
I did not see any carrying letters.

I only saw a small one, lying by the bank
This small fish handed me a letter.
I began to read it and began to cry,
How lonely it is for me to live in Canada

On The Other Side of the Atlantic
On the other side of the Atlantic there is a state,
Which is called the beautiful Lithuania.
There I was born, there I grew, there I was young,
After not too long I was separated from it. (2x)

When we arrived in the strange country,
I didn't find anyone of our own,
I didn't find my parents, my brothers and sisters,
Nor the neighbours or acquaintances. (2x)

Here are no friends of mine I used to go for a walk with
Nor is the flower garden where I have sown the rue
The paths I walked aren't here
Nor is the lad I loved so dearly.

Here are no friends of mine,

Nor do I hear the songs I used to sing,
And even if I sang them, who would understand
When my heart aches, who would feel for me? (2x)

I Remember that Morning

I remember that morning, when the sun was rising,
You woke me up, dear Mother, to get ready for the journey.
. . . .

The cuckoo called, the nightingale sang
And over there the field of rye was rolling so beautifully. (2x)
I went through the yard, past the garden of rue,
I heard my sister crying sadly in the garden. (2x)
"Shush, don't cry, sister, shush, don't cry, young one
Listen to what our dear mother is telling us." (2x)
"Overseas, there is a land of gold,
Where no one knows, no one sees the hardships." (2x)
When we arrived in the strange country,
Only then we learned to know, learned to see the real hardships. (2x)

"Tell us, dear Mother, tell us, Old One
Where are the mountains of gold; where is this happiness?" (2x)

"Dear Daughter mine, my beloved,
In Lithuania, in the homeland, there is true happiness." (2x)

The Wilno Boys

I'm a jolly old fella, you know my name,
I live at Wilno the village of fame;
For singing and dancing and all kinds of fun,
Sure the boys from Wilno they can't be outdone.

Now when on your patience I beg to intrude,
We hired with Fitzgerald, he was agent for Booth,
To go up the Black River, that's far, far away,
On the old Causewell farm to harvest the hay.

We packed up our turkeys on first of July,
Bronas Raczkowski, Joe Shalla, and I;
On the straightway to Pembroke our luggage we take,
There we boarded the Empress and sailed up the lake.

We arrived at Fort Collins, a place you all know,
We tuned our fiddle, we rosined the bow;
The warming strings rang out in a clear, tuning voice,
And the Oslo rocks echoed "Well done, Wilno boys."

But we left the next morning amid wishes and smiles,
From there to Causewell was forty-six miles;
On the north side of the mountain it was Joe led the route,
But when we got there we were nearly done out.

The board at the Causewell the truth for to tell,
Cannot be surpassed in Russell's Hotel;
We had beefsteak and mutton, hot tea sweet and strong,
And the good early carrots were six inches long.

We had custard, rice puddings, and sweet apple pie,
Good bread and fresh butter, that's much a surprise;
We had cabbage, cucumbers, both pickling and raw,
And the leg of a beaver we stole from a squaw.

When haying was over, we'll pack up our clothes,
We shouldered our turkeys, we went to the woods;
There we felled the tall pines with our axes and saws
Sure, we're terrified by animals, both Indians and squaws.

Us boys we were merry, we dance and we sing,
We lived just as happy as Emperor or King;
We had seven good fiddlers and none of them drones,
And I was the one, I can rattle my bones.

When the drive will be over, I wish it was soon,
So we'd intend to go home on the first week of June;
And if God spares our lives to get home in the spring,
And we'll make our hall at Wilno to ring.

The Gloomy Forest

I am alone in the dreary forest
My thoughts are anxious, my heart downcast;
I have found this place so contrary to nature
That all my poetic talents have forsaken me.
It prevents me from fashioning my songs
My Gaelic is no longer as fluent as it once was
In the old country across the sea.

It's no wonder that I am sad
Living here on the far side of the mountains
In the middle of a wilderness by Barney's River
Where only potatoes are made to grow;
Before I will have succeeded in planting and raising a crop
And clearing the terrible wood
By the strength of my own arms only
My health will have failed while my children are still young.

This country is full of hardship
All unknown to those still coming over;
How unfortunate we were to have encountered those deceivers
Who brought us here with their lying stories:
What profit they get will not last long,
It will not elevate them and that will be no surprise,
Considering how they are pursued by the curses of so many poor wretches
Who have been banished from their homes.

When winter comes and dark dismal weather
The snow piles up as high as the branches of trees
And thick and deep it comes past your knees
And even good quality trousers don't save you
Unless reinforced with double thickness stockings in comfortable moccasins
Severely fastened with leather thongs.
Another new experience for us too was bartering for such garments
With a skin flayed from a wild beast the day before.
When summer comes and the month of May
The sun's heat leaves me faint
But it revives all the animals
Which lie dormant in their dens;

The fierce bears rise out and do great damage to the herd
And the biting black fly exuding venom
Wounds me repeatedly with its sharp pointed lance.
I can't explain things properly to you in this poem
For it's beyond my skill to express myself fully
About all the things I would like to warn my friends against
Those friends I left behind in the country I grew up in.
Don't listen to the boasters
And false prophets who are fooling you;
Who care nothing for you, but are only after your money.

Song of America

When I was at home in the village
My mother kept me well
With all my brothers at my side.
But since, I grew up,
I passed over a great sea
I became very lonely.

At home I had no dollars,
But I had the oxen and the cart
So I whiled away my time
So I dragged along in bitterness.

Oh Lord, big is the dollar,
But you have to work for it, damn it;
If you are small, if you are sturdy,
To break your bones in the
factories.

Did I hear a lie,
That America is a good country,
A good and rich country
With enough money?
Indeed, the money has big figures here
And greedy is everybody,
How greedy I became myself
And left my village.

I left for a year or two,
To make my money and to return.
Years went along, one by one,
Working and gathering the dollars

But when I gathered some two dollars,
They went away for the hospital.

Song for Valparaiso

When I left the harbour
The wind alone cried for me;
And the kiss of the stars
Remained with the wind.

I will return to feel the spring
Climbing my native land—mine, yet not mine;
And that true hope
Is a love which is unforgotten.

Valparaiso, my harbour
Now let me sing to you,
To see your hills, to remember you,
To reveal the future in every child;
And that true hope is a love which is unforgotten.

Rent Money

Rent money, oy, oy, oy
Rent money we must pay
Rent money, a policeman!
We must pay rent money.

The superintendent arrives
And takes off his hat to you
But if you don't pay your rent
He hangs out a sign "To Let."

The landlord comes in
With his thick cane,

But if you don't have your rent to pay
He puts your beds out on the street.

Why should I pay him the rent
If the kitchen is in disrepair?
Why should I pay him the rent
If I don't have what to cook on?

The Red River Valley*

From this valley they say you are going;
I shall miss your bright face and sweet smile,
For they say you are taking the sunshine,
That has brightened my pathway awhile.

Chorus:
Come and sit by my side if you love me,
Do not hasten to bid me adieu,
But remember the Red River Valley,
And the girl who has loved you so true.

For this long, long time I have waited
For the words that you never would say,
But now my last hope has vanished
When they tell me that you're going away.

Oh, there never could be such a longing
In the heart of a white maiden's breast
As there is in the heart that is breaking
With love for the boy who came west.

When you go to your home by the ocean
May you never forget the sweet hours
That we spent in the Red River Valley
Or the vows we exchanged 'mid the bowers.

Will you think of the valley you're leaving?
Oh, how lonely and dreary 'twill be!
Will you think of the fond heart you're breaking
And be true to your promise to me?

The dark maiden's prayer for her lover
To the spirit that rules o'er the world
His pathway with sunshine may cover
Leave his grief to the Red River girl.

Un Canadien Errant*

Un Canadien errant, banni de ses foyers, (2x)
Parcourait en pleurant des pays étrangers. (2x)

Un jour, triste et pensif, assis ou bord des flots (2x)
Au courant fugitif, il adressa ces mots: (2x)

"Si tu vois mon pays, mon pays malheureux (2x)
Va, dis à mes amis, que je me souviens d'eux. (2x)

Ô jours si plein d'appas, vous êtes disparus (2x)
Et ma patrie, hélas! Je ne la verrai plus! (2x)

Non, mais en expirant, Ô, mon cher Canada! (2x)
Mon regard languissant vers toi se portera." (2x)

Once a Canadian lad,
Exiled from hearth and home
Wandered alone and sad
Through alien lands unknown.
Down by a rushing stream
Thoughtful and sad one day
He watched the water pass
And to it he did say:

"If you should reach my land,
My most unhappy land
Please speak to all my friends
So they will understand.
Tell them how much I wish
That I could be once more
In my beloved land
That I will see no more.

My own beloved land
I'll not forget till death
And I will speak of her
With my last dying breath.
My own beloved land
I'll not forget till death
And I will speak of her
With my last dying breath."

Notes

1. These lyrics appear in the McKenna brothers' CBC production *The Killing Grounds*, a World War I documentary, 1988.
2. Ellen Karp selected field recordings and published a number of immigrants' songs in a document entitled *Many Are Strong among Strangers* (Ottawa: National Museum of Man, National Museums of Canada, Mercury Series, n.d.). The oldest pieces in Karp's collection are the Irish broadside ballads, topical songs based on traditional melodies and sold on street corners since the seventeenth century, and Scottish songs which originated following the 1745 Jacobite Rebellion. Song lyrics taken from this collection are indicated by "K," followed by the page numbers.
3. "The Scarborough Settler's Lament," in Edith Fowke, ed., *The Penguin Book of Canadian Folk Songs* (Hammondsworth, Middlesex: Penguin Books, 1973). Set to a version of Robert Burns's *Of A' the Airts the Wind Can Blaw*, this song addresses feelings of nostalgia even after thirty years of absence. The words in this instance serve the text in that the lines musically and poetically line up, so to speak, as single phrases or single units of thought. Characteristic of the time in which it was written, the melody, given a spirited presentation, takes on a nationalistic, patriotic, and strongly military flavour. The sentiment of Sandy Glendinning's words of 1840, however, do not lend themselves to such a conceit, a fact which raises the issue of how the lyrics and melody serve each other (or do not).

   "Un Canadien Errant," in Fowke, *The Penguin Book of Canadian Folk Songs*, is a lament of another sort in that it represents a contrived and somewhat romanticized version of an exile, however longingly the writer/narrator speaks of home. In this case, the writer/narrator, himself not in exile, has set his words to a popular French song. Setting words to an existing melody, which we know to have been done in this example, imposes order on the words so that, in part, they serve the form into which they are set. This song, then, exists outside the given taxonomy, in that the impulse behind it is arguably apart from the other songs in this paper. It is worthy of note that in the original French, the song relies heavily on repetition, which Fowke, the collector, however well-intended, has managed to eliminate. Moreover, Fowke reduces the original five stanzas to three. She has also written English words with enough distance that they may not strictly be considered "translation," which is unfortunate, because the song is considerably more poignant, albeit understated, in French.

4. "The Forty-Five," 1745–46. Prince Charles Edward Stuart raised the Jacobite standard at Glenfinnan in August of 1745. This final "uprising" of the Jacobites in the Highlands ended with the prince's disastrous defeat on the moors of Culloden. See John Keay and Julia Keay, eds., *Collins Encyclopaedia of Scotland* (London: Harper Collins, 1994).

5. Margaret Atwood, *The Journals of Susanna Moodie* (Toronto: Oxford University Press, 1970).

6. Margaret Atwood, *Survival: A Thematic Guide to Canadian Literature* (Toronto: Anansi, 1972), 18.

7. The words "contrary to nature" heighten the drama of the narrator's feeling about the place in which he is attempting to make a life for himself and his family. I wonder if the intent of the words in Gaelic might have been closer, rather, to addressing the strangeness of nature in this new place.

8. Part of this song's charm is that it captures the unique speech patterns of an ethnic group of individuals for whom English is not the "mother tongue."

9. I have quoted from *Argosy to Adventure, Canada Book of Prose and Verse* (Toronto: Ryerson Press, 1961). The ongoing dispute over the origin of the words has been, and continues to be, the inspiration of many articles. The words have been set to "known" melodies as well as having been used in choral arrangements.

Acknowlededgments

I would like to acknowledge the valuable assistance of Dr. Dennis Cooley, whose thoughtful questions helped to shape this paper. I acknowledge, also, the more silent contributions through literary text, of Margaret Atwood (*Survival* and *The Journals of Susanna Moodie*) Dennis

Cooley (*Passwords*), Margaret Laurence (*The Diviners*), Eli Mandel (*Life Sentence*), and Robert Kroetsch (*But We Are Exiles*, and *The Man from the Creek*), whose narratives are migrations in various ways. Thanks are due, as well, to the National Museum of Canada for permission to use Ellen Karp's collection *Many Are Strong among Strangers*.

Contributors

Christopher J. Armstrong is an associate professor in the Department of British and American Cultural Studies at Chukyo University in Nagoya, Japan. His current research interest is modernity and the postcolonial situation in Atlantic Canadian fiction.

Joan Bryans divides her time between teaching philosophy at the University of British Columbia and being active in the theatre scene in Vancouver. She has just finished directing *Shadowlands* at the Jericho Arts Centre, and she is currently conducting research on women immigrants to British Columbia.

Kathleen Burke teaches in the History Department at St. Thomas University, Fredericton. She is currently conducting research into the impact of the Canadian experience on contemporary Canadian residents. She is also interested in the emergence of a distinct feeling of Canadian identity among early-nineteenth-century migrants from Britain.

Wendy Cameron is a partner in Wordforce and visiting scholar at the Northrop Frye Centre, Victoria University in the University of Toronto. She is co-author and co-editor of two forthcoming books: *Assisting Emigration to Upper Canada: The Petworth Project 1832–37* and *English Immigrant Voices: Labourers' Letters from Upper Canada in the 1830s*.

Karen Clavelle is a lecturer in English and a research fellow at St. John's College, University of Manitoba. A specialist in Canadian literature, she is conducting her doctoral research on the hybrid genre of the twentieth-century Canadian Prairie long poem/journal/travel journal and the constructed relationship of persons to place.

Tracey R. Connolly completed her Ph.D. thesis entitled "Emigration from Independent Ireland 1922–1970" at University College Cork, Ireland. She has written chapters on Irish emigration in the *Encyclopaedia of the Australian People* (Cambridge, 2001), *Ireland and the Second World War: Politics, Society and Government* (Dublin, 2000), and *The Irish Diaspora* (Longmans, 2000).

Duff Crerar teaches at Grande Prairie Regional College, Alberta. His current research involves the religious culture of the Scottish migrants to the Canadas after the Napoleonic wars. Previous research and publications have been concerned with Kirk session and parish discipline in Scotland and Upper Canada, with the religious culture of the Canadian Expeditionary Force in the First World War, and specifically with Canadian military chaplains.

John F. Davis was a senior lecturer in geography at Birkbeck College, University of London, and treasurer of the British Association for Canadian Studies. His contribution to the Edinburgh Migration conference was his last academic paper before his death in January 1999.

Richard Dennis is a reader in geography at University College, London. His main research interest is in the historical geography of housing, and he is currently working on a book on early apartment housing in Toronto and Winnipeg.

Bruce S. Elliott is a professor of history at Carleton University in Ottawa and a graduate of the Department of English Local History at the University of Leicester. He is the author of *Irish Migrants in the Canadas* and *The City Beyond: A History of Nepean*. He is currently working on a history of English emigration to British North America in the pre-Confederation period.

Sebastián Escalante studied international affairs and political science. He is a member of the Mexican Association of Canadian Studies, and his research interests include migration and human rights issues, globalization, and new identities.

Marjory Harper is a senior lecturer in history at the University of Aberdeen, Scotland. She has published several books on Scottish emigration, most recently *Emigration from Scotland Between the Wars: Oppor-*

tunity or Exile. She is currently co-editing a documentary source book of Scottish emigration to the Americas, 1650–1930.

Donald Harris was awarded a Ph.D. from the University of Birmingham, Department of American and Canadian Studies, for his thesis on the promotion in Shropshire of emigration to Canada up to 1914. Recent publications include "A Salopian Standard of Decency: Emigration to Canada Sponsored by Shrewsbury School's Liverpool Mission, 1907–1914," *British Journal of Canadian Studies* and "The Presentation of a British Canada in Shropshire, 1890–1914" in *Imperial Canada, 1867–1917*.

Gary L. Hunt is a professor in the Department of Economics at the University of Maine. He has co-authored several published papers dealing with the labour-market effects of United States immigration on native workers and has worked with colleagues for the United States–Mexico Binational Study on Immigration. He is researching the internal migration of natives in response to immigration and on the selectivity of immigration between Canada and the United States.

Peter Marshall is professor emeritus of American history and institutions at the University of Manchester and is currently preparing a study of the development of imperial law in the years before the American Revolution, with particular reference to the Quebec Act.

Terry McDonald is a senior lecturer in history and politics at Southampton Institute. His research interests revolve around nineteenth-century English and Canadian history, especially emigration from the West of England to Upper Canada, nineteenth-century elections, folksongs as historical source material, Newfoundland history, and contemporary Canadian politics.

Barbara J. Messamore has recently completed her Ph.D. in history at the Centre of Canadian Studies, University of Edinburgh. Previous publications concern the role of the governor general in Canada. She is currently teaching history at University College of the Fraser Valley in Abbotsford, British Columbia.

Richard E. Mueller is an assistant professor of economics and Canadian studies at the University of Maine. He holds a Ph.D. from the University of Texas and has published on Canadian labour-market issues. His current research investigates the migration of highly skilled Canadians to the United States.

Ronald Stagg writes on late-eighteenth- and nineteenth-century Canada, with an emphasis on Ontario history. As well as contributing extensively to the *Dictionary of Canadian Biography*, he has authored numerous articles dealing with the era of the Upper Canadian rebellion of 1837. He has also co-authored, with Colin Read, *The Upper Canadian Rebellion of 1837*. He teaches at Ryerson Polytechnic University in Toronto, and is the former chair of the History Department.